N

Bradt

Ballina

Castlebar

Westport   MAYO

Cleggan   Lough Mask
                 House
Clifden   Cong
                              Tuam

        CONNEMARA   GALWAY   Athlo

                 Galway   Loughrea

Inishmore   Ballyvaughan   Bir
ARAN ISLANDS   Burren
                 Doolin   National Park
Cliffs of Moher   Kilfenora
        Lehinch   Nenagh
        Mullagh   CLARE
                              Ennis
        Kilrush   Limerick
                              Boher   Thurles
        Tarbert   Cash
               Ballybunion   LIMERICK TIPPERA
Mouth of the Shannon   Tipperary   Fethard
        Listowel   Lough
               Charleville   Gur
Castlegregory   Tralee   Clonmel
Dingle   Mitchelstown
Blasket   Mallow   WATERF
Islands Dingle Bay   Lismore
Valentia   Killarney   Dungarva
Island
              Kenmare   CORK   Blarney   Midleton
Waterville   Yougha
        Sneem   Cork   Cobh
                       Bantry Blarney
Sheep's Head   Dunmanway Bandon
        Skibbereen

KEY
——— Part 1 route - see page
——— Part 2 route - see page
o ———— 25km
o ———— 15 miles

A Connemara Journey

A thousand miles on
horseback through
western Ireland

Hilary Bradt

About the Author

Hilary Bradt grew up in the Chilterns and trained as an occupational therapist, a profession she pursued in the USA and South Africa to finance her ever-longer periods of travel. Eventually the travel bug took over completely, and with her husband George she spent four years backpacking through South America and Africa, founding Bradt Enterprises (now Bradt Guides) along the way. She returned to England to concentrate on writing and publishing, punctuated by summers working as a tour leader. Her books include three Slow guides to Devon and 13 editions of the Bradt guide to Madagascar (with Daniel Austin). In 2020 she co-authored the first ever guide to the island of Socotra. She now lives in semi-retirement in Devon, dividing her time between writing, sculpting, and pottering around the county.

Hilary was awarded an MBE in 2008 for services to the travel industry and to charity and in subsequent years received four lifetime achievement awards including from the British Guild of Travel Writers and Travel Media.

First published in the UK in March 2021 by
Bradt Travel Guides Ltd
31a High Street, Chesham, Buckinghamshire, HP5 1BW, England
www.bradtguides.com

Print edition published in the USA by The Globe Pequot Press Inc,
PO Box 480, Guilford, Connecticut 06437-0480

ISBN: 978 1 78477 825 5

British Library Cataloguing in Publication Data
A catalogue record for this book is available from the British Library

Photographs:
p.i *En route to Killary Harbour*
p.iv *Peggy*

Print production managed by Sue Cooper
Printed by Zenith Media in the UK
Digital conversion by www.dataworks.co.in

The Adventures of this Book

Why wait 37 years to publish a book? Here's why.

When I got home from my two-part Ireland adventure in 1984 I could hardly wait to start writing. Although I hadn't set out with the intention of writing a book, I'd kept a diary that I wrote up each evening in my tent, listening to my tape recorder play-back to catch the immediacy of the moment. But on my return I had books to publish and correspondence to catch up on, so it wasn't until the following spring when I found the opportunity to start my book. My parents went on holiday, leaving me to house-sit. I sat at the scrubbed kitchen table on which I had spent so many childhood hours drawing, painting and modelling horses, and started writing. I wrote in pencil on thick A4 pads of lined paper.

I worked steadily, checking my route on the maps I had carried with me, and listening again to the tape recorder to catch bits of dialogue, absorbing the cadences of the Irish accent and hearing the clip-clop of my horse's hooves as we covered the miles. When my parents returned three weeks later I had got it all down, but it needed a lot of revising and polishing, and for this I wanted another period of isolation away from my desk. A house-sitting opportunity came up again, this time in Haringey. As well as solitude it had another advantage: an African grey parrot. I adore parrots.

I packed the two blue writing pads into a cardboard box, along with some maps and photos, put a few clothes into a suitcase, and drove my ancient car to north London, arriving at Julian's house at dusk. He had already left, but I let myself in and started unpacking the boot, putting the box containing the manuscript on the garden wall so I could take my case inside. There were lots of written instructions to absorb and a very cross parrot. The phone rang, Polly escaped and started walking determinedly down the stairs, and by the time I had got her back into her cage and found a sticky plaster for my finger where she'd bitten me, all I could think about was a nice cup of tea and then supper.

Next morning I cleared the table, cleared my mind, and prepared to start work on the book. But where the hell was the manuscript? It wasn't in my bedroom, nor in the kitchen. Nor, to my increasing dismay, in the car. As I traced my actions back to unloading the car, I felt that awful sinking feeling all too familiar to absent-minded people. I'd never picked the box up from the garden wall. And it was no longer there.

I was distraught. Remember, this was pre-computers, and the only copy of my precious book was the one I'd lost. I couldn't, wouldn't write it again. I cried for about an hour, and then found a sheet of white paper and a black marker pen. '£50 reward!' I headed it. Yes, a huge amount of money, but someone must have taken the box, been disappointed at the worthlessness of its contents, and could be persuaded to return it. I went to the photocopy shop and had 100 copies printed. These I put up on every telegraph pole and lamppost, and posted through all the neighbouring letterboxes for several blocks around. I was sure that someone would phone within a matter of hours, and certainly the next day, but I heard nothing. My despair deepened. I was alone in a strange house with a hostile parrot, and my whole purpose for being there had disappeared into thin air. Soon I had to leave not only London but England, being due to lead a trip to Peru where I would be out of communication for over a month.

Enter my knight in shining armour. Two knights. My friends Tanis and Martin Jordan heard about my loss – everyone I knew heard about my loss – and stepped in. "We'll find a dowser" said Tanis. "There's one who advertises in our local paper." I was easily convinced to leave it in their hands – I had run out of both time and options.

The Jordans contacted the dowser and visited him the day before I left for Peru. "Well, he was old and scruffy, maybe a gypsy," Tanis reported. "He had a pendant, some sort of crystal, and a grubby map of London. We found the house on Rokesly Avenue, and he dangled the pendant over the area and moved it slowly in all different directions. It started to go in a circle over a school, just at the end of that road. We watched. It was extraordinary – it just went round and round and he said 'That's where it is'. There were other possibilities that we circled on the map, then we paid him and off he went. My sister-in-law's going to help me with the search next week. I'll write to you in Lima."

I still have the letter.

"First, no luck so far. Ginny and I drove over to Hornsey, located the spot on the map and parked the car. The one thing I'd been dreading loomed in front of us – a builder's skip overflowing with rubbish. However, a quick check of the map showed it to be on the wrong road, plus the fact that it had probably only been there a few days made it an unlikely chance, we convinced ourselves, but we gave it a quick once-over just in case. We then located the exact spots on the map and these proved very interesting. One circle was over the school.

The other was a long, shrub-lined drive leading to some barrack-style buildings. The sign at the end of the road said 'Rokesly Road Kitchens. No Entry'. So we went in. The place seemed perfect for our search, full of rubbish under wildly overgrown weeds etc. Of course, being an explorer, I'd failed to bring a stick to poke around with and was wearing flip-flops. A few nettle stings and one bee sting later I waded out of the jungle, found Ginny, and peered through the windows of the buildings which were locked and deserted. So that's still one possibility.

"After that we decided to knock on some doors. I think they thought we were selling something since most people seemed to be out. And when they did answer the door they couldn't understand what we wanted. But one lady not only believed us but was very helpful. She suggested the YMCA round the corner. The woman there was the most unhelpful person I've ever met. Her only comment was 'Have you any scientific evidence to back this up?' She did allow us to put a message on the notice board, though.

"We were having too much fun to stop, so worked our way back to where we'd started from, searching drains and gutters, and paid particular attention to the school. We now had long sticks so went round the perimeter pulling out rubbish and examining it (fortunately it was quite a clean school). It was closed for the holidays but where the circle on the map was, we peered through the windows and saw – kitchens! So maybe there's a link with those buildings we looked at earlier. We managed to find the caretaker – a large lady from Trinidad – who was the first really helpful person we met. She even knew what a dowser was. She insisted that we memorise the names of all the schools in the neighbourhood, including 'Tottenham High at de back of de church'.

"So I'll follow up with some phone calls tomorrow. And who knows. . .?"

I was sure that this exhaustive search would be rewarded, but when I returned home there was a message from Tanis saying they still had no news. Weeks passed, then months. I stopped thinking about the missing manuscript every day and came to terms with my loss. Sort of. I didn't want to write it all again so that was that.

Six months after I'd set that box upon the wall I was having dinner at my house and the phone rang. "She's here if you want to speak to her," said my mother. "It's Julian," she whispered.

"There's a young man here with your manuscript," said Julian. "He wants to know if the reward is still on offer."

"What? How? When?" I spluttered. "I think it's better not to ask any questions," said Julian carefully.

So I got my manuscript back. And when I read it, after the six-month gap, I realised it needed a lot more than simple polishing. It needed a thorough revision. I put it in the loft and got on with other things.

By the early part of the 21st century we at Bradt had expanded our list to include travel narratives so I cautiously mentioned that I had this pencil-written manuscript in the loft. It was agreed that it was worth having it typed up and shaped for possible publication. After such a long gap I wanted to make a return journey (by car) to Ireland to revisit the people and landscapes that had made the trip so special. The result: *Connemara Mollie* in 2012 and *Dingle Peggy* in 2013. But why stop there? I wanted this single journey, though with two different ponies, to be combined into one book and to finally end its 37-year stop-start adventure.

This book is dedicated to the wonderful people of western Ireland who provided conversation, food and accommodation for Mollie, Peggy and me in 1984.

Mollie

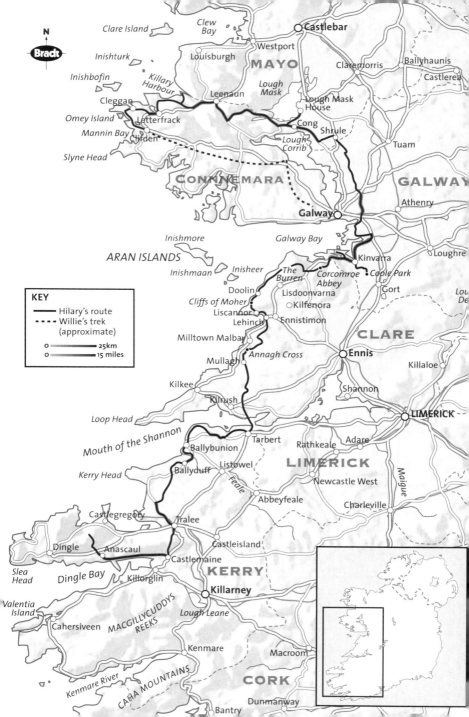

Chapter 1

It is noon in late May. The sky, washed by the rain of last night, is pale greenish-blue, and joyful with the song of skylarks. The sun is warm on my back. To my right, and a long way below, is the sea. The grassy track rises gently between grey stone walls, disappearing into a dip between domed hills which seem covered with silver-grey snow; for this is the Burren where the limestone bones of the landscape break through the soil. And I am seeing this view between the two grey ears of Mollie, my pony. My Connemara pony. I am living a dream.

☾　☾　☾

It began with a book: *Four Rode Home* by Primrose Cumming. As a pony-mad child I got through a horse book every week thanks to Harrods Children's Library. This was an extraordinary service. Every Tuesday a smart van would draw up in our drive, the front door would be pushed open and a uniformed man would shout "'arrods!" and drop a brown-paper parcel on the mat. Then he'd pick up the book I had hastily finished and wrapped that morning. I would supply a list of all the titles I wanted to read and I was very rarely disappointed. Only once, and I remember it vividly, they gave me *Little Women*. I was so outraged that I've never been able to bring myself to read it. *Four Rode Home* was different from the usual story of the impoverished heroine acquiring a pony despite fearful odds and going on to win rosettes at the local gymkhana. Here the children trek through the English countryside from the New Forest to their home in Romney Marsh, staying in youth hostels and having lots of adventures. The idea was born: one day I would have my own pony and do a long-distance ride through changing scenery. And have lots of adventures.

My parents said bluntly that we couldn't afford a pony, had nowhere to keep one, and what about my asthma? They had a point; I was so allergic to horses as a young child that I had to take to my bed following each riding lesson. So I read about ponies, dreamed about ponies, galloped an imaginary pony along the grass verges along the bus route on the way to school, and drew them all over my rough book (for which I was punished). And each year I cut my birthday cake with my eyes tight shut and my wishes screaming to an unlistening fairy godmother.

By forcing my younger sister, Kate, to wish for a pony on her birthdays I doubled my chances, and finally our wishes half came true with Johnny. Johnny was the outgrown, evil-tempered first pony of a school friend who not only lived in a large house with rich parents, but had enviable curly red hair which she used to flatten down for Parents' Day with lacrosse grease. She'd also inherited their commercial sense. One day, in response to my endless pony drone, she said "You can hire Johnny for a week, if you like." The charge would be 10 shillings. Conveniently, Johnny was accustomed to being tethered, so where to keep him was not much of a problem; a neighbour gallantly said she didn't mind him mowing their back lawn for a week. Johnny was by no means a dream pony. He kicked. Not just a casual one-foot kick, but a full frontal attack with ears flattened and teeth bared, then wheeling around and letting fly with both heels. We loved him anyway, and since there was only one of him and two of us we were happy enough for him to stroll along the Buckinghamshire bridleways while one walked and the other rode. And we enjoyed the fringe aspects of pony care as much as the actual riding; grooming, picking out hooves, and cleaning tack each day like the children in the books. I wheezed and sneezed for a week, but at least I wasn't bedridden.

Now I was 11 or so I was considerably braver – reckless, even. Near our home was a smooth-surfaced private road which was perfect for roller skating. A group of ponies grazed in the adjacent field, and Kate and I used to sneak sugar lumps or carrots from the larder to feed to them in between bouts of wobbling along on our clip-on skates. One day I was sitting on the wooden fence while the pretty chestnut pony below me nuzzled Kate's hand for titbits. On impulse I lowered myself onto her back. I felt her muscles bunching under me and she took off at a gallop. A small part of me thought 'Wow, I've never been this fast!' and a much bigger part screamed 'Oh my God, she's going to jump that barbed wire fence!' At the last minute the pony braked and swerved. I fell off and, both unharmed, we stared at each other wide-eyed. I should have recognised an unbroken filly from the blonde tips to her mane and short tail.

Like Johnny, Ricky and Tara were not the stuff that dreams are made of, but the chance to look after them while their owner was in Canada came as one of the high spots of my childhood. No longer restricted to walking pace, Kate and I roamed the countryside, played silly games, entered and failed to win rosettes at gymkhanas, and fell off. It was easy to fall off both ponies, although in Tara's case it was always she herself who fell. This piebald mare, half carthorse with enormous hairy legs and a droopy lower lip, was so clumsy that if urged to a canter she periodically fell over. And she had a funny saddle. Her owner, Rosemary, told us proudly that it was an old army saddle that she'd lined with wool fabric from Daddy's factory. Heavy to carry and difficult to clean, we hated it. We hated Ricky's saddle too. It was a 'felt pad' and we could feel his backbone through it. Little Ricky was only 12.2 hands high but could buck like a bronco and was so intelligent that keeping him became a battle of wits. He could get down on his knees and wriggle under the wire fence, leaving Tara neighing hysterically. Tara loved him and he repaid this affection by biting her at every opportunity. She would return from each ride with green slobber marks on her white bottom where Ricky had periodically grabbed a mouthful of grass then a mouthful of Tara.

When the sad time came to hand the ponies back I was 16 and suddenly grown so tall that at my last gymkhana it was I that knocked down the jump with my foot, not Ricky. But I'd learned a lot about pony care and found to my relief that my allergy to horses was diminishing with my increasing years.

After Ricky and Tara came Sonnet. When I left school at 17 I somehow persuaded my parents that they could now afford to buy us a horse. We'd earned the ponies' keep by working weekends at the local riding school which I was sure would continue to give us support. Besides, I said, I'd looked in *Horse and Hound* and a suitable animal need only cost about £70 (that was in 1958). Now that I fancied myself grown up, I wanted a horse not a pony, and I wanted one with all the qualities that Johnny, Ricky and Tara lacked: high head-carriage, keen, and a challenge to ride. 'Not novice ride' the advertisements would say, but these horses were still over £100. Then we were offered Sonnet. When she was led out of the stable I should have seen a 15.2hh bay mare with a too-large head, a ewe neck, a mean eye and sunken quarters. As it was I saw a proper horse with – joy-oh-joy – a normal saddle, and all for £70. We were assured that she was keen and not a novice ride and the horse-dealer confirmed that she'd do better out in a field all winter than in a stable where she might hot-up.

I rode her round the paddock and was thrilled to find that she was a comfortable ride, forward-going with smooth paces, and a nice high head. I knew we were going to buy her. "We held a paper chase yesterday," the dealer said, "so she's had plenty of recent exercise."

"How did she do?"

"She bolted. But the man riding her was an idiot." I laughed sympathetically. It's such a shame when a lovely horse like Sonnet ends up with an idiot.

During the two years we had her, she bolted regularly. She charged through a hedge out hunting, she cantered through red traffic lights in our local town, and she jumped a motorbike plus rider that happened to be in the way during one headlong flight. The problem, we soon realised, was that this mare couldn't bear any pressure on her mouth from the bit. Sonnet's reaction to a pull on the reins was to throw her head up, breaking my glasses, and to increase her pace. We learned alternative ways of stopping, until one day the brakes failed.

There was a large field near our house where the wheat had been cut. I noticed that the gate had been left open and wanted to take Sonnet for a gallop there, an enclosed field providing a great opportunity to let her go for as long and as fast as she wanted. I decided to use her old rubber snaffle in this brief excursion since it was the bit she was most comfortable with. We never got to the field. Approaching one of our regular cantering places Sonnet, as usual, broke into a trot and started throwing her head around. When I restrained her I felt something break – it was the bit itself, the rubber having rotted – and the reins hung uselessly in my hands. Surprised at this unexpected freedom, she started to canter but leaning forward I managed to grab the noseband and slow her back to a trot. Then the noseband also broke and I was left with the bridle dangling uselessly from her neck. As she galloped off down the

road I realised, sickeningly, that she was following the familiar route to
her previous paddock, 2½ miles away. The country lane would soon join a
major road which led steeply downhill, crossed the A313, and continued
down to Chalfont St Giles below. By the time Sonnet reached the first
junction she was galloping so fast that she skidded and nearly fell when
making the turn. There were no cars coming, but I could see them ahead,
lined up at the main road waiting for a gap in the traffic.

As Sonnet hurtled down the hill I could see a regular stream of cars
on the main road and I knew that she would go straight across towards
the village. I considered throwing myself off, then looked at the black
tarmac whizzing past beneath her flying hooves and decided not to.
Flying hooves resulted in flying shoes; they became loosened and I heard
two of them sail off and land with a clink behind me. 'Damn,' I thought,
'those were new last week.' Then we reached the main road. The line of
cars had diminished to one, and the driver must have looked in his rear-
view mirror. He just had time to bump the car up onto the pavement
as Sonnet careered past. I saw the cars moving steadily by on the main
road; one passed just ahead of me, another behind me. Miraculously I was
safely across and continuing on our headlong descent. The track leading
to her old field was on the right, opposite the village pond, and I saw a
black car pull over as this galloping apparition appeared in his mirror.
But Sonnet was going too fast to negotiate the turn, hit the car with her
shoulder and fell.

I lay on the ground until a very shocked-looking young man came
and helped me up. I remember his white face and his trembling voice as
he said "You alright, missy?" In fact I was. More or less. There was a crowd
of people round Sonnet (being British, the onlookers were much more
concerned with an injured horse than its shocked rider) who had a gaping
wound in her shoulder, but at least she was on her feet with no broken

bones. Someone gave me a cup of tea and a coin so I could phone home, tearfully explaining what had happened, and asking my ever-obliging parents to find a horsebox and a vet. I was just in time. A few minutes later an acquaintance rang my mother: "Ooh Mrs Cross, I've just seen your daughter galloping past our house on a runaway horse, so I was wondering if she's all right!"

I was uninjured apart from a chipped collarbone and the shock from which I never really recovered. My confidence was permanently affected and I no longer sought out difficult horses; I was happier on something quite docile and preferably small.

Chapter 2

"I travel, therefore I am." I don't know who said this, but what pretentious rubbish! Travel interests some people and not others, that's all. I travel because it happens to satisfy my curiosity and feed my various interests. And because I enjoy adventure which means travelling without fixed plans. And for this, nothing beats hitchhiking.

On a damp May morning in 1963 I set out with a friend to hitch from London to Dover and thence to the Middle East. At 21, Val and I had just completed our occupational therapy training and wanted a final fling before our first jobs. The couple who stopped for us a few miles from the ferry were from Peru. "Where's that?" I muttered to Val. "Africa, isn't it?" Well, geography was the first subject I gave up at school. Three months and £90 later I walked up the hill to my parents' house with a much better understanding of geography and politics. The lesson in frugality was long-lasting, but the real benefit was what I had learned about people. Hitchhiking teaches you that all over the world most people are astonishingly kind and generous, and even the dodgy ones can be dealt with diplomatically. And there's plenty of time for thought. Driving through eastern Turkey with two lecherous Cypriots I gazed at the unfenced hilly landscape laced with tracks trodden by laden donkeys and planned my long-distance ride. Some day, I told myself, I would buy a horse in the Russian Caucasus and ride it back to England through Turkey, Greece and Yugoslavia. Instead, I went to America, lured by the high salaries for OTs and proximity to Peru; I was now obsessed by the Incas.

While living in the United States I occasionally indulged my latent horsiness. Near Boston was 'Bob's Rent-A-Horse' where I rode an animal called Freeway which had a Sonnet-like tendency to bolt. At a fancier place in the Blue Hills the horses were stabled and full of oats, but you were still allowed out unaccompanied (inconceivable these days). Once, I fell off and spent the rest of my hour crawling around in the leaf litter looking for my glasses so I could be sure that I was catching a horse not a bush. Best of all was the week spent on a dude ranch in Wyoming. Here I learned to ride western style, wheeling my horse around with only one hand on the reins and spending all day on the many trails that led through the golden aspen forests and up into the foothills of Grand Teton. Hitherto I had only climbed mountains on foot and the advantage of doing it on someone else's legs was immediately obvious.

In 1969 I travelled to Peru in search of the Incas, found Machu Picchu, floated on a variety of vessels down the Amazon, and returned to England just in time for the NHS to treat my hepatitis. But I failed to settle down, went back to Boston and met George. He was an enthusiastic backpacker. No, he was an obsessive backpacker, spending three months every summer in some remote area of the US, hiking around on his own and carrying all his needs in a rucksack. I'd done some backpacking – indeed, I'd hiked 100 miles of the 2,000-mile-long Appalachian Trail – but tended to agree with some wag who said "Once you've seen two billion leaves you've seen them all". The eastern United States, I decided, had too many trees. To George I was an

obsessive traveller, willing to abandon my job and friends and head off
to such diverse places as Iceland and South America at the drop of a hat.
He'd done some travelling but considered there was no reason to leave
God's Own Country which had the monopoly of beautiful scenery.

We compromised when we got married and planned to backpack
round the world – with help from whatever vehicles were going our way.
After four years, with half the globe still unexplored, we called a halt and
started writing guidebooks. After all, no one else had described where to
walk in South America and Africa. Nor, so publishers told us, did anyone
want to read about such matters so we published the books ourselves.

∪   ∪   ∪

Writers learn as much from their books as their readers do. After a
while you start to believe you've always known exactly what to pack for
a ten-day trek in the Andes, where to go in Uganda, how to spot lemurs
in Madagascar, what sort of boots to buy, how to make a tent, and so
on. And you have a missionary-like zeal to spread the word. So not only
did we publish books, we phoned a company called South American
Wilderness Adventure and asked if they needed travel consultants. We
were a bit vague about what we could do for them, but were sure that
our boundless knowledge of the South American wilderness would
prove useful in some way. The two affable Californians who ran the
company were unimpressed at our consultancy idea but suggested that
we become leaders. A similar offer had been made the previous year by
the very charming director of an alarmingly up-market and expensive
company offering luxury treks along Peru's Inca Trail. His clients were
mostly male, said this elegantly dressed man with one gold earring, as
he leaned back in his executive's chair, and they expected the utmost in
comfort. The porters carried tables, chairs, chickens and wine. And if

the clients wanted their feet massaged – well, that was the leader's job. He suggested we might like to lead one of his trips; his present leader, a young man, was often troubled by nocturnal visits from his clients and a friend thought a married couple might have an easier time. He told us how much he paid and we accepted the job with alacrity. Then we got down to details. "What," George wanted to know, "do we do if a client arrives for a trek with the wrong footwear?"

"You take him shopping for suitable boots."

"You mean to tell me it would be my job to drag some asshole around Lima looking for boots, when he's too stupid to come properly equipped?"

The letter arrived later that week: "Dear George, the fact that you referred to my beloved clients as assholes reinforces some doubts that I had..."

Wilderness Adventures seemed much more down to earth. We weren't expected to provide foot massages or night services, so with some hesitation we accepted their offer. I still regard this as an astonishing turn of events, having always felt myself to be a natural follower. How can someone be a leader if she's usually lost and if she's too cowardly to tell a waiter there's a caterpillar in the salad? Receptionists at hotels terrified me (not that I'd been in many hotels with receptionists) and I couldn't imagine arguing my way onto an overbooked plane or dealing with lost luggage.

While I was making the change from being a follower to a leader, George was also changing. The left-wing American hippie I'd married eight years earlier, discovered that all this while he'd been a closet capitalist and now he ran a publishing empire he could 'come out'. While I wanted to write, travel and lead trips, he wanted to stay home and run the business. While I believed that absence made the heart grow fonder, he thought otherwise and in 1980 the marriage ended.

ʊ   ʊ   ʊ

My dreams of doing a long-distance ride intensified. Now that I was alone, riding a wild Russian mare through Turkey no longer seemed such a good idea and my years away from Britain had nurtured nostalgic memories of heather-covered mountains and bridle paths through beech woods. I would buy a Highland pony and ride home to Bucks. Or perhaps a Welsh Cob and ride to Cornwall. Having neither the time nor the money to do such a self-indulgent trip didn't stop me thinking about it as I drove around the country selling books, or waited on a Peruvian hillside for the slower trekkers to catch me up. And it was in Peru that I moved a step closer. When planning the horse tour in my imagination, the question of what to bring and how to carry it had long been a sticking point. I knew I didn't want a packhorse; apart from the expense of buying or hiring two ponies, there would be the worry and inconvenience of controlling a second animal on the busy British roads and being limited to walking pace. I'd heard about people using small saddlebags and planning routes and night stops in advance, but that wasn't my style – I wanted to be completely flexible, to go or stop as the mood took me, or as the landscape and people invited me. This, after all, is what backpacking is all about and I felt that my experience as a walker could be put to good use; I knew that a rucksack containing all one's requirements for a wilderness trek of a week or more need weigh only 40lb. The question was how to carry that amount of luggage on a horse?

Then came the phone call. "Hi, Bill Roberson here. Do you want to join us on a horse trek in Peru? You know Tiki from Lima? She's running the thing but we haven't done this route before so we really need an extra helper." When I arrived at the trailhead in the Cordillera Blanca and saw the gear that Bill had brought from California I was thrilled.

Instead of being carried in local-style hairy cow-hide nets suspended from wooden saddles, our heavy supplies were packed in smart panniers and our personal luggage was carried in saddlebags. "Put soft things such as clothes and sleeping bags in the middle section," said Bill, "and heavier things on each side. It's important to make sure that the two side bags are the same weight." He left us to get on with our packing but I was excitedly copying down the name of the manufacturer of this wonderful stuff: Morgans Horse Products. The saddlebags looked a bit like two large canvas handbags attached to each end of a duffle and were roomy enough to hold everything one would need for a lengthy solo trek. They were designed to fit over a western saddle but I thought they could probably be adapted for an English saddle, especially a military one like Tara's.

The first day was filled with drama. The previous evening, some boys had brought us two small owls they'd shot down with stones from their catapults. They wanted us to buy them for our dinner. Instead, we disinfected their wounds and put them on a nearby fence, hoping they'd recover enough to fly away during the night. One did, but on the morning of our planned departure the most severely injured of the two remained, eyes half shut but still alive and still with a small chance of survival, so we left it where it was. The muleteers arrived and started loading up their animals with much chatter and bursts of song. Suddenly there was silence. The headman walked slowly up to Tiki. "We can't go," he said simply.

"Why on earth not?"

"Don't you see?" he pointed to the little owl. "That means that someone will die on the trail." One of the men walked towards the bird with his machete, intending to kill it.

"Wait!" Tiki shouted. "It's only bad luck if you kill it, then someone will die. If you leave it alive everything will be all right." There was a long muttered discussion in the local Indian language, Quechua, before the men reluctantly agreed to continue.

We started our ascent towards the shining white peak at the head of the valley, the line of packhorses making their sure-footed way along the narrow trail cut into the side of the mountain. Suddenly, behind me, I heard a noise like a police siren. One of the elderly women clients was clutching the pommel of her saddle, looking down at the river a few hundred feet below, and screaming. Her *arriero* stared at her in astonishment, his hand on the reins of the stationary horse. He spoke no English but could understand the "No!" that she fitted in between screams. We also stared. If she had a fear of heights, someone suggested, perhaps she should dismount and walk. She did, and the screams only got louder.

Bill told her they'd better have a little chat. The path got considerably worse later on in the trek and if vertigo was such a problem she was in for a bad time. So were the rest of the group. "I didn't know," she sobbed, "I prepared for the trip by riding in the woods. I was fine there." It looked as though we'd have to turn back. This suggestion, however, activated her husband, who up till that time had been gazing at the scenery. "For Christ's sake, Martha, get a grip!" And to our amazement and her great credit, she did. Occasionally faced with a precipitous drop, her grip loosened and some screams escaped, but she learned to shut her eyes and allow her *arriero* to lead the horse. He was very kind: "*Venga, venga abuelita,*" he murmured soothingly as he patted her knee. 'Come, come little grandmother.'

I learned a lot about horses' capabilities during this trek. In England I'd never have dreamed of asking a horse to climb steps roughly hewn from rock, to ford fast rivers over slippery boulders, or climb a pass of 15,000 feet. Not, come to think of it, that there's much opportunity of tackling such terrain in Britain. And as well as finding out what horses can do, I learned what we can do for them in return. Less-developed countries are not known for their kindness to animals, but our Peruvian muleteers made sure that the horses, donkeys and mules had adequate grazing each night and an hour's break without their loads in the middle of the day. This consideration was balanced by their disturbing custom of cutting off a sick donkey's ear to allow the disease to run out, and shoeing a nervous horse by throwing it on its side, tying the unwanted legs together and banging the shoe on each outstretched hoof in turn, while an assistant distracted the animal with a cord twisted around its upper lip.

ʊ   ʊ   ʊ

This wasn't my first experience of horse management in the third world. George and I had hired two ponies in Ethiopia to transport us into the Simien Mountains. One was a pack animal and we were to take turns in riding the other. George had only been on a horse a couple of times before, so was more than willing to accept the guiding hand of Ephram, the owner. I, however, waved him away airily in the knowledge that with my experience of both English and western styles of riding I could control any horse. Not this one, I couldn't. It walked briskly off in the wrong direction while I tried everything in my repertoire to turn it around. Hauling on one rein had no effect, nor did neck reining. Humiliated, I had to accept help. It wasn't until I watched an Ethiopian steer his mule that I learned how the locals do it: whack the animal on the side of the face with a stick. It soon learns to turn sharply in the opposite direction at the mere glimpse of the whip.

Coming down the steep mountain trails where the path is made of boulders and deep mud, the Ethiopians didn't bother with steering. We always got off and walked these sections, not trusting ourselves to stay in a lurching saddle angled at 45 degrees. The Ethiopians just swung themselves back to front, gripping the high cantle of the saddle while the mule (valued well above horses) picked its own way down the slope.

Ephram demonstrated other local methods of horse management, though with no common language our miming abilities were put to the test. Most evenings, as we pitched our tent and cooked our dinner, he'd hobble the ponies by tying their heads to a foreleg – an effective and not unkind method that allowed them to graze with unrestricted movement but prevented them from throwing up their heads and galloping off. One evening I'd set up the tent and came to tell George that supper was ready, and I found him hopping on one leg in front of Ephram, the other leg hooked over an arm, while he pulled his head towards his knee. Ephram understood this extraordinary display much faster than I did. George was reminding him to hobble the ponies. The Ethiopian did his 'It's alright, don't worry' gesture (which he had come to use frequently) so we left him chewing his way through that day's ration of *injera* (Ethiopian bread resembling grey foam rubber) and went to our tent. Early the next morning George, up early as usual, came to tell me something was dreadfully wrong with the ponies. I crawled out of my sleeping bag and followed him a short way from the campsite to where they were both lying stretched out on the grass looking faint. Anxiously, I urged them to their feet; they were not sick but were dead lame. I interrupted Ephram's breakfast of more grey foam rubber and insisted he came with me. When I pointed out the ponies staggering around on three legs he gestured 'It's all right, don't worry'. I gasped when he produced a knife, wondering what gruesome demonstration of Ethiopian surgery we were about to witness. Within seconds of taking hold of a limp foreleg, he held up the source of the problem: a thin piece of cord tied tightly round the animal's leg just below the knee. The other horse was released from its 'hobble' the same way. He smiled at our consternation and shrugged off our anger. 'After all,' he was probably saying, 'it works!' Sure enough, by the time we were ready to leave the horses were sound again, but he never again used that method of restraining them during the night.

ᘐ ᘐ ᘐ

After the Peru trip I wrote to Morgan's for a catalogue. My plans took shape around the pictures of horses and riders fully prepared to spend several days or weeks in the wilderness, and I knew I would be able to do my ride. All that remained was when and where, and, to some people, why? Was I going to make it a feat? To ride from John O'Groats to Land's End, for instance? The answer was emphatically no. I've always disliked the publicity given to travellers who set out to beat some sort of record. For me it's the travel itself that is sufficient, the opportunity to see beautiful scenery, observe wildlife and, when I could get up the courage, meet new people; that was my Achilles heel as a traveller – I was shy and it always took an effort to talk to new people. So travelling alone, I was not at all afraid of any physical risk but the need to make contact with strangers was always an anxiety.

I couldn't decide where to go. I was ashamed to admit it, but I wasn't brave enough to do a solo horse trip in the developing world. There were just too many challenges, and the end of my marriage to feisty George had left me more shaken than I wanted to acknowledge. I still fancied Britain, with a nod at T S Eliot's lines: "We shall not cease from exploration. And the end of all our exploring will be to return to where we started from and know the place for the first time." But I hadn't come to the end of all my exploring. . .

I know, Iceland! It had all the requirements: lovely scenery, a tough breed of native pony and friendly people who generally spoke English.

I'd been there and loved it. I tried out the idea by rather casually mentioning in my Christmas letter that I was going to buy a native pony in Iceland and do a long-distance ride. I received a reply from a horsey friend: "Ireland! What a great idea. A Connemara pony would be strong enough and it's such a beautiful country. And they love horses." Oh. My handwriting. . . well, let's think about Ireland then. It had never come into my reckoning, perhaps because of a very wet family holiday there when we children had sulkily squelched up Ireland's highest mountain in mist and rain. All I could remember was sinking into bog up to the top of my thigh, and weeping with the misery of it all, while my father retrieved my missing plimsoll from the black, watery depths. But now, suddenly, everything fell into place. Ireland was an ideal choice. Scenic, safe, English-speaking. . . perfect!

I still didn't know *when* I would do my ride since I couldn't imagine ever having enough money. I needed enough capital to buy a pony. This, I thought, would be the only way to do the ride cheaply. I could sell the animal at the end of the trip and since it would, if all went well, be a fitter and more worldly-wise pony by then, there was no reason why I shouldn't sell at a profit. Hiring would be expensive and would force me to do a circular tour. Apart from the lack of money, there were other considerations that made me wonder if I was really ready for this. It was several years since I'd even been on a horse and nearly 25 years had passed since we'd sold Sonnet. It all became a bit overwhelming.

Then came a bit of Peruvian serendipity which served as a dress rehearsal. In 1983, when leading one of my Andean treks, I had to evacuate a sick client. Lynn wasn't dangerously ill, but she had acute mountain sickness caused by the thin air of the Andes and needed to get down to a lower altitude. Fortunately I had a co-leader (a new recruit who was learning the ropes) so was able to leave him in charge while an *arriero* and I escorted

Lynn on horseback down to the valley and a bus to Cusco. At that point she was feeling so much better I discussed with Faustino the possibility of my rejoining the group. They were an exceptionally nice bunch of people, the scenery was superlative and the weather fine. Peter, my co-leader, and the group could have managed without me but I wasn't sure that I could manage without them. Lynn encouraged this plan. She was happy to take the bus to Cusco and spend a few days on her own before we rejoined her.

Faustino agreed to rent me a horse so that we could ride together and intercept the group. If we left early, he said, the trip could be done in two days. At 6.30 the next morning he had introduced me to Flaco, a scrawny black pony of 14 hands or so. My luggage was in two flour sacks tied each side of the saddle, but what drew my eye was Flaco's head collar. Made from strong leather decorated with silver rivets, it looked practical as well as versatile. Not so the saddle, which was old and poorly padded, with stirrups of unequal length. I mounted and followed Faustino as we trotted briskly through the village. We trotted briskly towards the mountains, and we trotted briskly to the settlement that marked the trail head. I begged Faustino to slacken his pace and let me go on foot for a while. I could barely stand up. My thighs were rubbed raw, my knees felt as though six-inch nails had been driven through them, and my bottom was pulverised.

Faustino had told me he would find us lodging for the night on the way to the high pass, so when we came to natural hot springs I told him that I was going to have a bath. He settled down to watch with interest.

In a high valley surrounded by snow peaks, a one-room hovel stood alone under the white bulk of Mount Ausangate. This was our shelter for the night, the home of an alpaca farmer and his daughter. We were given a shy welcome and while Faustino caught up on gossip, I climbed a nearby hill to watch the setting sun give a golden outline to the woolly alpacas.

Returning to the *casita* in the failing light I ducked under the low door and groped my way to a seat in the corner covered by a sheepskin. It was surprisingly comfortable. The girl handed me a plate of tiny boiled potatoes, to which I added cheese brought from the town. When darkness came at 6.30 we prepared for sleep. The girl watched enthralled as I blew up my air mattress, stuffed a T-shirt with a sweater to make a pillow, and pulled my sleeping bag out of its stuff bag. Faustino, who spoke Quechua, relished his role as man of the world and explained the use of each item, but when she saw me climb into the blue cocoon sleeping bag, it was too much for her – she burst into giggles and little explosions of laughter accompanied the rest of my preparations. When she was ready for sleep she just curled up on a pile of sheepskins.

Faustino and the girl got up at 4.30 to round up the horses and start the cooking fire, fuelled with llama dung which was white with frost. I shivered in my blue cocoon until it was light enough to see my surroundings. That was when I discovered that the chair I'd reclined on the previous evening was in fact half a sheep carcass with a well-sprung rib cage.

We set off at sunrise and headed for the pass. I led Flaco and we both gasped for breath as we toiled our way upwards. At 16,000 feet every step is an effort, but the view from the top – a broken semi-circle of snow-covered peaks with a whipped-cream glacier below us – was breathtaking in the best sense of the word. And after that it was downhill all the way to my rendezvous with the group.

Back in Cusco I bought a head collar just like Flaco's. I had taken the first step.

Chapter 3

I put in my order to Morgans: saddlebag, nosebag and a single-stake hobble. In the absence of any advice, I'd given the subject of tethers and hobbles a lot of thought; it was fortunate that I'd seen so many varieties of horse restraints while travelling abroad since the English seem to have a blind spot on the matter. The horsey people I spoke to were shocked even at the idea of a nosebag, let alone something as gypsy-like as a tether or hobble. They were not much more helpful over gear for me. Since I hadn't been to a saddler selling riding clothes for about 20 years, I browsed through a smart shop in London. It seemed that nothing had changed since I was a teenager; there was no innovative, lightweight rain gear, no saddlebags and certainly no hobbles or tethers. The horse's comfort was catered for but not the rider's; appearance was put before utility, echoing the Pony Club dictum that 'the rider should always be smartly turned out'.

There was no illustration of how to use the single-stake hobble I was purchasing, but I assumed it was actually a form of tether, tying the horse by a leg rather than by the neck, which seemed a good idea. Horses' necks are designed for pulling, but not so their slender legs, so I assumed that a leg tether need not be as strong. We had tethered Johnny from a neck strap, using a chain and a heavy iron spike to drive into the ground with an equally heavy hammer. For this trip I had to reduce the weight wherever possible, so bought a nylon rope instead of a chain, and in a camping catalogue I found a light aluminium dog-tether which looked like a giant corkscrew and was almost impossible to pull out of the ground using brute force.

It was much easier visualising the horse's night-time arrangements than my own. I was planning to camp, which was fine. What was not fine was that I would have to ask permission to camp in farmers' fields and that brought up the spectre of 'batey' farmers. Kate and I, like most children raised in the country, had done our share of trespassing. Every now and then we were caught and roared at by the farmer. The conditioned reflex was so enduring that even in adulthood a glimpse of the landowner while mushrooming would send me quivering behind a bush, and cause me to turn back and quietly retrace my steps rather than follow a public footpath through a farmyard. So the thought of having to ride a horse up to a farmhouse each evening to ask for a field was dreadful. I mentioned this anxiety to an aristocratic Irish acquaintance. Suppose I trespassed without realising it? "Oh there's nothing to worry about," said Kieran, "they might threaten you with a shotgun, but they'd never hurt you." I was not reassured. Danger is part and parcel of adventurous travel, and there's something almost refreshing about rational fear; it's irrational fear that's so debilitating because of the feeling of foolishness that goes with it. It is hard to admit that someone who has survived detention in Uganda, with her nerves intact, quails at the thought of making a phone call, entering a crowded room or ringing a doorbell.

When I was married to George it was easy. He had no social fears and, in his company, nor had I. Now I was alone I wanted to learn to like being alone. To travel with a companion would have been a cop-out. My Connemara pony, I reckoned, would provide the company I needed.

As well as my conscious worries about farmers I had a variety of subconscious anxieties that surfaced in a rich crop of dreams. Many of them had elements of realism, as in the one where I had just bought a horse and had pitched my tent in a busy campsite. The field was full of tents, spaced as neatly and regularly as war cemetery crosses. Through this order my disorderly horse wandered, crawling into other people's tents and making a thorough nuisance of itself. I decided I must tether it with the new hobble. It was only after I bent down to attach the strap to its leg that I realised, to my horror, that I hadn't inspected all of the horse when I bought it. It was a fine looking animal – from the body up – but its legs were as tiny and slender as a sheep's. No way could it carry me and the luggage.

Another dream had me wandering in a maze of urban alleyways, and I was angry with my horse for sneaking up to the back doors of the houses and ringing the doorbell. Then I saw, walking across a field, a well-dressed man in a suit with a copy of the *New Yorker* magazine sticking out of his breast pocket. I asked my horse if it subscribed to the *New Yorker*; if so, perhaps we could share a copy? To which the horse replied, "I'm a *Daily Express* man myself."

I set a date. In 1983 I was offered four trips to lead, which would give me enough money to buy a horse in 1984. I was determined to set out at the end of April. By March I had most of my equipment laid out in my sister's house where I was living, and a rough idea of what I wanted to do. Since I planned to buy a Connemara pony it was logical to start in Connemara, which I learned was not a county but a region – a fat peninsula, really – in the west of Ireland encompassing most of Co Galway. But I still lacked the most important piece of equipment – a saddle. I thought longingly of Tara's military saddle and remembered ruefully how much we had hated it. Perhaps I could advertise for one in *Horse and Hound*? Then Kate mentioned casually that one of the other mums she chatted up outside the school had told her she had a saddle in the attic and didn't know what to do with it. It had been given to her husband by a landowner to 'get rid of' but they knew nothing about horses nor how to go about selling such a thing. Kate went to have a look. "It's a funny sort of saddle. A bit like Tara's. But it looks OK." I phoned Jenny and arranged to come over. Propped up in the corner of her conservatory was a brand new military saddle! I couldn't believe it. Designed for long journeys, its deep seat and high arch made it comfortable for both horse and rider. The suede knee rolls on the saddle flaps would add to my comfort and the plentiful supply of D rings on the extensions at the back meant secure attachment for the saddlebags. I was euphoric at this find. Neither Jenny nor I had any notion how much a saddle like this was worth, but she was happy with the £50 I offered. I took it home, saddled the back of my armchair, and gloated. Bored friends were brought to see it and I couldn't resist stroking it whenever I passed. I took my acquisition of such a fine saddle to be a sign that God was on my side.

Kate was a good antidote to all this gushing optimism.

"You think this trip will be fun?" she responded to some casual remark of mine. "You'll wake up to hear drip drip drip on the tent roof. You'll pack up in the rain, ride 10 miles in the wrong direction and it'll still be raining when you pitch camp. You'll be trotting along and there'll be 'clip-clop squidge clop' and you'll realise the horse has lost a shoe. You'll ask where the nearest farrier lives and they'll tell you 'We don't have one. There wasn't the demand, you know'. You'll be lying in your sodden tent and you'll hear," – and she did a passable imitation of a horse coughing

– "outside. Or you'll go to catch it in the morning and find it lying down looking ill. Or lame... I wonder how you'll get rid of it for insurance purposes... push it over the cliffs or under a double-decker, I suppose."

Kate had actually raised some points I had decided not to think about too much. What would I do if the horse went lame or became ill? I didn't know but wrote 'insurance' on my list of things to do when once I'd bought a pony, since I couldn't insure a non-existent animal. I knew shoeing would be a problem, but there was nothing much I could do there except contact local riding schools to find out which farrier they used; and as for getting lost, this was inevitable since I'm devoid of any sense of direction. I can't even find my way out of a house (usually opening the broom cupboard door as I say goodbye over my shoulder) let alone a town. I need a distinctive landmark, like a mountain range which I hoped I'd find in Ireland. And I know how to use a compass.

I was impressed with what I'd accomplished by the end of April. It had been the usual effort to get all my publishing work up to date and organised for my assistant to take over. A week before departure I needed one final piece of equipment. "What's that you're making?" asked six-year-old Nicholas as I sat sewing.

"It's a bag to carry everything I need during the day when I'm riding."

"Oh yes, I know, like perfume and cheese-and-chutney rolls." Just so.

I also had to adapt the saddlebags to fit my new saddle and it seemed a good idea to try everything on something a little more horse-shaped than my armchair. An acquaintance was willing to lend her pony as a tailor's dummy and I was relieved to find my design for the cheese-'n'-chutney-roll bag was perfect to attach to the D-rings in front of the saddle and could quickly be detached to carry as a handbag. The big saddlebags seemed all right, though I'd need to add some extra straps and an additional girth to prevent them bouncing up and down when

I trotted. The final adjustment would have to be made after I bought a pony. And that was the one item still missing.

I had no idea how to look for a pony in Ireland (remember, this was long before the internet). I didn't know if there was an equivalent to *Horse and Hound*, with its pages of advertisements of horses for sale, and anyway I wanted to buy a Connemara pony in Connemara, which limited the search. At least I had a friend in Dublin: Dorothy, who had shared the ill-fated Lynn's tent in Peru. Her cousin, John Daly, happened to be one of the best-known breeders of Connemara ponies and show jumpers in Ireland. Then there was Kieran who had once hired horses from a chap called Willie Leahy in Loughrea. "Try Willie," Kieran said. "Sorry I can't help," said John Daly, "but try Willie Leahy, and come and visit me when you're underway." So I wrote to Willie Leahy, found Loughrea on the map, not far from Galway, and knew that here at least was a likely source of good, strong ponies since Willie also organised horse treks.

My equipment was complete. For tack I had the saddle and girth, a snaffle bit and reins, plus little straps to attach it to my silver-studded Peruvian head collar, and an Ecuadorian sheepskin to guard against saddle sores. Then there were the two saddlebags (the small cheese-'n'-chutney-roll one for the front and the capacious American one behind), the tether rope ending in a strong clip, a nylon dog lead for leading the pony or tying up for brief periods, the hobble and corkscrew picket, a nosebag and a plastic collapsible bucket. That took care of the horse. I was equipped as for backpacking, with a rain cape designed for cyclists, waterproof chaps which I could put on over my hiking boots, a tiny 'Peapod' tent, ThermaRest mattress and a light sleeping bag, a water flask (which clipped to the saddle D rings, along with the tether rope), maps, books, compass, camera, binoculars, a change of clothing, and all the other things needed for safety, comfort and enjoyment, including a small transistor radio. Altogether it weighed about 50lb.

I'd given so much thought to what to bring and how the horse would carry it, I'd forgotten to consider how I myself would carry it to Ireland. I'd chosen to book a coach and ferry because the luggage is loaded on in London and doesn't have to be touched again until the coach arrives in Dublin. Or so I thought. But I still had to get it to the coach. Kate took me to the local train station in the afternoon of April 26th where three people were needed to load the five bags onto the train. And these weren't bags in the normal traveller's sense of the word, these were five plastic bin liners, supposedly extra strong but already starting to split.

Since the coach left Gloucester Road at 8am I thought it provident to spend the night with friends in London, even though it meant bringing all my luggage to Clapham. As the taxi driver helped me out at the aptly named Shamrock Road address, I thought I should explain this abundance of oddly shaped bags. "So you're goin' to be 'orsin' around in Ireland, are you? Well, that's summink, I suppose!"

Chapter 4

"Dear Kate," I wrote from Dublin. "No, I haven't got a horse, I've got luggage." The sheer awfulness of getting all those bags to Dublin and then to Galway pushed all other thoughts from my mind. The plan had been so sensible: book a coach direct from London to Dublin so I wouldn't have to carry my uncarryable luggage. The coach, I assumed, went onto the ferry. Not so, it turned out. The coach dropped us on the dock at Holyhead, seemingly miles from the boat, and we were told to remove all our luggage. Another coach would meet us on the other side, so they said. Of course there were no trolleys to be seen, but since I couldn't physically carry all my stuff I managed to find one lurking in some dark recess and was just piling my luggage on when an officious man appeared and said, "You're doing it all wrong." He took all my things off and loaded the trolley with cases belonging to a girl standing next to me. Then came my oddly shaped and already splitting plastic bags. The girl was most grateful and I was not particularly gracious as I pushed the thing towards the mass of people waiting to board the boat. Then, of course, I wasn't allowed to take the trolley onto the boat so I had to heave my stuff on board in relays, banging the backs of people's knees as I went. Some turned round to remonstrate but after a look at my furious face, changed their minds. I just left it all in a pile near the gangway.

At least the sea was calm, and so was I until I had to get the luggage off the boat and into the next coach. Fortunately someone helped me this time, but my troubles weren't over. Dun Laoghaire, Dublin's port, is so near the city they hadn't bothered to provide a proper coach. This one had no luggage compartment. I struggled inside with my five bags, clunking people on the head with the saddle, which was starting to emerge from its torn plastic bag, and swearing instead of apologising. After a short while the bus stopped by what looked like a bombsite and everyone got out. Or rather, most people got out. I didn't. After we were underway I learned from the driver that this was the only stop in Dublin (the bus was continuing to some other town) so he had to make a special stop while I heaved and clonked and swore my luggage down the aisle and traffic piled up behind.

I did manage to flag down a taxi, however, and had a lovely warm welcome from Dorothy. Then the whole process had to be repeated next day when I took another bus to Galway, except that there was no question of getting a trolley to take the bags 'five minutes' from the bus stop to the nearest left-luggage place in Galway station. It took me a good 20 minutes, again working in relays and just hoping no one would investigate the pile of bulky plastic bags apparently abandoned by the bus stop (in London, at that time, the area would have been cordoned off and a controlled explosion would have taken place – Galway was less IRA conscious). By that time I was so exhausted I just checked into the first B&B I could find. Serious horse-hunting would begin tomorrow.

I had a list of telephone numbers and stood in a Galway phone box, steeling myself to call these possible horse-dealers one by one. I'd already made an appointment to see Willie Leahy in Loughrea, but there were several other recommendations which I knew I should check out. None could help. The last one was Lady Someone who, I'd been told, knew all about Connemara ponies. I'd found two listings in the phone book, one for Lord Someone and the other *The* Lord Someone. 'Lord' without the definite article sounded marginally less frightening so, quaking, I tried that number. Then to the question "Who shall I say is phoning?" I had to go into a bumbling explanation of who I was and what I wanted. Her Ladyship was very nice but terribly busy with the trustees so couldn't really help. And that was enough. I'd made an effort to broaden my search, but it all came down to Willie Leahy.

Willie had made it clear on the phone that there was no point in my heading out to Loughrea until later in the week. All his ponies were out at grass, but he would be bringing them in soon to prepare for the first trek of the year which was heading out on Monday. Could I come on Thursday, when he should have something to show me? It was Tuesday, and I didn't want to fritter my time away in Galway, so thought I'd take a look at the Aran Islands, or at least the largest one, Inishmore.

It was such a beautiful morning that I decided to walk the five miles to the ferry, rather than take the bus. The landscape was an appetiser for the Connemara countryside that was to come: dry-stone walls, thatched cottages and fields full of flowers. Everyone said "hello" and at every step I felt better about travelling alone.

I'd expected Aran to be touristy, but far from it. On arrival, visitors had to climb up a vertical metal ladder to reach the pier. The Americans on the boat could hardly believe it. Lots of "Oh my"s. Then we had the choice of jaunting car, bike or foot to get around; I chose the latter because I thought I'd see more. It was still a cloudless day and I walked along a narrow lane with tiny fields enclosed in stone walls and absolutely choc-a-bloc with wild flowers: primroses, celandine, cowslips, violets, and several I didn't know including lots of lovely purple-coloured orchids. When I came across the first one I was hugely excited, thinking I'd found something very rare since it was so pretty. Then I saw fields full of them and realised that these early purple orchids are to the west of Ireland what dandelions are at home.

I ate my lunch on a natural rock bench overlooking a rock-and-sand bay. There was no-one around. Then I cut up through the fields, climbing all those wobbly stone walls to the upper road where I hoped to find a B&B. The first village was deserted, but as I walked on to the next one I fell in with an old fellow in a peaked cap who was quite talkative. I was relieved that I could understand him; most of the local folk who I'd overheard chatting to each other were speaking Irish. "The sweaters? You won't find people knitting them by hand these days. They have knitting machines. And the wool comes from the mainland. Not many sheep here any more." We walked on in silence for a while. I ventured something about the lovely weather. "'Tis awful dry. Not right for the time of year." I didn't share his gloom about the unremitting sunshine until Mrs O'Flaherty at the B&B told me I couldn't take a bath because of the water restrictions.

She showed me the route to the most important historic site on the islands, Dun Aengus, a prehistoric (1st-century AD) stone ring right at the edge of a 270-foot cliff. The fortress itself is very fine and the location stupendous. I walked along the cliff edge in the late afternoon sunshine and marvelled. The cliff is not just sheer, it's Shakespearean sheer, seeming to 'o'er hang and jutty his confounded base, swilled with the wild and wasteful ocean'. The wild and wasteful ocean is eating into the confounded base so dramatically that sooner or later it's all going to fall into the sea. Meanwhile there are clumps of pink thrift and other flowers, and geometric-shaped slabs of limestone looking hand-laid and levelled, with rectangular chasms going down to bottomless depths, and lots of noisy sea birds. I was entranced and walked for miles before realising that it was nearly nightfall.

It was 10 o'clock before I got back to the B&B so Mrs O'Flaherty was naturally worried, but after I'd apologised we settled down to a cosy hour by the fire watching a TV programme on the new Northern Ireland Forum. It was my first introduction to The Troubles from a local viewpoint. When I was talking about my proposed trip in England, some people were surprised that I would venture to 'such a dangerous country'. Hard to imagine now, but in 1984, only five years after Lord Mountbatten was assassinated by the IRA in Co Sligo, that was not an unusual opinion. However, I never met anyone in the Republic who had any sympathy for the IRA or who considered unity a reasonable goal, although I wrote in my diary that 'even after a week of talking to people and reading Irish history I feel that Irish unity is the most moral goal. Whether it can ever, or should ever, be achieved is another matter'.

"Isn't he good-looking, God bless him," Mrs O'Flaherty said, pointing at the screen.

"Who is he?"

She looked at me sharply. "The Taoiseach!" I still didn't understand but kept quiet; clearly I had a way to go before I could safely discuss Irish politics.

I'd arranged to meet Willie Leahy that morning in Loughrea. He met me off the bus and I explained my plans over a glass of Guinness, before heading out in the drizzle to look at some horses. Only look, mind you, they were loose in a huge field, and Willie said that catching them was not an option. Not until the weekend, anyway. Nor could I get any idea from him about how much a suitable pony might cost. It was all very frustrating. I spent the night in an icy B&B with no hot water (I'd taken the precaution of bringing my toothbrush and purse, knowing I'd probably miss the last bus back to Galway) and looked at more loose horses, and more rain, the next day. The experience was conclusive in one sense – I decided that without my own transport I was pretty much stuck in Loughrea, and since Willie had lots of horses and seemed willing to sell me one – eventually – I might as well collect my luggage and camp nearby until he was ready to do business. Eva, his assistant, assured me that with a trek starting on Monday, he would have to bring in the horses the following day.

I'd been dreading another tussle with the luggage, but for once luck was on my side. The bus left from just outside the station, where I'd stored my stuff, and had a spacious baggage compartment at the back. Eva was there to meet me, as promised, and after dumping my things we went straight to the field to help in the roundup. And roundup is the right word – the scene bore more resemblance to Texas than the British Isles. There were horses galloping in all directions pursued by whooping boys on horseback, sheep scattering, dogs barking, people shouting conflicting instructions and a happy air of confusion and chaos. Finally, as dusk came, the excited horses were all penned in a corral so the ones needed for the trek could be caught and loaded onto the waiting horsebox. Even this wasn't easy in the failing light with thirty or so horses milling around and occasionally making unsuccessful breaks for freedom. I kept an eye on the two grey mares that Eva had picked out for me, to make sure they were included in the selection. One was a very pretty dark dapple grey with a small head and slender legs – typical of the lighter build of Connemara pony that is popular now. The other was also Connemara but the old-fashioned type: heavier, stronger, not so elegant and with hairy fetlocks like Tara's. But I'd admired her general bearing and action as she trotted round the field with her head held high and long mane and tail flowing. I was glad they were both grey (the heavier one was almost white); apart from being photogenic it made for good visibility in poor light conditions. Both important qualities, I thought.

It was after 10 by the time the horses were crammed into the horsebox. A sheep and her crippled lamb were put in the passenger seat, a few dogs stuffed in behind them, and they were driven off to the stable. Eva and I, plus some other helpers, came by car. At midnight we were sitting in Willie's kitchen, ravenously eating good wholesome farmhouse fare of Mother's Pride bread and processed cheese while I wondered if I'd be able to pitch my tent for the first time in the dark. Willie lent me a powerful torch, which helped, and rather to my surprise I got it up easily apart from kneeling in a cowpat. And also to my surprise I felt safe and happy in the night although the field was some way from the house. It was the first time I'd slept alone in a tent.

Next day I was up bright and early, and expecting a clamour of activity by 8.30 in a farming household of five children, I knocked at the door. Silence. I knocked again and Willie appeared in his pyjamas and very kindly cooked me breakfast. I was in Ireland quite a while before it sank in that the Irish don't get up early. Even farmers would emerge from their rooms rubbing their eyes at 9.30, and when I first made the mistake of answering the B&B question "When would you like breakfast?" with "8 o'clock please" I was firmly put in my place. "We'll make it 9 o'clock, shall we?"

Most Saturdays are horse-show days so Willie and his sons were busy getting the show jumpers ready. The ubiquitous Eva was around, however, and helped me saddle the larger of the two grey mares for my eagerly anticipated try-out. I ran what I hoped looked like an expert eye over her and my hand down her legs, trying to remember choice bits of *Buying a Pony* advice from my childhood books. 'The pony should have a nice wide forehead and large kind eyes' – tick that one off – 'a broad chest, sloping shoulders, slanting pasterns and round hooves'. OK for these too.

'Avoid a horse with a neck like a plank of wood'. That one had Kate and me falling about with laughter since Sonnet's neck could have come straight from the timber yard. This pony, however, had a powerful arched neck like a Leonardo da Vinci horse, and with her white coat, dappled grey on the quarters and abundant mane and tail, she fitted her name: Belle. She also had a rather endearing military moustache.

I was pleased to find my saddle and the Peruvian head collar fitted perfectly and that my improvised bit attachment also worked well. I rode nervously out of the yard; it had been at least 10 years since I'd been in charge of a horse and several months since Belle had been ridden. Everyone had advised me that I must buy a fit pony or it would be prone to saddle sores and other health problems. They had also told me to get myself in shape for riding or I would suffer a similar fate. I reckoned Belle and I would just have to get fit together. I was already thinking in terms of 'we' after only about half a mile. Belle was very fresh from her months of inactivity and night in the stable. She walked briskly along, ears sharply pricked, eyes wide, nostrils dilated, ready to shy at any strange object. But when a car came, she passed the most important test of being quiet in traffic. She had smooth, comfortable paces and was responsive to the aids. I also tested her willingness to stand quietly when tied – a very important point – while I went into a shop to get something to eat (I hadn't liked to hang around Willie's at meal times but there were no restaurants nearby so I was getting pretty hungry by 3 o'clock in the afternoon). She was also the right height, given all the mounting and dismounting I was going to do: about 14.2hh.

When I returned to the stable yard I was almost sure that Belle would be my choice, but I still had to try her with saddlebags. She didn't seem to mind when I heaved them onto her back (although they were lighter than usual without the tent etc) and walked along quietly enough when I gingerly led her down the road. I had a hard time swinging my leg over the hump of the bag behind the saddle when I mounted, but Belle stood calmly and again walked willingly under the unaccustomed weight and encumbrance. I was hugely pleased and relieved to find the bags so trouble-free; all I had to do now was finish making the belly strap to prevent them from bouncing up and down when I trotted.

There was still the dark grey pony to try out; Willie had been particularly enthusiastic about this mare and so was I when I first saw her. She was prettier that Belle with more quality, but she was quite a bit smaller and lacked Belle's air of reliability and common sense. She had been nervous and difficult to catch in the corral and when I approached her to put on the bridle she threw up her head and rolled her eyes in fear. At some stage in her life she must have been roughly treated; I didn't want a head-shy animal. My early negative feelings were reinforced during the subsequent ride. The pony was nervous of cars and had a hard mouth. She was actually a very comfortable ride but I just didn't like her so wasn't willing to see any of her good points. I'd decided on Belle and all that was left was to find out whether I could afford her.

In Willie's bathroom, turned face to the wall lest it discourage customers, is a cautionary verse about buying a horse from an Irishman, 'Caveat Emptor'. In this poem there was no difficulty in getting the Irishman to talk about the deal in the first place, yet I spent the rest of Saturday trying to gain an audience with Willie. I sat in the yard sewing my saddle straps and hoping to waylay him during his brief appearances, or lurked in the kitchen where his hospitable wife fed me cups of tea while visitors and family came and went, wondering who I was and what I was doing there. I began to ask the same questions myself; it was a good lesson in humility. In England and Dublin my plans had excited interest and admiration, puffing my ego into a buoyant state. Here at Aille Cross people had other things on their minds; the first trek of the year was imminent with many preparations necessary: all the horses had to be shod, the tack checked and allocated, the hotel reservations confirmed and picnic food bought. No wonder Willie was hard to pin down. In the end I made an appointment for a business talk at 10 o'clock on Sunday. I felt so powerless that I looked on mutely as Belle was loaded into a horsebox with other trek ponies. It was Eva who gently told the boys that I was hoping to buy the pony so would want to go riding on her today.

Willie had suggested that I join his trek so that I could get to know the pony and the local terrain before heading out on my own. It seemed a good idea but I didn't want to commit myself until Belle finally became mine and that happy event receded further when the appointed 10 o'clock came and Willie was banging on horse shoes and obviously couldn't be disturbed. I hung around, clearing my throat and passing the wrong tools until he gave up and came to sit beside me on the bench. My heart pounded as I said that I wanted to buy Belle (he already knew that) and what would be the price. "I've already told you it would be somewhere between 700 and 800 (punts or Irish pounds (IR£))." "Did you?" I couldn't remember having that conversation. "Would you, um, consider 600?" Willie turned to look at me. "I can get more than that in the market," he said, "for horse meat." Of course that concluded the conversation, as he knew it would. "I can't possibly sell for less than 775 with the new set of shoes." I agreed. What else could I do? Translated into sterling his price was about £650, which didn't sound so bad, though it was well over the £500 I'd given myself as a ceiling. But she was a good pony, not just for my purposes but for anyone's, so I should be able to get a good price for her when I sold her.

So on May 6th 1984 I finally became the owner of the pony of my childhood dreams. I rode exultant down the narrow Irish lanes and all those birthday-cake wishes crowded together as I said aloud, "You're mine! You're mine!"

Chapter 5

I couldn't quite believe that I was a horse owner again after 24 years. I kept visiting Belle in her stable to make sure she was real. And I asserted my ownership by changing her name. She was now Mollie, named after the vain pony in *Animal Farm* that hides ribbons in her stall, runs away from the fighting and finally defects from the cause. Since this was 1984, a nod towards George Orwell seemed appropriate and I wondered whether my mare would stick with me through thick or thin. There was a touch of vanity about her: she obviously dyed her mane – why else would the roots be dark?

When I shook hands with Willie over the purchase of Belle/Mollie I also told him I'd like to join the trek for the agreed price of IR£10 since I would now be riding my own pony and would camp rather than stay in hotels with the rest of the group. The trek would begin the following day when the horses, including Mollie, would be transported to Oughterard, the beginning of the Connemara Trail, to be introduced to their riders.

There were five in the group: two couples and a single woman. All were experienced riders, and must have thought I was very strange, going off to sleep in a tent at the end of each day. I was in too much pain to worry about what they thought. My plan had been to get riding-fit gradually by walking on my own feet a good part of each day, so six to eight hours in the saddle was pure torture; I had stabbing pains in my knees and my bottom was so sore I considered a transplant. When we dismounted for a snack I had to stand for a while admiring the view while persuading my legs to straighten so I could walk normally.

On the first day we had a picnic in the grounds of a ruined castle, while the horses grazed the close-cropped grass. A sign said that it was Aughnanure Castle, but there was no other information. These days it is an established tourist attraction owned by Heritage Ireland, with helpful information boards telling you what you are seeing and a ticket booth – and no admission for horses. On our trek I wandered around inside the tower and through the tumbled ruins, making up the history as I went. As we munched our sandwiches Willie gave us a few facts, with embellishments from one of the group who knew his Irish history. The Norman part was extended by the O'Flahertys as a defence against rival clans in the 14th and 15th centuries. Supposedly the old gate into Galway carries an inscription which reads something like 'Oh Lord protect me from the fearsome O'Flahertys'. They were imaginative hosts: under the chair of the guest of honour in the long, splendid dining room there was a trap door, ready to open at the flick of a switch if the guest had not behaved appropriately. I liked the story about the lady pirate, Gráinne O'Malley, who married into the O'Flaherty clan. She was captured by the wicked English and brought before Queen Elizabeth I who, having heard of her exuberant dancing, commanded a performance. Gráinne danced her way out of an open window and escaped.

As the trek progressed I became a little more used to those hours in the saddle and appreciated this chance to get to know Mollie and discover what she could do. And that included dealing with bogs. This being the first trek of the season, Willie had to prepare the trails as we went, cutting branches to provide footing over the squelchy bits. I was amazed that the horses would walk over these and they also walked happily over a long rubber strip that Willie used to cover a particularly tricky stretch. It was a holy carpet, having been used to cushion the wheels of the Popemobile during John-Paul's visit to Ireland. Despite these bridges, two of the horses slipped off the prepared route and sunk up to their bellies in bog. It was terrifying to watch, so I couldn't imagine what it was like for the riders. One woman hopped off onto firm ground as the horse went in but the other stayed put, frozen with fear, and Willie had to tell her what to do. Once free from the weight of the rider, the horses managed to get out – after a struggle. Willie was very calm about it all so I suppose it happens fairly regularly. Thank goodness Mollie understood bogs and walked quietly and carefully over the branches and matting.

Apart from learning how a horse copes with bogs, I discovered that they can swim in the sea. Mannin Bay has a long, sandy beach and we had come prepared with our swimsuits. I was quietly sure that I wasn't going to immerse myself in the Atlantic Ocean in May, but it was a sunny day and no-one dared drop out. With Willie leading the way, we rode into the water until we could feel the horse lose its footing on the seabed and start swimming, with just its eyes and nostrils above the water like a hippo. A strange feeling, but not as cold as I feared because the horse's body keeps you warm. As well as this dip in the sea we frolicked up and down the sand dunes, galloped on the beach and generally had a good time.

The frolicking continued through our farewell dinner when we had a singsong in the bar. The barman was obviously used to Willie's groups and handed out song sheets so we could get the words right. My favourite was about the train that used to run from Ennis to Kilkee in Co Clare. This railway was built around 1860 and wasn't very reliable as the song points out. The Irish then, as now, were sensitive to criticism and the rail company sued the song writer, but when he failed to turn up at court on the appointed day because the train was late the judge dismissed the case.

At breakfast the next morning I learned what I had missed by retiring to my tent. One of the men, still in frolicsome mood, dressed up in a nightie, doused himself in his wife's perfume, and tip-toed into Willie's room to play a seduction scene. When Willie didn't see the joke he sneaked his clothes away and hung them from the chandelier in the hotel's reception area to be discovered by the other guests in the morning. Poor Willie, but I reckon it served him right for teasing me so much over an incident a few nights earlier when a very drunk man tried to find his way into my tent after the bar closed. It was actually rather scary, particularly after his friend said, "I'm not waiting for ye, Willie" and drove off, so the boozy voice outside said I'd have to let him in because he couldn't now get home. He stumbled around outside for a while, tripping over guy ropes and eventually went away, presumably to sleep in a ditch. When I told the group the name of my would-be visitor there was much hilarity.

Only someone with Willie's local knowledge could have devised this trek. He told me about the challenges and obstructions that were put in his way when he first planned it in the 1970s – and he is still leading it 40 years later. Little has changed. The route cuts through the roadless, watery wedge of land that makes up most of Connemara, running up mountains flaming yellow with gorse, through dark forests, and along the disused Galway to Clifden railway line which provided our best canters. Each day had its own highlight and, for me, its lesson in cross-country riding – a lesson I was afraid would be wasted, for how was I to find my way with only half-inch-to-the-mile maps and a compass to guide me? The maps had looked so detailed in the shop, but none of Willie's paths were marked on the Galway sheet. Nevertheless, I learned that Mollie would ford a river with water swirling above her knees, picking her way carefully over slippery stones, deal calmly with bogs, gallop on the beach, swim in the sea, and jump low stone walls.

For the middle few days of the trek the group stayed at Clifden, at the tip of the Connemara peninsula. The misty blue mountains known as the Twelve Bens or the Twelve Pins had been part of the view for a couple of days, but now we were close by them, drenched by sudden rain storms and then drying in the bursts of May sunshine. Last year's dead bracken coated their sides, contrasting with the bare grey rocks of their summits – quartzite, I was told, which had resisted erosion, hence their rugged outline.

Clifden marked a dividing of the ways. After our day on Mannin beach, the group had their final evening in the hotel, and I had my last horseless night in the tent. Mollie was also having her last night with equine company, although she didn't know it. She might have absconded if she had. The next morning I helped Willie round up the horses, saddled and bridled Mollie with her Peruvian head collar and detachable bit, retrieved the saddlebags from the luggage vehicle, and negotiated with the hotel for Mollie to share my tent space in the orchard. The plan was to ride with the group until lunchtime, then head back to Clifden for the night while they continued east.

After warm goodbyes and exchanging of addresses, the group went one way and Mollie and I went the other. I was brimming with mixed feelings: excitement, nervousness, relief, anxiety. This was it. Mollie's feelings were more straightforward. She was appalled. Without the other horses to follow, my lovely keen mare became a sulky plodder, only livening up when she realised we were approaching the field where she'd spent the previous night. When we passed the turn-off her disappointment was crushingly clear, and for the rest of the journey back to the hotel she tried to turn around in the road or shied at manhole covers and plastic bags. It was probably years since she was out without the company of other horses.

If Mollie was despondent, the enormity of what I had set out to do had me quivering with anxiety. I had never tethered Mollie before and had no idea how she would take to it, and my route plans had been kept deliberately vague. All I knew was that my next night would be in Cleggan, Connemara's most westerly town, followed by a loop round Lough Mask so I could visit John Daly, then head south along the coast with no final destination in mind. When I reached the hotel these preoccupations were replaced by a far more pressing problem: I couldn't get into the grounds. Cattle grids blocked both the front and back entrances, and there were no side gates. It was 7 o'clock at night and I couldn't think what to do. I had started rather vaguely leading Mollie back up the road looking for a field or a farmer (but too timid to ask the farmers I saw walking down the road) when I heard a shout. "Hi! How are things?" It was Donna and Peter, two Americans who were staying at the hotel and who had joined us for that day's ride. I explained the problem. "Well, did you ask the hotel manager?"

"Um, no, actually . . ." Within minutes Peter and the manager had returned with a couple of planks which they laid over the grid and Mollie walked placidly into the grounds.

The Americans took one look at my tiny tent and cooking stove, and invited me to dinner. "After you've settled Mollie." Time to try out the tether. The corkscrew picket went easily into the ground and felt firm. I attached the padded hobble to Mollie's foreleg, clipping one end of the rope to its ring and tying the other to the picket. Then I stood back and watched. Mollie was too intent on grazing to make a fuss, so I changed my clothes and went in to dinner. It was an interrupted meal. Each time I went out to check on Mollie she was standing pathetically, foreleg stretched out, obviously assuming from her previous experiences of such situations that she'd better stand still until rescued. Each time I had to lead her around to get her used to the idea that she could walk with this gizmo round her leg, and each time she made a major performance of it, lifting her feet very high and giving little snorts of anxiety. She also made a performance of rejecting my nice new collapsible plastic bucket after I'd scrambled down a muddy slope to collect some water for her. Even the hotel's metal bucket was eyed with suspicion.

During that first night of being a horse owner I felt like a new mother just home from hospital with her baby: 'Is she still breathing?' Or in this case 'Is she still munching?' I could hear the steady chomp chomp near the tent, and when it ceased I had to climb reluctantly out of my sleeping bag, put on my boots, and show Mollie once again that being at the end of her tether didn't mean she was incapacitated. She was a slow learner. Each time I found her with her leg stretched out and an accusing expression in her eyes; each time I had to lead her back to the picket while she did her little anxious snorts. Neither of us got much sleep.

I had agreed with Donna and Peter that they would come and see me off at 10 o'clock so I got up at 7 to be sure of being ready in time. I gave Mollie a nosebag full of oats – a parting present from Willie – and prepared my tea and porridge. The sight of all my stuff laid out on the grass filled me with dismay. How had I accumulated so much? The tent, sleeping bag and Thermarest mattress fitted nicely in the centre part along with my (very few) clothes, but then there was my little radio, a couple of books, maps, my stove and some food, and various odds and ends. When it was all in and zipped up I could barely lift the bag from the ground, let alone heave it over Mollie's back. "This isn't going to work!" I muttered, but of course it did, because it had to, and Mollie was very patient with all the uncomfortable banging and thumping.

I was pleased to have a send-off; as a lone traveller I missed being able to say something like "Here we go!" to a companion, yet something is needed when heading out on an expedition. More practically, I was grateful to have someone hold Mollie while I mounted; getting my leg over all that luggage wasn't easy. A few minutes after waving goodbye I had to dismount again, having forgotten the cattle grid. The planks were still there and once again Mollie walked over without fuss and I rode west through Clifden, taking the steep hill bordered by moorland, signposted 'Cleggan'.

Chapter 6

Nicky had been recommended to me as a possible source of a
Connemara pony. When I had phoned her from Galway she
explained that she had no ponies for sale, but the friendly welcome in
her voice when she suggested that I might like to camp at their place in
Cleggan shaped my plans. Cleggan is only a half-day ride from Clifden,
so a logical stop for my first night. Besides, how could I resist staying at a
farm with a single-digit phone number?

Riding out of Clifden I felt as though I was sitting on an armchair.
The soft middle section of the saddlebag partly covered the cantle and
made a nice back support if I adopted my favourite sack-of-potatoes
posture. It reminded me of a dream I'd had while planning the trip. I
was all saddled up and ready to go when the horse turned round and said
sharply "Don't you think you can do better that that?" I saw its point;
instead of a saddle there was a blue kitchen chair on its back.

People stared at my strange luggage or used the 'don't stare, dear'
technique – a quick glance, look away as though there's nothing abnormal,
then stop in their tracks to gaze at my departing figure. At least Mollie
disregarded all those strange lumps attached to her saddle, not to mention
the one in the saddle, and walked on cheerfully enough.

I took a minor road along a deep inlet – a fjord really – called Streamstown Bay. It was a sunny day with clear views across the blue water to the craggy green peninsula beyond. Mollie was in a reflective mood, probably wondering what she'd done to deserve such punishment. Every so often she'd wake out of her reverie to shy at rocks, drains or white lines painted on the road, and that woke me out of my own reveries. It was a side of her I hadn't seen when riding in company; then she was the essence of common sense, ignoring all the imaginary hazards that sent other ponies scuttling across the road.

This was rocky, gale-swept Connemara; a few hunch-backed trees leant away from the prevailing wind, but on this still, sunny May morning the little fields by the road were full of sheep or flowers; there were bluebells, plantains and cow parsley in some, a white blanket of daisies in others, and great bunches of king cups and marsh marigolds in rushy water meadows. The road ran between steep banks covered with primroses and violets. I didn't mind Mollie's slow pace.

"You really must go to Omey Island," Nicky had said. "You can have a wonderful gallop on the beach at low tide." And indeed, we arrived at a half-mile expanse of rippled yellow sand fronted by sea-weedy boulders being picked over by two oyster catchers. Mollie seemed to have forgotten all her seaside experiences and made a terrific fuss about stepping onto the sand and rocks, although completely unfazed by a hysterically barking sheepdog. I was tempted to take the saddlebags off and have a really good gallop, but the memory of the effort needed to heave the pack back into position, stopped me. I contented myself with cantering in the direction of the island, with the dog in hot pursuit, before making a large circle and galloping back.

I arrived at Cleggan in the afternoon; an attractive village of a few shops lining the waterfront, with the farm, backed by mountains dotted with white sheep, clearly visible across the bay. The family were out, but Nicky's mother-in-law showed me a large field for Mollie and the back lawn for my tent. To my relief there was no sign of any saddle sore or rubbed place under the bags so obviously the sheepskin and towel were doing their stuff. Mollie was thrilled at being turned loose after her tethered night, and walked off with that funny bent-leg walk that horses adopt when planning to have a roll. I watched her kicking her feet in the air and grunting with pleasure, before leaving to put up my tent. There were still hours of daylight left so I went off to explore the neighbourhood and in particular to look for a 'megalithic tomb' marked on the map. These dolmen tombs are fairly common in this part of Ireland and are some of the island's earliest archaeological remains, dating from around 3000BC. The purpose of the structure – side stones supporting a huge capstone – is not clear, but I wondered how on earth the builders managed to lever the giant stones into position. Probably there were more large trees around in those days.

When I got back to the house the family had returned and I was immediately enveloped into the easy atmosphere of farm life. Nicky's husband, Hugh, inherited the farm in a semi-derelict state and was gradually restoring it to productivity; a race against time as he was losing his sight. A peat fire burned in the grate and blocks of peat were stacked up on each side of the huge fireplace. "I don't suppose you ever have to buy coal?" I asked. "Well, not yet, but turf is still a fossil fuel, you know. And they've already used it all up in the Aran Islands, so it won't last forever." The phone rang. "OK," said Hugh, "I'll be right there."

One of the neighbour's cows was stuck in a ditch. By the time we got there the cow had been hauled out but the calf, which she had tried to reach when it fell in a drainage ditch, had drowned. The poor cow walked miserably along, bellowing for her lost child, but the farmer was quietly relieved to have saved her. "A few more hours and she'd have been dead," he said. "Cows don't last long in water." I was fascinated by his singsong accent, so different from the flatter tones of Galway. He went on to discuss what animal was killing the newborn lambs. "I wouldn't wonder if it wasn't a pine marten," he said but he pronounced it "paine mairrten".

Crawling into my tent around midnight, glowing from hospitality for the second consecutive evening, I reflected that it was a good thing I was going to start trekking properly tomorrow or I would get soft. My destination was a youth hostel at Killary, about 20 miles away, at the tip of a peninsula. Yesterday I'd been told by a cyclist that it was one of the prettiest hostels in Ireland; there was no phone so I couldn't check whether grazing was available.

Mollie had also enjoyed the hospitality and had no intention of leaving her spacious field the next morning. Most horse owners are familiar with the rage and despair that accompanies the trudge around a large field of long, dew-soaked grass in pursuit of their animal. Mollie kept on with her eating, an ear cocked for my soothing pleasantries and a sneer on her lips, until I was 10 feet or so away, then took off at a brisk trot. I'd left her head collar on, just in case, but she understood the just in case perfectly well and made sure I was never within grabbing distance.

"Come on Mollie, good girl!" I said in gentle horse-loving tones as I walked towards her with equicide in my heart. After half an hour I realised she was not going to get bored with this little game and I'd have to resort to bribery. The family was out, but fortunately I had spotted a sack of horse nuts outside the kitchen door. I'd discovered during the trek that Mollie didn't know what to do with a titbit, having tried her with apples, carrots, barley sugar, Polo mints and sugar lumps, all thoughtfully purchased from shops along the way. She'd inspect each one, smelling it carefully with a look of astonishment on her face, then throw her head up with a 'you can't fool me' gesture and refuse to have anything more to do with it. She liked recognisable food in a recognisable container and no messing about.

Filling a bucket with horse nuts I went back to the field and got exactly the same reaction. Mollie let me get a little closer and showed interest in the bucket's contents, but however stealthily I reached out my hand she always saw it coming and trotted off. However, my arrival with a bucket hadn't gone unnoticed by the herd of bullocks in the neighbouring field and they galloped up and down the fence bellowing encouragement whenever I seemed to be approaching them. Eventually Mollie's greed got the better of her and I managed to take hold of her head collar. Typically, once caught she accepted the situation with equanimity and I was able to clip on the lead rein and start for the gate. Here I was confronted with a new problem: Mollie's gate led into the bullocks' field where another gate, at right angles to the first, opened onto the road. Both were secured by the same piece of rope so either both were closed or both open. The bullocks were clustered excitedly by the gates, waiting for me to deliver the goodies in the bucket. I had to tie Mollie to the gate-post and leave her eating her horse-nuts while I unfastened the rope securing the two gates. Then I propped both gates shut and started to climb back over the stone wall into Mollie's field. The top boulders gave way. I fell heavily with a squawk of pain, Mollie took fright, pulled back and broke her lead rein, the gate swung open and three bullocks escaped into the road. I was near to tears. My attempts to drive the bullocks back into the field only resulted in the escape of two more; I had a bruised arm, a gashed ankle, Mollie was once again enjoying her freedom and I'd committed the cardinal sin of damaging a fence and letting out livestock. The wall was easily rebuilt but I could see that I'd never drive the bullocks back without someone else stopping the rest of the herd oozing through the open gates. I returned to the house and was fortunate to find that a friend of Hugh's had just arrived. Together we succeeded in driving the animals back in their field.

Mollie was even less willing to be bribed a second time. It was two hours since I'd first gone out to the field and rain was now falling steadily. I cursed horses and Ireland and childhood dreams until Mollie suddenly got bored with the whole business and allowed me to take her head collar and lead her (successfully this time) through the gates to the house, while I told her what I thought of her and reminded her of the price of horse meat.

It was raining hard as I rode out of Cleggan. "A grand soft morning!" exclaimed an old farmer as I plodded past, scowling, with the rain dripping down my neck. I'd meant to buy lunch provisions in Cleggan but was in too bad a mood to make the diversion to the shops so trusted to luck that I'd find a grocer along the way. Which I did, though the notice outside the general store-cum-post office said 'Closed for Lunch 1–2'. It was 1.50. I tied Mollie with a long rope so she could graze (not that she deserved it), hunched myself in my leaking anorak (promoted as a major breakthrough in rain gear) and settled down to wait. At 2.15 someone ambled along and opened the shop; I bought a yoghurt and apple and ate them in a growing pool of water near the door. I also had a parcel of unwanted maps and other odds and ends to send off – I had to lighten my saddlebags. While the post mistress was helpfully looking for brown paper and string, a small child came running in excitedly with the news that there was a white horse outside. Everyone went out to look while I tied up my parcel and then went outside to retrieve the post mistress so she could weigh it and take my money. I emerged just in time to release Mollie from a tangle of rope round her legs; she was starting to panic and use brute force. At least I'd had the sense to tie her with a slip knot.

I rode around Ballynakill harbour in improving weather and better spirits. "Lovely day!" called out a farmer as he approached. "That's a grand way of seeing the country." We chatted about my plans and he admired Mollie and asked how much I'd paid for her. Then he looked at her teeth to check her age. Irish countrymen find it almost impossible to admire a horse without looking in its mouth. Our meetings took on a set form: "Beautiful day, lovely mare! What did you pay for her?" followed by speculation on her age. By the end I expected Mollie to open her mouth automatically when anyone approached. I gave up saying she was nine. No-one agreed with me; estimates varied between five and 15. And I gave up giving the true purchase price since I got tired of suggestions that I'd been done.

When we turned northward away from the sea the scenery became austere. Peat bogs stretched away towards low hills dramatically backed by grey clouds. Mollie was stodging along and we needed some variety so I took a turf cutters' track across the moor, hoping it would link up with the road the other side. It was even bleaker in the middle of the moor; green-brown bogland with a rain-filled sky overhead. The only splashes of colour were provided by the wrecks of cars discarded along the way and those belonging to a group of turf-cutters who stopped their work and watched me in astonishment. I asked them if the track joined the one to Tully Cross. "Sure it does, but you'd do better to go back." Once I persuaded them that I wanted to be away from the road they gave me directions.

Turf cutting seemed to be a family affair. Men and women worked at it together and their children played around the wrecked cars or sat around with their parents in chilly groups drinking tea from thermos flasks. I learned all about turf during a pub conversation a few days later. I still had difficulty remembering to call it turf; peat is what they call it in other parts of the world. Someone told me about the visitor who asked "Are you going to get peat?" and got the reply, "No, Pete's got the flu, I'm going for George." My informant told me that peat is only used in gardens; turf is cut from a peat bog. Most rural houses are sold along with their turbary rights or sections of bog. Householders can either cut the turf themselves or pay someone to do it. First, the top six inches of heather, grass and other vegetation has to be removed before the potential fuel is reached. Although machines are used now, in the 1980s many people still cut turf by hand, using a slane or spade with a wing which cuts neat bars of the chocolaty peat (the dictionary definition is 'decomposed vegetable matter partly carbonised'). A bar of turf is about 14 inches long, with the best quality found near the surface, one to three bars down, although it's still good to 10 bars but this is poor fuel. The bars are left to dry for a week then stacked into neat pyramids of eight, and left for a further two weeks to dry out completely. Horses and drays (a type of toboggan) or donkeys with panniers were still used in some parts of the country to collect the turf. Turbary was worth about IR£1,000 an acre. My pub friend estimated this would yield 12,000 trailer loads of turf at a total cost of 5p per year.

The threatening rain kept off and with the help of my compass I joined my intended road just as the sun broke through. Climbing a heathery hillock, I came upon such a beautiful view of sea and islands, I decided to give Mollie a rest from the saddlebags and ease my aching body. Despite my six days in the saddle with Willie I still felt stiff and sore after a few hours of riding, and needed a break from time to time. Mollie's bridle arrangement worked well; I could quickly undo the side straps and remove the bit so she could graze more comfortably. It was rather nice of me, I thought, to ease Mollie's back at the expense of my own. Although the mailing of that map parcel had rid the saddlebags of some of their weight, it still took a huge effort to lift them into place. Out of view of passing cars and their curious drivers, I could relax completely, propped up against a sun-warmed rock. I shut my eyes. . . Waking with a start I saw Mollie's receding figure as she walked briskly back towards Cleggan, but I'd left a trailing rope so it was easy to retrieve her and give her a lecture on gratitude before saddling and bagging up again.

Killary was still a good seven miles away and it was now late afternoon. I urged Mollie into a trot (she was becoming very idle) and made good progress along the little-used lane that ran past lumpy green headlands of short-cropped grass, shingle beaches and a dark blue sea. It was all incredibly beautiful in the evening light. Just as I was wondering where I'd find provisions for supper I passed another of those handy post-offices-cum-shops found in remote areas of Ireland. "Jesse James rides again!" said the boy with a giggle as I paid for my bread, milk, eggs and sausages.

I led Mollie the last few miles to the youth hostel. We both needed a rest from the saddle. The road dropped steeply down to Killary Bay through tall trees and past a manor house just visible up a long drive, bright with rhododendrons. There were lush green fields on my left and heathery hills on my right, cropped almost bare by sheep. A farmer stopped to talk and I told him that I was looking for grazing. "You won't find any around here."

"But what about those fields there?"

"Oh no, an English lady owns those. You won't get permission, definitely not."

The youth hostel is a converted coast-guard station picturesquely set by a small harbour full of fishing boats. I tied Mollie to a railing and went to look for the warden. He was surprised and a little depressed by my mode of transport and confirmed that I wouldn't get permission to put Mollie in one of the lush fields; they were green because the grass was being grown for hay.

Above: Me aged 15 on Tara
Below: Flaco in the Peruvian Andes. I purchased a similar head collar in Cusco

Above: At first Willie was too busy on the farm to discuss selling me a pony. Here he is with a ewe and her new-born lamb.
Below: "You're mine!"

Above: Trekking with Willie over the rough landscape of Connemara
Below: Swimming with the horses in Mannin Bay. Mollie is on the far left

Above: Mounting to leave on the first day and pleased to have a send-off from Cleggan
Below: Killary Harbour and its youth hostel, with Mollie in the tiny garden

"I'd let you put her in the garden," he said "but I'm trying to grow the hedge. I've been trying for three years." I looked at the garden; it was tiny – about 15 by 30 feet – with a few blades of grass struggling through the hard ground and a washing line at the far end hung with jeans and damp socks. It had one asset: it was completely enclosed by a wire mesh fence against which a few leafless twigs were attempting to become a hedge. The warden agreed that Mollie and the hedge could probably coexist and suggested I talk to the fishermen who were mending their nets on the jetty. Most had small farms nearby and should be able to let me have some hay. I went out and found Mollie standing in a huge pool of urine with some giggling hostellers hovering near the shallows. I disclaimed any association with her and approached the fishermen who glanced up briefly with bored 'Here come the silly questions' expressions. They became more interested when I explained my problem. "There's not even enough grass this year for the sheep," one said. "We've had no rain since Easter." That morning's downpour in Cleggan hadn't reached Killary, apparently. A fisher-farmer agreed to sell me some hay, and while he went to collect it in his van I settled Mollie in her night's accommodation. Getting in was tricky; there was a small gate leading off the rocky beach and then the washing line to duck under, but she followed me willingly enough in the expectation of peace and plenty. Explaining about the imminent arrival of best Connemara hay, I left her crossly ripping up blades of grass while I went to fetch water. I knew she was thirsty but the wretched animal once again refused to drink out of a bucket; it wasn't even plastic, it belonged to the hostel. It appeared that she'd led such a natural organic life that she could only drink from streams.

The farmer returned with hay, which cost me IR£1, and Mollie refused to eat it. As for me, it was past 9 o'clock and I was hungry. While I cooked and ate my eggs and bacon, I chatted with the other hostellers

from Switzerland, Germany and the USA. Every now and then, out of
the corner of my eye, I'd see a white form pass in front of the window.
Mollie was pacing up and down and I was sure she was looking for water
so went out with a Swiss girl to have another go at persuading her to
drink. When I approached her she gave me a scornful look and turned
away, but the Swiss girl talked to her in German, dabbled fingers in the
water, and lifted the bucket to the pony's nose. 'Oh, water!' said Mollie's
expression and she had a drink.

Next morning I found Mollie standing sulkily by the untouched and
expensive pile of hay, but when I tied her up to prepare her for the day's
work she realised it was her last chance to eat for a while, and started
tucking in. I decided to go for a walk and leave her munching.

The cyclist who'd told me that Killary was the prettiest hostel in
Ireland had good taste. It lies on a narrow peninsula south of the nine-
mile-long fjord, Killary Harbour. Across this narrow strip of water, the
Mweelrea Mountains, which include a 2,600-foot peak, rise abruptly
from the rocky shore. It was a brilliantly clear and sunny morning and
from my viewpoint near the tip of the peninsula I could see the islands
of Inishturk and Inishbofin in one direction and a skyline of mountain
silhouettes in the other. Red and blue fishing boats rested in the harbour
below the hostel where, picked out by the sun, I could see my white
horse. I felt almost euphorically happy and adventurous and looked
longingly at a grassy track running close to the sea's edge. To get onto
it with Mollie I would have to dismantle a stone wall and I didn't want
to risk riding several miles only to meet an impassable obstruction. I
now know (2011) that this track follows the shore for about five miles
down the southern bank of the Killary fjord; it would have been a lovely
ride. The hostel is closed for renovations and Mollie's tiny field is now
carpeted with long grass. There is no sign of a hedge. On the wall a

new plaque proudly commemorates Ludwig Wittgenstein's stay there in 1948. This gloomy Austrian philosopher lived alone in the cottage for four months: thinking, writing, tearing up his notes, and learning the names of English seabirds.

Mollie refused to leave the garden. Not because of the remaining hay and five blades of grass, but she jibbed at the idea of ducking under the washing line and then squeezing through the narrow gate. In the end I had to take down the line. I wondered if we'd ever make a smooth start in the morning; despite rising at 7 it was 10.30 before we left, taking the road inland rather than risking the coastal path. The weather was still cool and sunny and my euphoric mood soon returned with the views across fields of bluebells to craggy, seamed mountains. After an hour the first car passed and screeched to a halt in front of me. A man jumped out and announced that he was Tom from Gowlaun and that he'd seen me yesterday. What a grand way of seeing the country and how much had I paid for the pony? Hmm. . . about seven years old, he'd say. . .

I like lakes with names like Lough Muck, particularly when their unpolluted waters are fringed with bluebells and yellow gorse. The small lake dwindled into a river then expanded into the long sausage of Lough Fee. Time for a leg stretch. I considerately loosened the girths and walked along the side of the road with the lead rope loose in my hand, singing 'Molly Malone'. "Cockles and muss-els, alive, alive. . ." Mollie stopped dead. "Come on you stupid old cow," I said, hauling on her rope. No response. Looking back I saw that the saddle and saddlebags had slipped and now hung below her belly.

Oh heck, would I be able to undo the many buckles before she realised the unpleasantness of her situation and took off? But Mollie didn't look panicked, she looked resigned, and stood still while I fumbled with the straps. Once the saddle and bags lay in the road she started to graze. I patted her and told her she was quite sensible after all, and that I was fairly stupid not to consider the effects of a rolling walk and gravity on unevenly weighted saddlebags. I was glad this wasn't a busier road as I went through the saddling order of sheepskin, towel (put under saddlebags to absorb sweat), saddle, do up girth loosely, saddlebags, seven straps fastenings, then final girth tightening. Except that I forgot the latter so after five minutes or so the whole thing happened again. This time Mollie gave the sort of sigh that my parents gave when I phoned to say I'd missed the train. But she stood still.

Actually it was her fault, since I couldn't tighten the girth when I first put on the saddle because she always blew herself up like a white balloon when she felt me pulling at the straps. I don't know how horses do this – whether it's by taking a deep breath or tensing their stomach muscles – but it causes a dramatic increase in waist measurement and, in Mollie's case, a fearsome storm in her digestive tract. "Rumble thy bellyful!" I quoted, with my head under the saddle flaps. I gave her earfuls of Shakespeare, Yeats and other poets as she plodded along. One ear would flick back – appreciatively, I thought.

I mounted again and we continued through a great baaing of sheep. A lamb had escaped through the fence and was standing on the far hillside bleating for its mother. Mum was standing her ground, some way inside the fence, calling back. They seemed to have reached a stalemate. "No, you come to *me*." I thought that I should do something but didn't know what, so left them to their own devices.

Approaching the pretty village of Leenaun I was intrigued to see a sign 'Shellfish training programme' and wondered what they were being trained to do. Leenaun was set a-buzzing by my arrival, especially when I tied up outside a shop to buy a snack. This was the gateway to 'Joyce's Country' which I'd always thought referred to James Joyce but has no literary associations; it got its name from an ordinary landowner. Heading south, the very lovely road follows a deep river valley between two mountain ranges and is on the tourist itinerary. I was passed by several coaches with most of the occupants asleep. Joyce's river flows through green fertile fields with prosperous-looking farms tucked into the lower folds of the mountains. One appeared to have a long purple-blue wall edging a copse; my binoculars revealed a field crammed solid with bluebells.

The beautiful views and open countryside made me ambitious and I decided on a short cut over the mountains. If I rode due east, I reckoned that I should intercept my intended road on the other side. At first Mollie was thrilled to feel grass beneath her hooves but then she realised she was going uphill and this was hard work. I got off to prove to her that at least one of us had the willpower to keep climbing despite shortness of breath. I'd planned to cut diagonally across the hillside but was stopped by a fence which apparently ran from the summit to the road. Mollie had been reasonably willing to traverse the hill, but she saw no sense at all in following a fence up a 1,400-foot mountain when there was a perfectly good road running round the base. She made such a fuss I was afraid she'd have a heart attack, so gave in to her demands that we abandon the idea or at least stop for a snack. We did both and the view across to the bluebell field and mountains beyond made our efforts seem worthwhile. For me anyway.

After another hour we came to such a perfect campsite I decided to stop for the night. I'd turned off the tourist route onto a minor road running between a cleft in the mountains. Close by the road a noisy shallow river ran through pasture which gave way to the dead bracken and heather of the hillside. There were plenty of dry flat places for my tent and good grazing for Mollie who was hungry after her deprived night. The ground was firm enough to hold the corkscrew picket, and Mollie could drink from her favourite source of water: a river. There were no houses nearby so I didn't feel too guilty camping without permission.

Eating my soup beside the tent, warm in the evening sun, with my white pony grazing against a backdrop of river and mountains, I was aware of the rightness of the scene. This is what I had imagined my journey would be like, not a horse in a garden under a washing line.

Chapter 7

Mollie clearly believed in leprechauns. We could be slopping along, happily lost in our own thoughts, when suddenly her head would go up, her ears prick so they almost met in the middle and she'd snort and jump at every sound or movement. She'd keep it up for a mile or so, then get bored and slump back into an even plod. By the evening I swear that if she could have found a way of crawling on hands and knees she would, and even when I got off and led her, I had to haul her along like a toy tractor.

Providing her with sufficient water continued to be a challenge. She was quite maddening: except when desperate she'd only drink from natural water sources. Helpful housewives would come running out of their homes in slippers, slopping full buckets of water, and she'd just turn her head away. I was trying to persuade her to approach a lovely rustic water trough and urging her on with uncouth language when I heard "You can lead a horse to water but you can't make it drink!" coming from a tiny bent old man who'd been posing as a hawthorn tree in the shadows. That proverb should be 'You can lead a horse to water but you can't make it think'.

Mollie specialised in making me feel humble and guilty. She was still difficult to catch although I left a long rope trailing so I wouldn't have a repeat of that first morning, and I would be lying if I said there had been much bonding. Sometimes she would stare at me with an air of surprise, as if to say "Goodness, are you still here?" And she sighed a lot. Or she'd look at me, shut her eyes and look away. This is bad enough in people and just not acceptable in a Companion Animal.

That night in Joyce's Country was only the second time I'd used her hobble tether so I was doing my new-mother act of sleeping fitfully, listening out for her cries of distress. Not that you could call Mollie's 'This is the absolute limit!' snort, a cry. It was a noisy expiration of breath through half-closed nostrils, and she did it when she had reached the end of her tether, literally or metaphorically. But at least she'd come to terms with the hobble, although she still walked with an exaggerated high step when it was attached to her leg. The corkscrew was bent in the morning, but still firmly in the ground and I was pleased to have worked out that this is the best way of tethering a pony.

The early morning was clear, but by the time I was ready to leave I could see patches of rain sweeping over the mountains across the valley. It never reached me and I remained dry as I followed the route I'd selected the previous night on the map. There had been a choice of two roads, but how could I resist the one running by rivers called Fooey and Finney? My next night would be spent at Lough Mask House, on the eastern shores of that lake, with John Daly, an expert in all things horsey. He bred Connemaras, rode show jumpers, trained race horses, and owned the house which his cousin, my friend Dorothy, told me was once the home of 'the infamous Captain Boycott'.

The narrow road ran between two mountain ranges where sheep with curly horns grazed the golden-beige tussock grass, then dropped down to Lough Nafooey. Now I was inland it felt warmer. Cuckoos were calling, larks trilling and a pair of dippers bobbed in courtship on the half-submerged boulders of the lake. All morning I'd been looking out for a phone box so I could ring John to warn him of my arrival, and now I saw a shop displaying one of the little green 'Post' signs that indicate a public phone as well as a post office. An old man with a pale cadaverous face and shining blue eyes stood behind the counter. Above him was a hand-lettered sign 'Let nothing disturb you – all things are passing'. I bought my lunch-time snack, which those days mostly consisted of chocolate. And why not? I seldom ate a proper meal. One day I devoured an entire packet of Jaffa Cakes for lunch, and nothing else, but at other times I'd be a paragon of virtue eating brown bread and marmite, fruit and yoghurt. I munched my Crunchie while the postmaster slowly and carefully added up the bill on a scrap of paper. I told him I wanted to make a phone call and wrote down the number. He pointed to a phone box near the shop door where I waited for him to connect me.

John's wife Pat answered the phone. Yes, they were expecting me sometime and this evening would be fine. I told her I should arrive around 7 o'clock. When I paid for the call I asked the postmaster if he had to work long hours. "Oh yes," he said, with his serene smile "if someone's sick you're going to help them out." This tiny post office seemed to be the local telephone exchange and was clearly the hub of this area where many people had no phone. As I was leaving, a customer entered and greeted me like an old friend. "I saw you last night camping. Weren't you afraid?" I could truthfully say no. I was proud of that.

ʊ   ʊ   ʊ

On my return visit I found what I hoped was the right post office, but I wasn't sure. Above the door was a bold sign 'Duffy's Finny'. A delicious smell of fried onions greeted me, and a young woman emerged from the kitchen. "Children's lunch." she explained. "Thought I'd better make a stew while things are quiet." I told her about my 1984 visit. "Was this once a telephone exchange?"

"No, that's over the hill that way." I felt a stab of disappointment.

"What I remember most," I said, "is the almost radiant face of the old man who ran it. And there was a sign, something like 'Let nothing trouble you, all things pass'. The woman pointed – and there was the sign, just as I remembered it, handwritten in magic marker on a piece of cardboard cut from a box. "Paddy was my dad!" said Margaret. "He died the year you were here, in 1984. He was 74. I was one of nine children, and he was in his fifties when he had me so he always seemed old. I remember, he got one of us to make that sign. Not everyone liked it – some would say that it wasn't true. But, yes, he was always there if people needed help." We beamed at each other, each with our own memory of him.

U   U   U

The mountains were now at my back and the road to Lough Mask was flat and dull. I felt bored and cold; Mollie was bored and sluggish. She couldn't even stir up the energy to look for leprechauns. I had a brief frisson of excitement when we crossed into Co Mayo and another when we crossed back into Co Galway on a bridge over a narrow part of Lough Mask. Now I could see the main lake; it's huge (over nine miles long) and full of little islands, some sporting shrubs or trees like fancy hats.

I'd scribbled down John's directions and eventually we reached a formidable set of stone pillars by a little white gate lodge. Bypassing the cattle grid through a side gate I rode down about a mile of curving drive between fields with cattle-pruned chestnut trees in flower and splendid groups of beeches protected by mossy stone walls. What a contrast with Connemara which has few trees. A grey pony came galloping up and I was terrified that it would be a stallion and want to have his wicked way with Mollie. I waved my whip and it kept its distance, rather to Mollie's disappointment. When I reached the house there was another cattle grid and I couldn't find a gate so I tied Mollie to a tree and went to announce my arrival.

John and Pat and two bouncing Jack Russell terriers greeted me as though I was an old friend. John is taller than I imagined an ex-jockey to be, with all-knowing grey eyes. Pat wouldn't hear of me sleeping in my tent: "I've already made up a bed for you."

"And the mare can spend the night in the orchard," added John. Being such an expert on Connemara ponies I was dying to hear what he thought of her. "Well," he said. "Pat told me she'd passed you on the road about half an hour ago and that you had an absolutely beautiful pony." I smiled smugly. "But she's not, you know. Her head's too big and her back's too long. But the thing is, with that fancy bridle and all the saddle bags those faults don't show." I felt a bit crestfallen but I can't pretend I hadn't noticed Mollie's big head; I thought it might contain a large brain. I turned her loose in the orchard and John and I leaned over the fence and watched her as she had a vigorous roll. "She's not really tired, you know. And she can easily carry the weight." I think he thought I was a bit soft on her. He also told me that the spring grass has as much nutrient in it as oats and that Mollie didn't need any extra food (she'd been telling me she was faint with hunger and close to collapse).

I ate an enormous supper while the family sat around and watched in awe. Of the two children only Alan, a very polite red-headed teenager, was at home. He was a keen and successful show-jumper and showed me the beautiful Connemara stallion he rode in competitions. I asked John whether a stallion wasn't a problem in the show ring. "No, he knows when he's at a show and just concentrates on the work in hand."

While I was eating, John told me stories of his life with horses. Like Willie Leahy, he started horse-dealing at an early age. "My first pony cost IR£2 10s. When I was 15 he won the championship at the Galway show. We sold him for IR£225." Since then John has been involved in every possible horse activity. He's been a jockey and a top-class show jumper (when I heard that he'd competed against Pat Smythe I nearly stopped eating in admiration), has bred and trained race horses and jumpers and a film has been made of his technique of breaking wild Connemara ponies. He can make an animal that has never been touched by a human quiet under the saddle and bit in a couple of hours. He just oozed horse magic.

For as long as the Dalys have lived in Lough Mask House, they have been making money with horses. "When my grandfather was 21, about 1887 that would be, he walked the horses all the way to Dublin and then took them over to England. About 15 or 20, there were. He used drovers' trails – I think he went across the Welsh mountains. He used to stay in tollhouses, turn the horses loose, then round them up the next morning. He took them all the way to Barnet Fair where he got three sovereigns for each horse. He told my father he was terrified going home with all that money in his pocket in case he was robbed."

I asked John about Captain Boycott and why he was infamous. "It's where the word boycott comes from," he said. "He had a tough time of it; he was only doing his job, you know." I didn't know but decided to research it later. It's an interesting story, and provides a little nugget of history highlighting the strained relationship between the indigenous Irish population and the English colonisers.

Captain Boycott had a lease on Lough Mask House and 300 acres of land, and was also employed by Lord Erne – an absentee landlord – to collect the rent owed by the tenant farmers of the area. This was no mean task – the land encompassed over 1,500 acres worked by 38 families. This was in the early days of the Irish Land League, founded by Michael Davitt, with Charles Stewart Parnell as its president (he went on to campaign for Home Rule). The aim of the League was to transfer ownership of the land to the families who worked it – a precursor to the 20th-century political struggles in Africa and South America.

Harvests had failed for several years at a stretch due to bad weather and many tenant farmers were unable or unwilling to pay their rent. Captain Boycott was reportedly unpopular because of his inflexibility and adherence to petty rules (although John says that he was well liked. "Otherwise he would have been shot.") When, in September 1880, he served eviction notices on 11 families, the area was ripe for rebellion. As the process server, accompanied by local constables, started the eviction process, a booing crowd gathered and pelted the officials with mud and manure, driving them to take refuge in Lough Mask House. Parnell had suggested that local people 'shun' greedy landlords and his advice was taken up by the local priest. Boycott's servants and farm hands were persuaded to leave, shop keepers refused to serve him, and even the little post boy was intimidated. To make matters worse, it was the grain harvest time, and the Boycott household, including the women, had to roll up their sleeves and get the harvest in. But the root vegetables, including turnips and potatoes, remained in the ground, so Captain Boycott wrote a letter to *The Times* explaining his predicament, and describing, in colourful language, the 'howling mob' and the damage they were doing to his land.

This produced a flurry of sympathy from the English and Protestant Irish readers who were already uneasy about the rebellious Irish Catholics, and money was raised for the Boycott Relief Fund to hire a band of Ulster volunteers to bring in the remaining harvest. The press was thrilled at this turn of events, especially in America, and reporters started to gather at Lough Mask. Meanwhile some 50 Ulstermen marched the 14 miles from the train station in Claremorris (no transport, of course, was made available to take them to the house) in pouring rain and settled in tents, haylofts or wherever they could find shelter. Boycott could have coped with a workforce of 50, but his heart must have sunk at the arrival of hundreds of army chaps to protect the volunteers, not to mention the press reporters from England and America, who between them reduced the garden to a quagmire.

In some ways both sides won. The harvest was safely gathered in ('one shilling for every turnip' as Parnell remarked bitterly) and Captain Boycott and his family left Lough Mask House, accompanied by his dog, a parrot in a cage, and little else. He would no doubt have preferred his name to live on in another context. "You see, the farm labourers were Irish-speaking and couldn't say 'ostracise' so they said boycott. And the word stuck," said John. "He was a good horseman, you know. My great grandfather bought this house in 1886."

ʊ   ʊ   ʊ

It was lovely to sleep in a real bed without worrying about Mollie. All John's talk of horse-breaking brought on a dream about a group of cowboys dressed in black leather mounted on carousel horses and practising neck-reining and lassoing as they went round and round. In the morning John said that Mollie had succeeded in getting rid of her head collar and I was filled with gloom at the thought of trying to catch her in this horse haven and of finding a black head collar among so many fallen black branches. But John and Pat told me not to worry, to eat my bacon and eggs and they'd find it.

By the time I'd finished packing up, Mollie was standing by the front door dressed in her head collar, and John had cast his expert eye over her and seen something that had escaped me in the daily search for sores: she was scraping her upper hoof with the opposite shoe and had worn away all the hair on her coronet. "You need to see Paddy McDonagh in Shrule. He's the best blacksmith in Ireland." John smiled. "He's a great character. Won all those awards but he's no airs and graces. Rides about on his bicycle. I went to see him once and had a pain in my chest so I mentioned it to Paddy. 'Oh I knew a man who had that,' he said 'it's called angina. But he lived another three weeks, you know.'"

Next door to the house there's a ruined 14th-century castle. Apparently when they built the house in the 1800s they were wondering whether to restore the castle instead but decided against it. Thank goodness. It's a beautiful ruin all covered in ivy and crows, with a grand view of Lough Mask from the top of the battlements. Alan showed me around it and I thought how nerve-wracking it must have been for Pat knowing that whatever she said the children would play there, with sheer drops of 100 feet or so and some very narrow walkways.

When we were chatting over dinner, I'd asked John about scenic rides in the area. I couldn't believe that there were no bridle paths or similar. "Why don't you go to Cong and ride in the grounds of Ashford Castle? Ronald Reagan's going to stay there in a few days' time. They'll be too busy to bother about you."

Cong is a pretty village with a row of pastel-coloured houses, a ruined abbey and tourists. One stopped me and said, "See here, I can't find the entrance to this hotel." I suppose he thought I was just part of the village life. Huge machines were digging a deep hole near the castle gates; presumably a fallout shelter for the American president. Mollie didn't like the machines at all but allowed herself to be led past by one of the workmen. It seemed almost a foolish act of bravery to go in through that arched entrance in the imposing turreted gate lodge. The grounds were full of un-Irish-looking men with short hair and coats and ties,

pointing strange devices at the rose bushes. No one asked me what I was
doing. I just said "Mornin'!" in an upper-class sort of way and rode up to
the castle, which is huge, grey and menacing, along the golf course and
through the forest. I was so rigid with nerves I felt like a chunk of wood
nailed to the saddle with a grinning mask for a face; my bowels turned
to water so I had to get off, tie Mollie up, and go into the woods to dig
a little hole. I imagined there was a secret serviceman behind every tree
and they'd all rush forward after I'd finished to see what sort of explosive
device I'd buried.

The grounds are lovely: a big rushy lake, bluebells, sunshine, birds
and plenty of paths to choose from. I thought I'd done rather well to
complete a semi-circle to the back entrance without getting lost, but
found it had a cattle grid and no visible gate so I had to go back past
the castle and say "mornin'!" to the groundsmen and secret servicemen
all over again. Later I chatted to locals who were amazed that I'd been
allowed in. I suppose I was such a strange sight that everyone assumed
that someone else had given me permission.

I had to follow a boring busy road to Shrule. It was cold and cheerless
and Mollie was slow and cheerless after her glimpse of high society.
Heavy lorries roared past and a man on a bicycle stopped to say I must be
a very wealthy woman. A red pick-up truck loaded with wood screeched
to a stop. A tinker got out and said he had a beautiful brown pony at
home and how about doing a swap? Heavens, why would I want to swap
my lovely white pony for a brown one, even if she does only go at two
miles an hour? I declined politely while he asked her age, looked at her
teeth, and queried her price. Before leaving he asked, "You waiting long in
Ireland?" I had to get him to rephrase it before I understood.

It was easy enough to find Paddy McDonagh in Shrule; I heard a
neigh before I saw the forge and found him putting the last shoe on a

racehorse. He was straight out of a Real Ireland postcard, with shiny red cheeks, shiny brown eyes, and so strong an accent I could only understand about half his conversation. It didn't matter; it was lovely being in a blacksmith's shop again with the smell of burning hoof and the clutter of old shoes, bits of wrought-iron work, and the ping ping ping of the hammer and whoosh of the flames when the bellows were applied. Paddy took off both Mollie's back shoes and reshaped them so they were less curved on the inside. And he talked. John was right about him being the best blacksmith in Ireland. In fact, in 1959 he was the best in the world, having won an international gold medal against 17 competitors, each the best in their country. His speciality was surgical shoeing, and to win the competition he made 42 different shoes for different hoof problems. He showed me one he'd made for a horse with a foot infection which had pulled its hoof away from all the gooey mess underneath. The shoe was hoof-shaped and he was able to pack it with gauze dressing between the gooey foot and the shoe and attach it with wood screws to the half inch of hoof that was left under the coronet. Nowadays, he said, the apprentices don't want to bother with such skilled work; they expect to buy ready-made shoes. He also showed me a plastic shoe that is being tried out in America but he said they'll never find a substitute for iron. Mollie's shoes looked almost worn down although Paddy said they'd last three more weeks.

He charged me IR£2 for 1½ hours' work, and would take no more. By that time it was after 7 o'clock so I asked him if he knew someone in the village with a field. He suggested the pub down the road and I plucked up courage and knocked at the door.

Chapter 8

It must be alarming to open the door and find yourself face-to-face with an English woman accompanied by a gloomy white horse, but the young girl who answered my knock didn't seem in the least taken aback at my request. She took me to an enormous field of luscious green grass and fresh cow pats next to the pub. Mollie cheered up immediately and I found a good place for my tent in a hollow where I couldn't be seen from the road (I was slightly anxious camping so near to a town). I asked Madeleine if the pub did food (there didn't seem any point in cooking up my meagre soup so near civilisation) and she said she'd make me a sandwich. When I'd got the tent up and Mollie settled, I went to have a Guinness and my sandwich. A group of silent old men stared at me from the bar, but Madeleine brought me through to their living room to serve me a large salad with ham, potatoes, brown bread and coffee. And she would accept no payment. Nor would her mother when she came in. The Hylands were a delightful family. I lost count of how many children but I think it was five; or maybe seven. Or was that the age of the youngest who worked quietly at his homework while we talked?

I had a late start the next day, needing to hitch into Galway to go to the bank (I was still processing the payment to Willie) and to buy some dried meals for my future camp dinners, so it was late afternoon before I was on my way. Riding through the flat countryside beyond Shrule I felt as though I'd ridden into summer. Big fields of summer grass, summer flowers and butterflies and summer smells. The sun was warm on my back as we walked past baaing flocks of newly sheared sheep and I tried to summon the courage to ask for a field for the night. At about 8 o'clock I knew I couldn't procrastinate any longer and stopped a woman walking down the lane. "No, I can't say I know of anywhere," she said rather evasively. An old woman with an arthritic sheepdog was more helpful. "No, sorry, but go back to the two-storey house on the left. They'll help you." The door was opened by the woman I'd stopped in the lane. We were both embarrassed, she explaining that she couldn't say yes without her husband's permission and he was off with the sheep and me apologising and saying I quite understood. She now seemed happy to show me to a large field with plenty of grass, piped water and all mod cons for Mollie and I accepted the offer of a cup of tea once my tent was up. I went to the house in the twilight and found Mum, still apologising, by a table laden with bread and jam, cakes and tea. The rest of the family came in; a newly married couple who were building a house next door, the youngest daughter dressed to the nines for a party, and father who arrived tired from the day's sheep shearing. The television was on with the news of the latest shooting in Northern Ireland. Father turned down the sound decisively and conversation turned to The Situation. "You'll hardly meet anyone who supports the IRA down here. They've set us back a hundred years, they have. Now the English won't come here anymore. It's no good talking about a united Ireland, this just frightens the Protestants. We must win them over slowly. It'll take years but it's the only way." He went on to talk about the Irish Civil War. "'Twas brother against brother. Tragic. When you leave tomorrow, go and look at the cemetery down the road. There are 14 boys buried there who were shot by the Black and Tans and seven who were killed by their own people. 'Tis a desperate shame."

It was raining again in the morning. "Lovely soft morning!" went the greetings. I wouldn't be surprised if the weatherman announced "Lovely soft weather spreading from the West." Mollie was fresh after those acres of green grass and found the road full of life-threatening situations; there was a fierce sparrow, an ominous puddle, a lethal plastic bag, a terrifying flock of geese, a horse-eating terrier, and an ogre of such horrifying aspect that the poor woman had to remove the raincoat held over her head before Mollie would go past.

It rained all day. The scenery was flat and dull, the only excitement being my arrival on a new map. There's always a sense of accomplishment in reaching the edge of a map; it's a destination of sorts in an unplanned journey. I sat hunched in the saddle under my leaking rain cape and listened to Radio 4 on my little transistor while Mollie plodded along with her ears back. She hated the rain – inappropriate, I thought, for a pony born and bred in the west of Ireland. At least there were plenty of farms with large fields, but once again I couldn't bring myself to stop at one until we were both almost dropping with exhaustion. The rain had now cleared and I rode up the driveway to a farmhouse in time for a family crisis. A small child, about two years old, was standing in the track screaming. Facing him was a cow with lowered head and bulging eyes. Behind the cow the child's mother yelled instructions. It was hardly the right moment to make my request so I waited until an older boy had shooed the cow out of the way and led his little sister to safety. Yes, they had a field. It was rather small and scrubby but at least I'd be able to catch Mollie in such a confined area. The farmer's wife said she'd make up a bed for me. "No, no, I'm fine out here," I said, regretting it immediately. But I hated the thought of causing extra work. Besides, I liked the quiet solitude of an evening spent cooking my own meal and writing my diary, with Mollie grazing close by. While unsaddling her I found that she was covered in ticks, so I spent the cocktail hour picking them off with tweezers. Then she found a handy low branch and gave her back a good scratch before kicking over the bucket of water the farmer had kindly brought from the house.

As I packed up the next morning Mollie strolled around waiting for me to notice that she didn't intend to be caught, but by the time I was finished she was bored and allowed me to come up to her and clip the lead rope onto her head collar. That was a sort of break through, but paled beside the event later that day. As always, I had offered her my apple core at lunch time, but this time, instead of turning away disdainfully, she absentmindedly ate it. I laughed out loud at the shocked expression on her face as she chomped it with her lips drawn back and foamy apple juice dripping from her teeth. 'Hey, it's good!' With pricked ears she nuzzled my pocket for more. I stopped at the next shop I came to and wheedled a free carrot out of them. And she ate it. She learned fast, and soon became quite tiresome, stopping dead outside grocery shops and peering into the doorway in the hopes of a handout.

After lunch the flat, monotonous landscape gave way to sea vistas and distant mountains. We were back near Galway Bay with a good view over Dunkellin Estuary and its ruined castle, then open grassland and the dark grey skeleton of a large mansion standing on high ground overlooking the sea. I wondered whether it had been burnt in the Troubles. A few miles down the road I met an elderly man out for a walk. He had an erect posture, a red-veined face, and wore tweeds and two hearing aids. Before he spoke I could guess his accent. "Yes, I can tell you about that ruin. It's Tyrone House. It was built by a black Protestant, Christopher St George. Back in the 1700s. The St Christophers were great huntsmen, you know – they say that one of their horses was buried in a bronze casket. Don't know if that's true, though. Yes, the house was burned by the IRA in the 1920s." He went on to talk about horses. He'd been in the Indian cavalry. "We had 520 horses and mules in each regiment. They were only shod in front, not behind. The hooves soon toughen up, you know." I explained that I was doing too much road work to risk going without shoes, much though I'd love to. "Do you have horses now?" I asked. "I used to, I never stopped riding until just the other day and now I'm too old. Used to hunt three days a week. I did my own horses, too. . . That's a lovely saddle. Army type. They cost a lot of money these days. Very comfortable, ideal for long days in the saddle." Then he raised his hat and wished me good luck. A very charming Horse Protestant.

By taking a circuitous route near the coast I avoided the long stretch of main road to Kinvarra. I had planned to continue to the youth hostel a few miles beyond the town but by 6 o'clock neither Mollie nor I had the will power to go on. It was cold, I badly needed a bath and I thought it was time I treated myself to a B&B. I found a nice-looking place overlooking the harbour with an enclosed grassy area behind a high, locked gate next door. "Would you also have accommodation for my pony?" I asked, indicating the enclosure. "Oh, I should think so. It belongs to the pub so ask Michael." Permission granted. It was pure heaven lying back in a guilt-free hot bath, after consuming numerous cups of tea, with a hot meal to look forward to and knowing that Mollie was safe and happy in an enclosed field. Later I went to the pub to have a Guinness and thank Michael for Mollie's B&B. The bar was very dark, very smoky, and full of men. When I entered, everyone stopped talking and looked at me. I asked if there'd be music that evening and one gave an imperceptible shake of the head and continued staring. So I ordered a Guinness, sat down and drank it very fast, smiling with lowered eyes, then slunk out. The physical dangers of travel are no problem, but pubs are just too frightening.

Well fortified by my comfortable night and satisfyingly greasy breakfast I decided to go in pursuit of literary Ireland. I was carrying in my luggage a slim volume of poetry by Yeats, and learned from my two fellow bed-and-breakfasters, a couple of highly educated American women, that nearby Coole Park was associated with Yeats. "It's a beautiful place. Lovely grounds and the famous Autograph Tree."

"The what?"

"All sorts of literary men carved their initials there." They showed me their guide book: 'The house is in ruins, but the yew walk, garden, woods and autographed copper-beech tree are well kept. Lady Gregory, whose home it was from 1880, was one of the founder members of the Abbey Theatre. One of Yeats's closest friends and literary allies, she immersed herself in Irish traditional life and literature and her house became the centre of literary life in the period.'

I decided to leave my bags at the house and ride like a normal horsewoman to Coole Park (16 miles round trip), then continue on to Doorus House Youth Hostel which completed the Yeats/Lady Gregory connection since the two were introduced there in the days when it was privately owned.

I thought Mollie would be bounding along like a yearling without the saddlebags, but she didn't seem particularly grateful. I was strict with her, however, and did a good amount of fast trotting and cantering which she enjoyed. So did I; she had a lovely comfortable canter. Coole Park was indeed beautiful. Its long tree-lined drive was bordered by forest with inviting woodland trails radiating from it. A pair of friendly hedge-trimmers told me I could ride anywhere I wanted. Tethering Mollie I went to look at the Autograph Tree and eat my lunch in the formal gardens. The huge copper beech stood a little apart from its neighbours, on the fringe of the lawn, its bark deeply inscribed with the initials of the literary giants the period. There's a typically flamboyant GBS (George Bernard Shaw), a subtle SOC for Sean O'Casey, and WBY for Yeats himself.

Later I read about Lady Gregory and liked her. Her rather boring-sounding titled husband at least had the sense to let her follow her enthusiasms; she was a folklorist and a dramatist, and had studied the Irish language from a Bible borrowed from Edward Martyn, a wealthy Catholic landlord. It was he that introduced her to the poet because he couldn't think how to entertain Yeats on a wet afternoon. How satisfying it must have been for Martyn when he saw how well they were getting on and heard their plans for an Irish theatre. To realise the importance of this meeting one must know how uncultured Ireland was in the 19th century. While England was nurturing Dickens and the Brontës, its neighbour, caught in the grip of poverty and famine, was unfruitful. Coole Park became the centre of the literary revival that produced such a high proportion of Irish writers and playwrights at the turn of the century.

After lunch I explored the various trails. Grassy tracks led through woods full of bluebells and pungent with wild garlic; perfect for a gallop except that they were so lovely it seemed a shame not to enjoy it slowly. I did both and managed a serpentine ride that brought me out near the gate.

ʊ   ʊ   ʊ

I went back to Coole in 2011 and found it little changed. The woods are still lovely, dark and deep, suffused with the smell of wild garlic, and you can still wander – or ride – for miles along the forest paths or visit the small museum to learn about the former inhabitants. From a distance the Autograph Tree looks the same, its deep maroon colouring standing out among the neighbouring greens, but now it's protected from modern autograph carvers by a fearsome iron railing. The passing years have had surprisingly little effect on the 19th-century initials, but now there is an interpretation sign to help you match the literary figure to the autograph. On my earlier visit I hadn't spotted John M Synge, nor the artist Augustus John who has snuck in there amongst the literati.

☾   ☾   ☾

On the way back to Kinvarra I stopped to visit Lydacan Castle. It was typical of so many Irish ruins, impressive but apparently uncared for, standing lonely in a field full of cows. The solid Norman tower has five floors connected by a spiral staircase. I turned Mollie loose and climbed up to the top, from where I could see the ocean and also Mollie, munching away, surrounded by a surging sea of mooing black and white. Worrying that she might get fed up and kick them, I scampered down again and mounted to return to the road. "Shoo, shoo!" I said feebly at our escort of 20 or so bellowing cattle. But I'd neglected to take any bearings when entering the field, and now that I couldn't see the road I had no idea where it was. Nor had Mollie, I was disgusted to discover. When I dropped the reins and said "Home" she walked briskly back to the castle and started eating.

Back at Kinvarra I succumbed to the offer of a cup of tea, then bagged up and headed for the youth hostel. It was marked on the map but none too accurately, I later realised. A herd of cows was being driven up the lane by an irresponsible sheepdog which took one look at Mollie and fled. The cows scattered and I had to round them up and send them on what I hoped was their way. My way was equally vague; the road dead-ended at a gate opening onto a grassy track. Across the bay I could see a white building which must, I rightly concluded, be Doorus House.

The track led temptingly along the shore towards the hostel, skirting the bay with its glinting blue water. It soon petered out into seaweed, mud and rocks, but it's hard to turn back even after you know you've made a mistake. After all, Doorus House was only just across the bay, the tide was out and the mud/sand looked firm. But a stone wall stood in the way. I didn't think it would be too difficult to take off the top stones and lead Mollie over the lower ones. I dismounted and started heaving the boulders out of the way while Mollie tore ravenously at the scant grass. She stepped over the remaining stones willingly enough and I rebuilt the wall feeling pleased with myself. It was good to use a little initiative at last. I mounted and rode to the mud. Mollie took one step, sank nearly to her knees, and scrambled back onto dry land. Damn, it wasn't going to be easy. But further down I could see where cows had crossed the mud, so saw no reason why Mollie shouldn't be led across. For a while she stood on the edge looking mulish while I hauled on her rope, the mud slurping over the top of my boots. She eventually gave in and we reached the other side with sandy mud sticking to our legs up to the knees. I was now in a field with a herd of cows galloping eagerly up to make our acquaintance. A high stone wall separated us from the road and I could see no gate.

A man sauntered past on the road. "Excuse me," I shouted in some embarrassment, "do you know if there's a gate out of this field?" He looked at me severely. "I don't think so. And farmers won't like you tampering with the walls." He walked on. I was sure they wouldn't, but I was equally sure I wasn't going to retrace my steps. By that time it was 8.30 and I'd phoned the hostel to ask for grazing (yes, it was possible) and said I'd arrive at 7.30. Once the man was out of sight I chose the lowest bit of wall and started dismantling it. The boulders were bigger and heavier than in the earlier wall and the meadow was below the level of the road so that even when I had the top stones off it was not possible for Mollie to step over the large unmoveable lower ones. The best I could do was to reduce the wall to a bank about

2 feet high. I wondered if I could lead Mollie over. She knew I only wondered, that I lacked courage in my convictions, and did her mulish act. I mounted and trotted her at it. She pricked her ears and jumped over without hesitation. I was enormously impressed and pleased with her. I never really believed she would jump with the saddlebags. The grass was certainly greener on the other side which probably helped. She munched while I made a skilful job of rebuilding the wall. I don't think even the beadiest-eyed farmer would have noticed it had been tampered with. I rode up to Doorus House at 9 o'clock feeling very tired, having ridden around 22 miles that day.

"That's an unusual request, you know" said the warden looking at me rather accusingly. "When I said we had grazing I'd forgotten about the weed-killer. You can't tether the pony in front." She paused. "But I'll let you put her in our orchard. It doesn't belong to the hostel but we've been thinking of putting an animal there to keep the grass down."

The orchard was enclosed behind a high wall like Mollie's previous night's lodging, with the same lush grass. This one was like the Secret Garden, approached down a path through head-high cow parsley leading to elegant wrought-iron gates. Once again I could turn Mollie loose to eat her fill and rest after the long day. After I'd removed the saddle she had a vigorous shake and stood haloed in dust and flying white hairs. She was fast losing her winter coat.

I joined the other hostellers in the kitchen to heat my tinned stew and to listen to discussions on where to go next. They seemed to travel so fast – several had been in Killarney the previous night, a place I hoped to reach in two or three weeks. Hitchhiking was easy, they said, but they got tired of answering the same questions again and again, and even tired of drinking Guinness. As a way of meeting people and getting to understand a country, hitchhiking is excellent, but I realised how little these young people saw of the countryside. They had to stick to the main roads, and although many walked several miles a day it was the hitchhikers' walk overlaid with anxieties about the next lift and night's lodging. But they had Ireland at their feet; any part of the country was accessible in a day and the discussion turned to next week's music festival at Ennis. The tourist in me would have liked to go but how could I cavort to music with a pony by my side? And, to be honest, I shrank at the thought of all those drunken crowds. Each day of solitude made it an ever more desirable state.

"Did you see the Burren?" I asked.

"I think so." How could she not be sure? The Burren, described with lyrical enthusiasm by Kieren Guinness, had become one of my goals. The name describes a type of landscape rather than a clearly defined region, taking its name from Boireann meaning 'a rocky place'. Appropriate enough. From a distance the rounded hills seem to be producing some grey-coloured crop. This is limestone: compressed sand and shells heaved up from the ocean bed and smoothed by glaciation into the characteristic Burren 'paving stones'. It is the youngest landscape in Europe, a treeless world, scoured smooth and clean in the ice age. The Burren is described in images of death. As William Trevor in his irresistible book *A Writer's Ireland* puts it, 'The very bones of Ireland's landscape break through its skin on the Burren', and Cromwell's surveyors described it as 'yielding neither water enough to drown a man, nor a tree to hang him, nor soil enough to bury him'.

A good map, one inch to the mile, hung on the hostel wall, the first Ordnance Survey one I'd seen in this scale. It was only in black and white but showed all sorts of possibilities missing on my smaller-scale maps. I bemoaned to the warden the difficulty of getting decent maps. "It's for security reasons. Suppose the Russians got hold of them!"

Chapter 9

The morning was perfect. Sunny and clear; much too beautiful for me to leave the coast without some further exploring. The large-scale map in Doorus House had suggested that I could ride west along a beach for a couple of miles, so I set out eagerly, longing for a gallop along sand. But this wasn't really a beach. Mollie's hooves sank into the shingle, slipped on the rocks, and skidded on the seaweed. I dismounted and led her over the surf-smoothed pebbles, content to amble along watching the changing light on the sea while Mollie shoved me in the back with her nose.

We left the coast at a small, sheltered cove and followed a narrow lane inland. Ahead were the grey domed hills of the Burren, with Abbey Hill the most easterly bump on the horizon, and there was the green road that I'd spotted on the map, contouring the side of the hill. I found it easily and my heart lifted to hear the soft print of Mollie's hooves on turf instead of the clip-clop of iron on tarmac. Ahead, between her pricked ears, was the curve of the hill, with the sun glinting on the wet limestone, and to the right, beyond the bay, the blue mountains of Connemara where I'd started my trek 10 days ago. The Burren seems to grow boulders instead of crops; to produce food, or even grazing, the farmers have to pick up every stone, by hand, and create a wall. So the fields are tiny and the walls are many, for what can you do with all those stones except make a wall?

Back on the coastal road, at Bell Harbour, a sign pointed to Corcomroe Abbey. Yeats had set his one-act play *The Dreaming of the Bones* here, a place where 'even the sunlight can be lonely'. I decided to take a look. The abbey is still as lonely as the sunlight which bathes the ruins. Small ferns have found footing on the walls and wild flowers grow in profusion around the graves. Even the incongruous plaster Jesus with its plastic flowers has its place here, a modern expression of devotion which has prevailed over 800 years. The Cistercians built this place early in the 12th century, a massive undertaking in such a remote spot. Where did they find the stonemasons to carve those human and dragon heads which adorn one of the arches? They called the abbey St Mary of the Fertile Rock, revealing that these Burren valleys produced sufficient food for a large religious community.

Near the abbey is a small, ruined house abutting a meadow. The gate was open so I decided to let Mollie have a proper lunch break, untethered and without the luggage, while I ate my picnic nearby. I unbuckled the little straps that linked her bit to the head collar, and she plunged her head down to graze while I unfastened the saddlebags and heaved them onto the ground and took off the saddle. It made a convenient back rest while I ate my sandwiches and watched Mollie tearing up mouthfuls of grass. Later I wandered through the peaceful ruins, taking in the elegant Romanesque arches and the carved foliage atop the capitals. And the effigies; staring upwards with a pained expression was Conor O'Brien, grandson of Donal Mor O'Brien, the King of Munster who founded the abbey. More serene is an ecclesiastical gentleman with a massive folded tunic and a dinky little mitre, and the smiley face surrounded by flower petals could have come from a modern greetings card.

My map showed a path running across the saddle that lies south of Moneen mountain, suggesting a perfect short cut to Ballyallaban where I hoped to find a field for Mollie with a horse-breeder friend of John Daly's. Perhaps this would be another green road. As I rode up a narrow lane serving a few farms, I kept scanning the hills in front of me. I could see the saddle between the two peaks but no sign of a track. A new road had been cut into the limestone, just wide enough to take a tractor, but it ran in the wrong direction. At the last farm I dismounted, tied Mollie to the gate, and went for advice.

A tangle of children came to the door, giggling and hiding behind each other. It seemed that the road was the only way, and never mind that it went steeply up hill and south, not west. Mollie puffed and panted and I felt sorry for her, and dismounted. I puffed and panted and finally, after climbing about 800ft, reached the top to find a desolate view of barren rocky hills with no sign of habitation. The road even managed to climb higher. Before I got to the true summit the clouds closed in and swathes of mist obscured the view. We plodded on and on, downhill when possible, at each break in the clouds hoping to see the valley. It started to rain.

I was lost, and fed up. I'd give up on Ballyallaban, set up camp, and hope the weather would improve. I always had enough dried food for the odd night of wild camping, but both Mollie and I needed water. I found a food trough which had a little rainwater in the bottom but, needless to say, Mollie wouldn't go near it, despite my loud and eloquent arguments.

Scooped out of the grey hillside was a good campsite, protected on three sides by cliffs, with flat places for the tent and decent grass for Mollie. Perhaps I could risk not tethering her. Under the cliffs was a small copse of stunted hazel trees with dead branches lying around. I heaved them through the rain and made a reasonable barrier, finishing the effect with Mollie's tether rope. It was only an effect, she could have easily pushed her way through or even stepped over, but I hoped she'd take the hint. I remembered a man on Willie's trek telling me "At best a fence is only a request." A horse, he said, could jump virtually anything – if it wanted to. I needed water for cooking so took my plastic bucket and drinking cup back to the rain-filled food trough. The water was full of debris but otherwise clean and I scooped it up into the bucket. While I cooked my rather meagre soup dinner inside the tent I could hear Mollie chomping the lush grass outside.

In the Burren, farmers drive their cattle up to the highlands during the winter so they can feed in these grassy hollows. It's the reverse of the practice in other parts of Europe where cows are brought down from the mountains in winter to the valleys when the first snows appear. But climatically the Burren is the reverse of other mountainous areas: here the temperature is actually warmer on the hillsides and grass grows well throughout the winter so cattle need no extra feed. The limestone acts as a storage heater, absorbing warmth during the day, so the temperatures rarely drop below freezing at night.

I was uneasy in the tent that night, concerned that Mollie might make her escape and head back to Connemara. While it was still light I kept the tent door open so I could see her, and after dark I listened for her blowing her nose, a comforting horsey sound. The rain pattered gently on the fly sheet all night and at 6 the next morning I put on my glasses, unzipped the door and looked out at her blurry white dozing figure, dripping in the mist. I liked early mornings in the tent. On my own I had no reason to pretend that this is the best time of day, nor that the sounds of nature were preferable to the BBC. I switched the radio on and snoozed through the stock reports, *Yesterday in Parliament*, and other gloriously faraway subjects. It was still raining when the 7 o'clock news

Connemara
Above: Joyce's Country
Below: Wild camping

Hospitality – I received a warm welcome in a variety of homes
Above: John Daly of Lough Mask House (2011). "He just oozed horse magic."
Below: Farmer Tom and his mum

Co Clare

Above: The ruins of Corcomroe Abbey
Inset: An 800-year-old smiley face
Below right: The Autograph Tree, Coole Park
Below left: Entry into Jerusalem, Kilfenora (see page 92)

Above: Mollie enjoys a lunch treat in the Burren
Below: At the Cliffs of Moher

came on, and still raining at 8. I thought I'd better get up anyway. I still couldn't cope with the guilt of staying in my sleeping bag half the day, sensible though it might have been.

Mollie was particularly tiresome that morning. There was nowhere to tie her and she kept walking away with a determined expression on her face while I followed her, soaking my boots in the wet grass and cursing her in tender tones. The rain seemed set for the day, falling through a thick mist, and I knew I would have to steer by compass. I was completely lost but it didn't seem to matter; I knew the lane would lead somewhere. Eventually.

As we crossed from one farmer's land to another, gates barred our way. The first was a challenge: the catch was stiff, the wind blew my rain cape over my face, and Mollie jibbed. I hated dismounting in the rain. Not only did the saddle get wet but my carefully arranged limbs let in the water. By the eighth gate Mollie had learned her job and co-operated fully. It's not difficult to open a gate from a horse's back as long as it doesn't run backwards just as you're pulling the catch up.

The lane kept dividing, but using the compass I chose the forks to the west and eventually, two hours after leaving the campsite, dropped steeply downhill, passing some new barns which suggested that I was reaching civilisation. A black figure with two dripping sheepdogs appeared out of the mist and stared at me in astonishment. I asked him if we were near the road. "Sure but you are, there's a gate just down there. But 'tis locked," he added as an afterthought. "Ye'll get over the wall," he said comfortingly and went on his way. You bet I will, I thought grimly. I wasn't about to retrace my steps to the farm with the giggling children. The gate was indeed padlocked. I tied Mollie to it and cast around for a low section of the wall to dismantle. I didn't have to look far, the top stones were missing and the lower ones were easily removed to make a gap that Mollie could step over.

I didn't really know where I was but guessed it was not far above Ballyallaban. The rain continued to fall steadily, driven by the blustery wind. Mollie hated it and walked with her head almost touching the ground, and her face turned sideways away from the wind. She looked silly, like a peevish camel, and I pulled her head up when cars approached. Despite – or perhaps because of – my rain gear, everything was wet: my boots, trousers, arms (the seams of my jacket leaked), hair. I sat hunched in the saddle and even passed by a sign to the dolman tomb which I knew I wanted to see. I was too wet to dismount.

I had to get off when I reached the entrance to Ballyallaban and a cattle grid. Some cement-filled barrels blocked the gap in the wall that provided the only access for Mollie and me. Behind them, among the cows, I could see a chunky black bull. Keeping an eye on it, I pulled the middle barrel towards me and the pool of rain lying on top of the concrete sloshed over the remaining dry part of my trousers. The bull raised its head. I nervously led Mollie into the field and hauled the barrel across the gap again. The bull watched placidly while I remounted and then continued grazing.

The house seemed closed up. There were no cars in the drive, the curtains were drawn, and no barking dogs rushed out at me. I wondered what to do. I felt too wet and depressed to continue riding, and too wet and depressed to find somewhere else to camp. Mollie didn't share my feelings; she had seen other horses and her head was up and her eyes bright with anticipation. I tied her to a dripping chestnut tree and, without any hope, rang the doorbell. I was quietly shocked when I heard footsteps and the door was opened by a young woman who interrupted my prepared statement with "Oh hello, we've been expecting you, do come in."

Mary soon cleared up the mystery. John Daly had visited the family a few days earlier and told them I might turn up. I stood and dripped in the porch and Mary suggested I spend the rest of the day there and stay the night. "You can turn the mare loose out here," (you can always tell genuinely horsey people – they talk in terms of geldings and mares) "and dry your things by the fire." Better and better. It was a marvellous old-fashioned kitchen with a huge fireplace and hooks above the range for suspending kettles and pots and giant hooks on the high black ceiling for hanging bacon. Mary bustled around with admirable energy, finishing off the cleaning while I attempted to converse with Dad, who sat with his head in his hands by the fire. I had every sympathy. Why would he want to chat to a strange, sodden Englishwoman? I watched the steam rise from my clothes, while trying not to stare at Dad's attire. He was dressed in threadbare corduroys and a manure-coloured tweed jacket whose sleeve was making a bid for independence. Just a few threads still connected it to the main.

"I thought I'd hitch into Kilfenora this afternoon," I told Mary when she joined me by the fire. "The cathedral is interesting, isn't it? And the Burren Centre?"

"Oh, I'll drive you in – there are some messages I have to get." I must have looked puzzled. "You know – groceries." We sat down to an enormous lunch which I devoured with my usual greed, gushing my appreciation between mouthfuls, and then Mary drove me to Kilfenora via a roundabout route so I could see some of the Burren in the clearing weather. Strange to be in a car again and cover 20 miles in half an hour instead of a day. I thought what a waste it would be to do all your Irish sightseeing like that.

I described my visit to Kilfenora Cathedral in a letter home:

The cathedral is as usual, in ruins (not surprising, it was built around 1190).
It has some nice carvings, but these are nothing compared with the Doorty

Cross, which is what I most wanted to see. It's in the churchyard, set around with the usual vulgar modern gravestones, and of typical Celtic design but carved with the most imaginative pictures. None of the descriptions I've read tells you what they're of, except the 'Entrance into Jerusalem' on one side, so I'll give you my interpretation. Well, the entrance into Jerusalem is fairly straightforward if you accept that the donkey is either wearing size 13 wellingtons or has sea lion flippers not legs, and that Jesus's upper body has completely disappeared in holy squiggles and curlicues. It's a bit weathered at the top, near the cross part, so it's hard to see just what is going on, but the other side, protected from the prevailing wind, is clear enough. Except that I still don't understand it. There's a figure wearing a rather trendy embroidered tunic and a glum expression. He's sporting the same dunce's cap that Donal Thor O'Brien wears in Corcomroe Abbey so perhaps it's a Celtic version of a bishop's mitre. Except that his expression fits a dunce better than a bishop. In his left hand he hold a curly-topped crozier, while two parrots use his shoulders as springboards. This holy man is standing on the heads of two faceless hooded characters that maybe have their arms entwined or maybe the Celtic carver just gave way to his curlicue yearnings. They're also holding staffs with which they're prodding the creature below them. Impossible to say what this is – a dragon, maybe? Or a griffin? It's got two legs, anyway, and is standing on a pair of skulls. Or perhaps urns. All in all there's a lot going on.

In 2003 the Doorty Cross was moved to a new, less atmospheric, position under cover. And cleaned up, so more detail is exposed and it's lost some of its mystery. I'm glad I saw it in 1984 when imagination could take flight.

Mary dropped me off at one of the few established tourist sites in the Burren. Ailwee cave is a long, deep, heavily commercialised limestone cave with a few stalagmites, stalactites and claw marks from bears. Also on display were the antlers of one of my favourite extinct animals, the

Irish elk, designed while God was going through his Celtic curlicue period. And I learned that the last Irish wolf was killed at the end of the 18th century in Co Sligo. So sheep may safely graze, and wolfhounds have become redundant. I've only seen one Irish wolfhound in Ireland; it was sitting morosely outside a pub in Dublin.

I woke to one of those lovely washed mornings with a green/blue sky and birds singing from every tree. Mollie had been turned out in the huge field with the brood mares so I wondered if I'd be able to catch her. No problem, by the time I'd finished breakfast Mary already had her tied up outside the house, and I was able to groom her using a proper dandy brush instead of my mail-order pet brush with retractable bristles that didn't really work. I loved grooming Mollie, running my hands over the curve of her shoulder and along her back, pulling burrs out of her mane and brushing all the mud and manure out of her thick, long tail. I loved the soft, folded skin between her front legs and the way the dapples on her quarters were emerging now she was shedding her winter coat. By the time I had finished there was a heap of white hair on the ground and she looked sleek and summery. As always I checked her back for sores and picked out her hooves. Her shoes were looking increasingly worn but I reckoned they'd last another couple of weeks before I needed to find a blacksmith.

Mollie was in an obliging mood; the half-day's rest in aristocratic company had obviously done her a world of good. Perhaps she'd enjoyed boasting about her exploits:

"I come from Connemara."

"That's nothing, I was born in Tipperary."

"Bet you got here in a horse box."

"Well, how else are you going to travel?"

"I came on hoof."

"You mean you *walked* all the way from Connemara?"

Mary and I peered at the map spread over the kitchen table while I munched my last bit of brown bread. Ballyallaban House was there, and I could see my route down into the valley then up to Feenagh. "See that green road? It'll take you over the col to Formoyle and you should be able to get across the hills on that track." This is now the Burren Way, but in 1984 it was just a speculative route on the map, made all the more seductive by its uncertainty.

The track was rough and stony, with yesterday's puddles still lying in the ruts. At the top of the pass the view was so perfect, and the sun so warm, I decided to have a long lunch break and again undress Mollie completely so we both could relax for an hour. I also had a special treat for her, a nosebag full of oats that Mary had given me. There was no-one around except a man on a tractor who came to pass the time of day and admire my pony. I loved it when people asked "Where did you hire the horse?" and I could say "She's mine!" After I'd eaten my home-baked bread and marmite, and Mollie had finished her oats, I left her to graze and wandered around photographing flowers. My information booklet told me that the Burren is a meeting place of flowers from northern and southern Europe. It is thought that before the last ice age this area had a warm climate and southern plant species flourished, then seeds from the north arrived trapped in the glaciers – along with boulders and other debris – which spread over the Burren. When the ice receded it scraped and smoothed the limestone hills and left a mixture of northern and southern plants. 'There is nowhere in Europe where Mediterranean and Arctic-alpine plants grow together in a similar way.'

Early purple orchids were still in flower and plentiful, and between the boulders, clumps of primroses, celandine, and delicate mountain avens brought splashes of yellow and cream, along with magenta from bloody cranesbill and the pure blue of gentians. While I was looking for flowers I wandered over the limestone paving stones. These are quite extraordinary. They run in fluted dimpled rows with deep gaps separating them. The gaps, grykes, run pedantically from north to south, and I could just imagine God with his compass and spirit level laying out this huge rock Garden of Eden and getting so carried away with the civil engineering he forgot that apple trees won't grow here (nor snakes, come to that).

From my lunch spot I could see a track running between stone walls over the opposite hillside. Mary had thought it might be blocked by a wall but my binoculars showed it to be clear at least to the col.

As we dropped down to the Caher valley I spotted a couple of walkers gazing at the turbulent river. The two women told me they were from Ulster and holidayed regularly in the Republic. "Splendid, splendid! What a marvellous thing you're doing! No, we haven't been all the way to the top, but the path's clear for the first part. No wall." A grove of stunted hazel trees partially blocked the entrance to the track, but Mollie and I pushed our way through and panted up the steep hill. Stone walls ran on either side of the track, the flat boulders placed on their edges to create a filigree design. Stone walls encircled fields of stones, and ran up the grey limestone hillsides in long, wavy lines.

There was indeed a wall at the top of the pass, but it was hardly an obstruction; I could easily make a gap for Mollie to step over, and after that it was simply glorious – a wide grassy track where I could canter whenever I, or Mollie, felt like it. And, obviously thrilled to be off the tarmac, she felt like it. Even at a gallop she seemed able to ignore the bouncing saddlebags. Sometimes it was too beautiful to gallop; the sky was full of larks, flowers lined the track and the grey domes of the Burren contrasted with rugged blue hills to the south – the mountains of Kerry! My next destination seemed a long, long way away, but so did the bens of Connemara where I'd started from.

After that first wall, there were no obstructions apart from an occasional gate. The track ran high on the flanks of Slieve Elva, a hill quite out of keeping with the Burren, with incongruous conifers and a shale summit, before dropping down to farms and tiny, stone-walled fields on the road to Doolin – 17 miles of perfect riding.

Chapter 10

I wanted to spend the night in Doolin because everyone kept telling me that this is the centre for Irish music, but the glories of that day in the Burren had wiped all practical thoughts from my mind. So when I rode past a 'Hostel' sign it took me a while to register that this was a Good Thing; I turned round and rode back again, tied Mollie outside, and went to look for the warden. Up until then I'd stayed in a few YHA places, but this was the first independent hostel I'd seen, although I'd been told they were more relaxed than the official places with fewer rules and a wider variety of users: couples and older people. People like me, in fact.

There was no accommodation for Mollie and the Australian girl looking after the place didn't know of anyone with a field. "You'll have to ask around the village. I'll keep an eye on the pony." First I enquired in a rather raucous pub and they all said ask Mr Brown, then fell about laughing. So I found Mr Brown who was lurking behind a cottage, so run down it was almost indistinguishable from the surrounding countryside; the walls were sprouting plants and most of the thatched roof seemed to have reverted to mud and grass. Mr Brown was also sprouting. Poor man, he had some awful infection on his pendulous lower lip. Having found him, I felt I'd better press on with my request but I never found out if he had a field since I couldn't understand what he said. It seemed unlikely, so I thanked him profusely and left. My next effort was a farm surrounded by well-fenced fields. A group of men were cutting silage so I walked up and asked them if I could graze my pony in one of the fields. They told me to check with a large woman who was standing rather vaguely in the farmyard. She stood with her hands on her hips, looking at me out of one eye while the other wandered over the surrounding hills. "Well, I'm not sure... the calves wouldn't like it, they've never seen a horse... no, I don't think so." I tried hard to persuade her that Mollie was indifferent to other animals, had spent plenty of nights with cows, and needed somewhere secure for just one night. "No, I don't think so." So I gave up. I'd spotted a grassy area by the river as I rode to the hostel and had thought at the time that this would do at a pinch. I tethered Mollie close to the bridge where she could reach water to drink as well as the grass. But I worried about her incessantly as I cooked and ate my supper. Suppose she was stolen by tinkers or molested by the children?

The hostel was almost deserted, but the few people there were in Doolin for the music. A Swiss girl and I headed off to the pub that's reputed to have the best players, and already there were more visitors than locals. The music was excellent – if you like traditional Irish music. I realised I don't. I like everything about it except the actual sound. I like the old toothless cloth-capped men playing tin whistles, the younger equally toothless boys playing fiddles, the atmosphere, and the fact that the tradition of Irish music is alive and well and – from what I was told by a music group in Dublin – played for pleasure, not just for tourists, but... not the music itself. So I left after an hour or so and made my way back down the pitch-dark lanes, getting lost in the process, and finally coming to Mollie's bridge and stumbling down the bank to give her a goodnight kiss.

I was up horribly early to check on her. She was fine, which was more than could be said for the weather. I found a phone box and called the recorded weather forecast. "Rain clearing by noon," they said, so I moved Mollie's tether and left her to have a leisurely breakfast, while I sat in the warm, dry common room, writing letters and planning the next stage of my journey.

'A great, undulating wall of rock.' That's how my guidebook described the Cliffs of Moher; nearly 700 feet high, they were obviously a major tourist attraction since even the girl who wasn't sure if she'd seen the Burren was quite certain she'd been to the Cliffs of Moher and that they were spectacular. And even better, my map showed a green road running close to the sea between Doolin and the highest point, O'Briens's Tower.

As I was riding up the hill out of the village, a tourist coach drew up behind me and its occupants jumped out to take pictures. I wonder how their guide explained this quintessentially Irish scene? One particularly large lady panted along the other side of the road trying to get a photo from the front; by the time she'd got her camera focussed I was too close and she had to run ahead again. This happened several times until I softened and stopped for her – which I would have done at the beginning had she, or her fellow passengers, spoken to me.

We soon left the tarmac to follow a classic green road, skirting the shore and rising steeply ahead to hug the cliffs. It was even lovelier than yesterday; the wide track followed an inadequate fence that kept cattle and Mollie from the cliff's edge where pink thrift grew in clumps over pockets of green sea, and sea birds were speckled white against the black rock. I gave Mollie a break while I sat on the cliff edge with my binoculars, identifying great black-backed gulls, fulmars, terns, and guillemots while a couple of choughs wheeled overhead shouting 'ch-ang!'

This beautiful old road continued for about a mile with only views to delay me. The first river was crossed by an ancient stone bridge but the track stopped at the next stream which had cut its way through the pasture to the sea in a deep channel, bridged by a single wooden plank. I dismounted and considered my options. The river banks were about five feet deep and white water cascaded between large boulders. Impossible. A path of sorts veered off to the right, following the stream, so I led Mollie along it looking for a crossing place. Frustratingly there was a ford that had obviously been used by cattle, but beyond it the fields separating us from the resumption of the track were divided by three high and solid stone walls. Leaving Mollie to graze I took a close look at these. The first two were well built with huge boulders and the last had a gap, but blocked with a plank piled with gargantuan stones. I couldn't get through that way. I turned my attention to the river. Perhaps if I cleared the boulders Mollie could be persuaded to jump down the bank into the water and scramble up the other side. There was a place where the drop was only about three feet. I heaved the boulders to the side and made an inviting landing pad at the bottom. "Come on Mollie!" She dug her feet in and looked down in horror. "It's only a little jump," I said, pulling her. No go. I slid down the bank and hauled pointlessly on her lead rope. She stood firmly on the bank three feet above me, leaning back against the rope. I felt like a climber scaling a rock face and cursed Mollie's chin; she looked particularly irritating from that angle. Climbing up the bank again I mounted and rode her at it. When we got to the edge my nerve gave out. Of course she was right! It was a stupid thing to attempt. I apologised, let her get on with her eating, and heaved the rocks back into their original position.

Perhaps the area by the bridge would be easier. There was a boulder-free bit of bank she could descend safely, then a short walk down the river bed, and up the other side. It was worth trying. I spent ages preparing the way, taking down the bridge, clearing the riverbed, but Mollie wasn't having any of it. She was becoming fed up with my ambitions; while I reconstructed the bridge she tried to sneak back to Doolin. The only possible course (apart from returning the way I had come which was unthinkable) was to try to get over the walls.

Leading Mollie over the ford to a new patch of grass, I started lifting the top stones off the first wall. They were very heavy and I found that rock dropped on rock with a finger in between hurts. There was no question of removing the lower boulders – they were much too large – so I was left with a three-foot-high wall. It was jumpable but higher than anything we'd attempted before. It was worth a try. I cleared the approach and landing area of rocks and stones, mounted and rode up to the wall so Mollie could look at it and see what was expected of her. Then I pushed her into a canter and she jumped it without hesitation. I was thrilled! It must be harder for a horse to jump with an extra 40-pound dead weight; I wondered if she'd be less willing to do the next wall. She trotted up with pricked ears and popped over. What a splendid pony I had for this job! She was too sensible to agree to my doing anything dangerous. All that was left now was to clear the giant stones from the plank blocking the last gap. They were huge, but by this point I just had to move them, and after I'd passed through I had to put them back again. As with all the walls, I had to try to leave them exactly as I found them.

My relief at being back on the track was short-lived. There was another wall; smaller stones this time, but with a strand of barbed wire along the top. This I was able to unloop and pull back. And so it went on: between the stream and the end of the green road there were eight fences. Some were straightforward walls, others were fiendishly complicated wire fences with a dozen spiky strands to be untwined, or a combination of stone and wire. One took me half an hour to deal with but by this time I'd reached the point of no return; I couldn't bear the thought of undoing all those fences I'd so carefully reassembled behind me. I dreaded meeting one that couldn't be taken down or undone.

Eventually I could hear traffic and see it racing along the main road. The track rose towards it, skirting the edge of a large ploughed field. I could see the final gate opening onto the road and prayed hard that it wouldn't be padlocked. Two farmers were walking slowly through the field, deep in discussion. Would they tell me off for trespassing? I gave them a cheery greeting as I rode up to the gate which, to my immense relief, was easily opened and I passed through to the main road.

I had ridden a little over four miles that morning; it had taken me just under four hours.

"Hello!" A suntanned girl, on a bike loaded with luggage, greeted me enthusiastically. "Oh, that is so good! I have a horse in Switzerland." We discussed the relative merits of horse versus bicycle but of course it was no contest. She longed to do what I was doing, and I enjoyed answering her questions. I was proud of my gear, the distance I'd covered (about 300 miles so far) and of course my pony. I told her about all the fences and walls, and how Mollie jumped them. And I showed her the two swollen fingers which would soon develop black nails where I'd dropped the stones. And I stroked Mollie's neck in appreciation.

I wondered what it would have been like travelling with a companion. It had been a tough day, full of anxiety, the sort of day that would have been merely an adventure with someone to share it. But although a trouble shared is a trouble halved, it's not the same with beauty. I'm not sure that my spirits would have soared to the same heights if I had discussed those sea views with a friend.

A number of coaches passed me as I rode up to the Cliffs of Moher Information Centre, a small white building perched on a grassy hill, and I soon found myself surrounded by excited Americans and clicking cameras. One girl was overcome. "Oh my, this has just made my whole trip! I can't believe it!" It was cold and windy, I'd eaten an early and inadequate lunch, so I thought a cup of tea and a few cakes in the tearoom would slip down a treat. There was excellent grazing for Mollie outside, so I led her up to the highest part of the hill, away from the path, screwed the picket into the ground and tethered her from the head collar; the hobble was too deep in my saddlebags. I sipped my tea and wrote postcards, half listening to other visitors discussing a white horse in excited voices. Then, with rain threatening, I went out to look at the cliffs, leaving Mollie eating her tea on the hillside.

The Cliffs of Moher are indeed impressive, but not, I thought, as beautiful as the cliffs I'd gazed at earlier that morning nor those of a similar height in Aran. Few tourist sights can retain their impact when the viewpoints are crowded with visitors. However, I learned that Mollie and I were perhaps lucky when we visited the more dramatic cliffs to the north. They are not horse-friendly. The Irish name is *Aill Na Searrach*, which translates as The Cliff of the Foals. Many, many years ago, they say, Ireland was ruled by the Tuatha Dé Danann. Perhaps they were kings, or maybe gods, for they arrived on a cloud and had magic powers. One king feared for his daughters, that they might be taken by his enemies, so he shut them in a cave in Kilcornan. Years went by before the girls, understandably frustrated by their incarceration, transformed themselves into young horses – foals – and burst from the cave. Dazzled by the unaccustomed light they galloped blindly to the west, towards the setting sun, towards the sea, to the very edge of the Cliffs of Moher where they leapt to their death. But the force is still with them, or with those cliffs. In 2004, surfers discovered Ireland's greatest wave at the foot of these very cliffs. It is popularly known as Aileen's Wave, a corruption of *Aill Na Searrach*.

I was the only person venturing along the cliff path, most being content to climb up to the viewpoint and take their photos. I wanted to look for puffins which are said to build their burrows in the cliffs. There were plenty of other sea birds and I was sitting happily with my binoculars spotting kittiwakes and guillemots when I saw something out of the corner of my eye. Something white. Mollie was in difficulties. I was too far away to see clearly, but I could tell what had happened. Her rope had become wound round her back leg and by struggling she had not only made it tighter but it was pulling her head between her forelegs. It all seemed to happen in slow motion – I watched appalled as she battled the rope until something broke and she was sent cart-wheeling down the hill; the rounded bulk of the saddlebags over her back and sides made her almost circular. When she reached the bottom Mollie got to her feet and continued grazing as though this was a perfectly normal method of descent. By that time I was running towards her with mingled dread and relief; she obviously wasn't badly hurt but would I find her lame? "She's fine, don't worry," said the man holding her rope. In fact Mollie seemed much less shaken by the incident than I was, although I suppose it's difficult to see if a white horse has turned pale. I walked her around and she was indeed fine; the saddlebags hadn't even slipped, so I rode her up to O'Brien's Tower and asked a German tourist to take our photo. Then I left the cliffs and headed south for Lehinch where I was to pick up my mail.

U   U   U

In 2007 the Cliffs of Moher had a makeover. The little information centre on Mollie's grassy cart-wheel slope has been replaced by The Cliffs of Moher Experience, created inside the hillside, and hordes of tourists pay their €6 to enter and marvel at the cliffs from behind safety barriers. However, by the time you read this, a new path will have opened following most of the route that I took with Mollie, but without the walls and without the ankle-deep bog that I squelched through on my return visit in 2011. It will continue beyond the Cliffs of Moher, via Hag's Head, to Liscannor, a walk of 14 kilometres. And it will be wonderful!

U   U   U

Mollie and I walked along narrow lanes past large fields. Silage cutters were out in force, the lush green grass being scooped up by giant machines and transported to the farmyard to mature. The evening sun slanted through the grass giving it that peculiarly Irish glow. In the tropics I was used to seeing the sun shine directly over the landscape, giving a flat shadowless look to the scenery, at least at noon. Here the sun was always low, and in the evening, when it was just above the horizon, it shone through the vegetation and even blades of grass were lit from behind. Then the grey clouds blew across the sun and the first spots of rain began to fall. I pulled on my rain chaps (no need to dismount to do this) and got out my yellow cycling cape. It poured. Huge chilly drops of rain slammed against us. Mollie put her head down, ears back and face sideways, away from the wind, her whole posture expressing misery at being subjected to such discomfort. We passed a farmyard with a large hay barn. The door was slightly open and I could see the farmer working inside. On impulse I turned into the yard, the farmer pulled back the sliding door and Mollie and I walked inside out of the rain. I didn't quite know what to say, but it wasn't necessary to say anything. The farmer helped me off with the saddlebags, and I asked if Mollie could spend the night in one of his fields. And perhaps I could sleep in the barn? No problem. I was rather pleased. In books, people often sleep in hay barns, but I'd never managed it before. The rain stopped as suddenly as it had started and I put Mollie into the field with some calves and a donkey.

The farmer got on with mending a fence and I went for a walk to dry off and fill in a bit of time. I was near the village of Liscannor, and could see the white houses of Lehinch across the curved, sandy bay, picked out by the setting sun. A few yards from my barn I came to a sign announcing an independent hostel half a mile away. What a temptation! A hot shower, company and a comfortable bunk. I stared at the sign and pondered. I didn't really want to talk to anyone, nor make the effort of sorting through my saddlebags for the items I'd need for a night there. I turned away from the sign and walked along the road to the beach. The tide was out, which meant it would be low in the morning so I should be able to take Mollie along the sands to Lehinch. I crossed a mini rubbish dump and trod down some rusty barbed wire which made a half-hearted attempt to block access to the beach. The bay was patterned with wavy ridges of hard sand and trapped sea water reflecting the evening sky. Flocks of redshanks and dunlin waded in the shallows near the river which bisected the bay, and oyster catchers picked around the smooth pebbles. I was glad I hadn't gone to the hostel.

Back in the barn I prepared my bed for the night by spreading the unfolded tent over a nice heap of straw and rolling around until I'd made a hollow for my sleeping bag. Then I found a large flat stone for my candle. I knew I shouldn't even think about lighting a candle in a hay barn but since I had to have light I would just have to be very careful. I found a plank of wood as a base for the cooking stove and filled my bucket from a water butt. It was wiggling with mosquito larvae. No bath tonight; I wasn't even going to undress. Then I sat on a hay bale near the door, in the fading light, and wrote my diary, measured my mileage (only nine) and planned the next day's route. And felt chilly and lonely. But I managed not to set fire to the barn. It was a comfortable bed, and I slept well. When I packed up the next day I found the nice fresh straw I thought I'd been sleeping on was impregnated with cow dung and that my legs were covered with itchy bites.

Mollie walked up to me with a little whicker, and nuzzled in my pocket for a titbit. Gone were the days of chasing her around the field in the morning. I had her groomed, watered, saddled and bagged by 8 o'clock and set off for Lehinch before the farmer was up, leaving a thank-you note in the barn. Mollie stepped over the rusty barbed wire onto the dunes leading to the beach and quickened her step in anticipation of a gallop. It was the first time I'd ridden her on sand since that first day by Omey Island, but I was content to walk and look at the morning light on the ribbed sand and the surf, and the wading birds. I took out my binoculars but bird watching on horseback is not satisfactory; I could never convince Mollie of the importance of keeping still. We came to the river and Mollie gazed at it with bulging eyes and a 'You cannot be serious!' snort. I saw no reason for such a fuss, considering she'd actually swum with me in Connemara, so urged her on vigorously. Reluctantly she waded in to the deep fast water in the centre. Here the riverbed was composed of slippery seaweed-covered stones and the water swirled well above her knees and splashed over my boots. Halfway, though. Silly to go back at this point. I kept up my encouragement, Mollie kept up her snorts of complaint, and we emerged the other side with mutual expressions of relief. There was still a mile of firm sand between the river and Lehinch and I urged Mollie into a gallop, kicking up chunks of sand and scattering the gulls. Can anyone gallop on a beach without grinning euphorically? I know I can't. It's a wonderful feeling. Then the cheese-'n'-chutney roll bag thudded to the ground because I hadn't secured it properly and I had to pull up, dismount and fret over my camera.

I rode down Lehinch's high street just as the shops were opening. Having skipped breakfast, I planned to collect my mail and have a cup of coffee, so found an out-of-the-way telegraph pole to tie Mollie to. Hearing the hoof beats, a woman peered out of a door near my selected tethering post. "I'll throw an eye on her," she said, when I explained that I was going to be gone a while. "You go and have a good breakfast." A good breakfast – why not? I deserved it. The tiny post office had a couple of poste restante letters for me and I asked the girl behind the counter to recommend a place that would serve a decent breakfast. The Atlantic Hotel did look a bit posh, but I went in anyway. The receptionist looked at me in disgust and, not trusting herself to speak, nodded in the direction of the dining room. A loo was the first priority. Catching myself in the mirror I thought the receptionist's expression of distaste was quite generous: my nose was peeling, I had straw in my hair, sand on my boots, horse grime on my baggy trousers, grease on my cheese-'n'-chutney roll bag cum shoulder bag, and purple patches on my fingernails from wall building. I looked dreadful. I tried to enter the dining room with poise and dignity, easing my way round the tables of staring tourists, and ordered a huge breakfast from surly waiters in red jackets that matched the tablecloths. The food was uninspiring and I thought again how lucky I was in my chosen mode of travel, never normally having to pay so much for so little. I read my mail then studied the map.

Lehinch marked the end of the Burren and the most interesting part of Co Clare. Had I been a normal tourist I would have motored to the Killimer–Tarbert car ferry across the Shannon, and been in Kerry in a couple of hours. On horseback I hoped to be there in a couple of days, but would they allow me to board the ferry? It was a question that had been occupying me for some time. Mary Davoren had said, "If you can't get permission to lead her on then you've a good chance of catching a lift in a cattle truck. Lots of farmers go to Kerry to buy cattle so drive over with empty trucks." I would keep my options open. One thing I did know was that there was no alternative. The nearest bridge was in Limerick, an 80-mile journey on main roads. I planned a route to the ferry that avoided all busy roads, included a few *bohreens* (narrow lanes), and took me through the most interesting-looking countryside.

Mollie was drooping patiently by her telegraph pole. I'd felt very guilty about leaving her with nothing to eat but the neighbouring woman said she'd given her carrots and brown bread. "She's been as good as gold. Had lots of visitors." She looked as good as gold and so beautiful. I couldn't stop admiring her lovely clean sea-washed legs; they were usually assorted shades of brown. I felt one of my surges of love when I stroked her and fed her more carrots. I was so lucky.

Chapter 11

It just wasn't fair; whenever I tried to get off the busy roads I ran into trouble. Heading south from Lehinch I attempted to take a short cut along a newly surfaced track marked vaguely on the map in little dots. Perhaps it was just a glint in the cartographer's eye, since it meandered around, visiting farms, and lacked all sense of purpose, while our arrival caused great excitement with the local cattle. I kept thinking of the riddle 'Why did the cow slip? Because she saw the bull rush.' There were bulls rushing (or bullocks, anyway) and cows slipping all over the place in the mud. I didn't much like it when they rushed and slipped around me, especially when the road passed through their field. I closed the last gate behind me with relief. Then I heard a strange squeak and saw the most pathetic-looking donkey. Its hooves were so overgrown they curled up in the front like Turkish slippers, and a rope was tied so tightly around its throat that its bray was reduced to a noise like furniture being dragged over a polished floor. It was desperately lonely, and trotted along its side of the hedge with open mouth, squeak-braying at each breath. Mollie was a snob and ignored it completely, while I hastened to get away because it upset me so much.

The next hazard was a patch of peat bog. Two men were cutting the turf and stacking it into neat blocks. Beyond them was the road I was trying to join. They walked over and were full of chat and helpful suggestions. "Can the horse jump?" "Yes," I said, so they took down some wire at the top of the bank bordering a stream. I had to slither down into the water and ask Mollie to jump up the bank on the other side. She made a pointed demonstration of the absurdity of the idea by resting her chin on the top of the bank. She was right; it was much too high. The men, both of whom seemed to be called Michael, had a consultation and agreed there was an easier place further down. The bank was lower here, and after the trouble the two Michaels had taken to dismantle the wire fence, I drove Mollie at it with determination and she jumped up without hesitation. Mollie could always tell whether I believed in what I was asking her to do, and more and more I was trusting her with safety decisions. One of the Michaels escorted me to the road, explaining it was time for his tea anyway. I rode along, chatting, although I knew that it wasn't the road I wanted to be on. Instead of the five-mile *bohreen* round a mountain that I'd planned, I ended up with an eight mile slog along a main road. It was cold and cloudy and boring. I was angry and bored and Mollie was stodgy and bored. I kicked her along the grass verge, cursing cars and horses and Irish maps, and she looked for things to shy at. When I trotted the saddlebags slipped, but I was too bad-tempered to try to balance them. A silver strip of sea appeared on the horizon and this reminder that I was heading west not south made me even crosser. Then it started to rain and Mollie did her rain act – head down and sideways. "For Christ's sake, you're a Connemara pony!" I shouted. "You can't tell me you're not used to rain."

Suddenly the sun burst out from behind a cloud and a rainbow sprang up behind me. I found my turning off the main road; it was all so beautiful I stopped being cross and gave Mollie a tea-break on the grass verge while I let the usual feeling of tranquillity settle over me again.

I watched the sea turn from silver to blue, and a couple of hares frolicking in a close-cropped field. The Irish hare is thought to be sub-species and they have a special reason to be frolicsome: in times past it was believed that monks' souls entered into hares, so they were protected.

It was time to think about stopping for the night. As usual it took Mollie's decisiveness to end my procrastination. Each evening I rode along making up excuses: this house is too posh, that one's too poor, I'm sure there's no-one home here, or too many people home and looking at me there. Mollie knew the routine and when she reckoned it was time to stop for the night she'd snatch at grass on the roadside and try to turn down promising-looking driveways. Today it was quite late and she was sulking along having suggested various farms that I'd vetoed (the excuse – too early and why not enjoy the evening light) when we passed a pub standing by itself at a crossroad. 'Crosses of Annagh' was painted on its white walls. There was a family sound about it (my maiden name was Cross) and I waved at the people crowding the doorway as I went by. A pub would be full of farmers with fields and a Guinness would be good consolation for my unsatisfactory day. I turned back, tied Mollie to a gate and went in.

It was still early in the evening but a few men were quenching their thirst at the bar. Yes, several of them had a suitable field and yes, I'd be welcome to stay there. But first they had to finish their pint. And the next one. I fretted about Mollie who'd had a long day and meagre grazing last night. "Tell you what, try Sara across the road. She's got a garden that's all overgrown. You could put the pony there – and camp there. Sara wouldn't mind." And indeed she didn't. I led Mollie through the little garden gate and found a flattish place for the tent before turning her loose in the long grass and weeds with some apprehension. I didn't want her gazing through the window and embarrassing the occupants or manuring the garden path. I gave her a drink in a borrowed bucket and headed for the pub. The publican's wife showed me into a smaller side room, served me my Guinness, offered me sandwiches and introduced me to the sole occupant, a small, toothless man called Joe.

Now, as I've explained before, I'm not a pub person. Not even in England with friends. But it's part of the Irish scene and if I was to get to know the Real Ireland, slake my thirst, and have somewhere warm to go in the evening, I had to learn to be at ease in pubs. So there we were, just me and Joe, and we were both too shy to talk. We sipped our Guinness, and smiled, and kept our eyes lowered or gazed at the fire, and I wrote my diary. After that drink I went back to my tent, but returned to the bar when it was too dark to read. Two men, Michael and John, had joined Joe. John was a man of the world, having worked in Bournemouth and the Channel Islands, and he knew how to talk to ladies like me (I found out later he has a pub himself down the road). And because he was so friendly, jovial and funny, everyone began to talk and I felt properly part of the scene. I learned all about turf and silage, giggled over a lot of risqué jokes about women and mares (my feminist friends would be horrified) and heard what it's like to be an Irish construction worker in Bournemouth. Undiluted pleasure, apparently! John did most of the talking, with Joe and Michael listening and nodding. But Joe became much more forthcoming as the evening wore on. His bird eyes got brighter and brighter and he had a delightful toothless grin, especially when romantic suggestions were in the air. Joe was the sort of traditional Irishman that American anthropologists study. He'd suddenly come out with little snippets of folk-wisdom, like: 'Horses like Guinness. Did you know that? A man can drink, and come to a horse and it'll do anything for him. A horse likes a man with some drink inside him. A cow now, or a bull, it hates it.'

The evening ended with me stumbling off into the night to test Joe's theory on Mollie, and with a promise to visit John the next day at his pub in Mullagh, the next village.

It was Sunday. I arrived in Mullagh just before noon and found the high street full of tractors and other agricultural vehicles. I thought it must be a farm auction or something, but no, it was Mass. That's how you get to Mass if you're a farmer in these parts. With all the faithful in church the town was deserted, so I tied Mollie to a lamppost and went into John's pub. While I was drinking coffee and chatting, a crowd of men, dressed in their Sunday best, surged in talking about the horse outside. That made conversation easy – I just answered questions.

When I left the pub the street was full of little groups standing around gossiping, and a tight group of admirers were talking to Mollie. When I returned from my search for groceries I found that a man had untied Mollie and was giving pony rides to the local children.

I loved the straightforward Irish adherence to Catholicism. As I wrote later to Kate:

People here are so open about their faith. None of our Church of England defensiveness about Christianity. It's part of life and sacred pictures are part of the home décor. I was in a delightful house last night which had the usual religious painting with its own broken red light giving eternal illumination. Jesus was staring down at his dripping sacred heart with a horrified 'What will Mum say?' expression.

I think of Ireland as a Third World country, but in an entirely complimentary, happy way. If I'd come here from England without seeing Peru, etc first, the culture shock would have been much greater. It's the friendliness and hospitality, the lack of any consciousness of time or efficiency, and the grumblings at the government which seem so familiar. There are also the negative aspects. There's real poverty – the farmer I stayed with last night has no car yet lives miles from the nearest town and there's no bus service – rubbish is dumped in beauty spots and dead cars litter the countryside. They lie peacefully in their green graveyards like so many dozing cows; they're up-turned in hedges, nestling in bracken, dumped in fields and nose-dived in ditches. Many old cars refuse to die, however. The MOT test seems to be just a formality, with no relationship to actual road-worthiness, so cars have no bumpers, or have holes in the floor, as in Africa.

And talking of holes, the Irish must have the worst teeth in the world. One frequently finds young people in their twenties with a full set of false teeth and I'm no longer surprised to be greeted with a gummy smile from women my own age. Teeth-pulling seems to be part of the Irish way of life. I thought I was getting a clue last night when the subject of high dental fees came up. 'What do they charge?' I asked.

'Jesus God, it's seven punts an extraction!'

'How about fillings?'

'Oh, I don't think he does those.'

A landowner told me about his farmhand who complained, 'I'm getting neither ease nor pleasure from my teeth. And when I went to the dentist to have them drew, he told me to come back in six weeks when the stumps was well rotted.'

Our amble south from Mullagh was lovely. No spectacular scenery but sunny weather with no wind – the first day I'd been able just to wear a T-shirt – and I could clip-clop along, thinking my thoughts, greeting the occasional passer-by (cars often stopped for the drivers to have a chat) and looking at flowers and butterflies. The hedgerows looked and smelled like my childhood. The grass and the flowers aren't cut back and I remembered the names I learned as a child: speedwell, potentilla tormentilla, scarlet pimpernel – and orange-tip butterflies. There were geese and cows in the fields instead of sheep, and a warm feeling of summer. I say I was thinking my own thoughts but usually they were non-thoughts. I'd anticipated that on a trip like this I'd work out the Meaning of Life or My Place in the Universe, but instead words arranged themselves in my subconscious to the rhythm of Mollie's hoof beats. One day it was relentlessly 'What'll we do with the butter mountain?', and I generally found myself singing either 'Molly Malone' or 'It's a long way to Tipperary' – which I expected to reach in a month or so.

I did reflect on God from time to time. How could I not in Catholic Ireland, where every day I passed a wayside shrine or shared a living room with a devotional painting? But as an agnostic I have no faith myself, though I've always been moved by the poetry of the King James Bible. That day of warm sunshine and flowers, and Mollie's pricked ears in front of me, I felt a new understanding of 'God is love'. I was travelling in a pool of love, love for the sun, the flowers, the colours – and above all, for Mollie. "For love is of God; and everyone that loveth is born of God, and knoweth God". Yes!

My warm, happy feelings continued into the evening. We were walking down a very narrow lane when a man herding cows stopped me to have a chat. Tom had dark curly hair, well-patched trousers, and was so friendly and interested that we talked for quite a while until Mum appeared in her bedroom slippers to find out what was going on. Although it was only 6 o'clock I asked if I could stay in one of their fields. They were delighted and removed some calves from the paddock near the house, and then of course I was invited in for tea. After I got the tent set up I asked to use the loo. "Ye'll find a place!" they both said laughing. The house was the sort that's described in books as 'simply furnished but neat as two pins'. There were three rooms, so the kitchen/sitting room was also a storeroom, with bags of potatoes and farm implements stacked by the walls. The only furniture was a table, two or three hardback chairs and a settee. The floor was cement and tea water boiled on an ancient turf-burning stove. Apart from a religious painting and a calendar there was a 1940s wireless that didn't work and an even earlier clock with a loud tick. We spent such an agreeable evening together, drinking tea and eating brown bread. Mum sat snapping sticks for kindling while we discussed hospital care ("Oh God, I thought my heart would stop there and then"), the evils of television ("Oh Lord I wouldn't have one in the house!") to farming, marriage and whether politicians should tell the truth.

I also discussed my current preoccupation – whether I would be allowed to take Mollie onto the ferry across the River Shannon. "Ah, ye'll have no problem, just chat to them first," was the consensus here. I'd read about an earlier traveller who had reached the Shannon and been unable to get across. O'Sullivan Beare, an Irish chieftain, was impeded by the river when fleeing from the English in 1602. His men were starving and there were no boats, so he neatly solved both problems by killing his horses, eating their meat and using the hides to make curraghs.

I arrived early at the pier before there was much traffic, tied Mollie to a lamppost, and when the first ferry arrived I tripped nimbly up the gangplank to talk to the husky ferryman. "Absolutely not!"

"But. . . but there's a notice there saying 'Livestock carried at your own risk'. Well, I'll take the risk!"

"They have to be in a cattle truck."

"I'll buy you a glass of Guinness at the pub!"

"Listen, I said no and I meant no. If my boss found out we'd all lose our jobs."

He turned away and started directing the waiting cars.

I took off Mollie's saddlebags, attached the long lead rope to her head collar and sat down to wait for an empty horsebox or cattle truck to arrive. Now I'm used to hitchhiking – indeed, I've hitchhiked all my adult life – but this was the first time I'd tried hitchhiking with a horse, and it wasn't easy. Two more ferries came and went, and around noon I made a decision. I tied Mollie to the lamppost again, heaped the luggage beside her and went back to talk to a just-back-from-living-in-Canada publican who I'd chatted with on my way down to the ferry, when the urge for a loo hit me. His name was Pierce and he owned the pub that served beer to passengers waiting for the ferry (this charming place has now been replaced by a pseudo castle selling coffee and souvenirs). The pub was crowded and I hated asking him to pause from pulling pints to listen to my problem, feeling anything but reassured when he said he'd see what he could do. He was clearly too busy to do anything; I'd hoped that he would just point out a horsebox owner in the pub. I tried to take matters into my own hands and asked some of the more accessible-looking men nearby if they were local. They all said no, winked at their friends and burst out laughing, so I sat in a corner and drank Guinness, ate crisps and worried about Mollie and my gear abandoned by the river. I went out to check on them both, gave Mollie a consolation carrot, and returned to the pub for a sandwich and gloomy contemplation. The 1-o'clock ferry came in, the drinkers drained their glasses and left, and suddenly the pub was almost empty. I asked the barmaid where Pierce was and she said he'd gone out. My gloom deepened. Why should I think that a busy publican would bother to help a complete stranger?

Then I looked out of the window. Outside was what looked like a large orange-crate on wheels attached to a rather smart red car. Pierce got out of the car, walked into the pub and said, "Ready?" I was almost speechless. Here was an actual horsebox – of sorts – and despite all my fretting, less than an hour had passed since I'd arrived with my problem.

Pierce apologised for the delay – apologised! – and said it was his cousin's trailer but they'd had difficulty finding a car to tow it so Pierce would use his own and drive across. "But what about your customers?" I spluttered. He shrugged and looked at his watch. "We've just got time to catch the 2-o'clock ferry." So I raced ahead, found Mollie and the gear still intact, led her up to the ramp of the orange crate, heaved the luggage into the back of the car, and got into the passenger seat with Pierce's young son for the short drive onto the ferry.

"Only in Ireland!" I heard an American tourist say as I fed carrots to Mollie during the crossing, then we drove down the ramp into Co Kerry, quickly unloaded Mollie and my gear, Pierce turned around and joined the queue of cars waiting to board for the return journey to Co Clare.

Chapter 12

At last I was in Kerry. I'd looked forward to my arrival for some time. After all, it's the county that attracts the most tourists because of its mountain scenery, and despite my teenage misery-memories of squelching through bogs in the rain, I also remembered the wild rocky hills and deep valleys of the Dingle Peninsula where we had stayed. I could see the mountains of Slieve Mish across the flatness of northern Kerry.

After the ferry crossing I headed for Ballybunion (at the request of my right foot) along a gentle road running between large fields. It felt quite different from Co Clare. More prosperous somehow, with larger farms, more cattle, no sheep. But the Real Ireland was never far away and we met our first ever pony and cart – much to Mollie's delight, and mine, since she quickened her pace to catch up. "That's a grand pony!" said the tinker. "How old?" But he was already out of the cart and looking in her mouth. No, I said firmly, I really didn't want to swap her for his little chestnut gelding.

Since much of that day had been spent trying to get across the Shannon, I'd planned to ride well into the evening but Mollie had other ideas. She slowed down hopefully at every driveway, while I told her it was much too early to stop. I gave in when we passed a really beautiful farm; its long drive was bordered by trees shading large fields of very green grass, and I rode up to the farmhouse under the speculative gaze of two boys. Although I was getting a little braver about asking farmers for hospitality I still hated that initial approach, and sat stiffly in the saddle until they were within earshot.

Mollie ended up in the best field of the trip, with the cows safely in an adjacent field and a water trough should she design to drink. It was a dairy farm and Mum had told me to come to the house for milk, but first I sat outside the tent and wrote up my diary, pausing at intervals to watch Mollie grazing. Considering the amount of exercise she was getting she looked remarkably fat. Oh gosh, I wouldn't be surprised if Willie had absentmindedly let a stallion into the field. I was an accomplished worrier, and every day I checked her obsessively for sores or lameness. While preparing for the trip I had bought a little book about horse problems, and read in horror about poll evil, spavins, windgalls, laminitis, and navicular disease. With four legs to go wrong, there was plenty to worry about, yet I had to admit that Mollie was in perfect physical shape. She looked lovely, and I was so proud of her.

Time for supper. I went in for a bucket of water for my morning ablutions and a bottle of milk and was offered a chair and *Dynasty*, along with tea with masses of brown bread and biscuits.

I was woken the next morning by rooks cawing in the trees above the tent, had my usual muesli and coffee (with fresh milk), then hearing heavy breathing poked my head out of the tent to find Mollie a few yards away being investigated by a herd of white Charolais bullocks which had just been let into the field. When they saw me they stampeded but Mollie didn't give a damn, being intent on catching up with her eating before it was time to go. She knew the day's routine so well now. I could spy on her through the tent flaps when I first unzipped the door from the warmth of my sleeping bag, and see her dozing in the morning sun. She generally stayed near the tent during the night, and would watch my movements as I got dressed and heated water on the little stove for coffee. Then she would have her own breakfast, determined to eat as much as possible before hitting the road. She didn't have to worry today. Sheila beckoned me from the house and asked if I'd like a cup of tea. On the kitchen table was not only tea but sausages, bread and butter and marmalade. While I ate (I'm never one to be put off a meal because I've just eaten one) Sheila talked.

I learned that she was one of 14 children. "When I was a child there was no free secondary education in Ireland. My parents sent me to America to live with a childless aunt and uncle. I was so miserable! I was only 14 and I missed all my brothers and sisters. Aunty wasn't used to children and everything seemed so strange at first. But I settled down, went to college, and got a good job in New York. But we Irish always come home, you know. I never intended to stay there. I came back and married and here we are." I remarked what a beautiful farm it was, how its well-fenced green fields and white-washed buildings had caught my eye from the road. "But you should see it in the winter! Mud everywhere. It's terrible then." The conversation turned to the North. "You won't find many people who want a united Ireland. In many ways the Catholics across the border are better off than we are. Child allowance, for instance. They get more family allowance in one week up there than we get here in a month!"

Ballybunion was described in my guidebook as 'a popular holiday resort on a dramatic coastline of cave-riddled cliffs on the shores of a bay warmed by the Gulf Stream. Dividing the golden strand in front of the town is a promontory with the remains of late 16th-century Ballybunion Castle, a Fitzmaurice stronghold. . . and a golf course considered to be one of the best in the world.' We arrived around noon and found a path leading past some caravans to the beach. It was all as described, caves carved into the cliffs by the pounding surf, a long stretch of the deserted golden beach, and some golfers high on the cliff top who didn't even look up as I galloped by.

I pulled up by some dunes and decided this would be a good place for lunch. I could get out of the wind and there was a little grass for Mollie. These days I didn't tether her; I took her bit out and let her wander around, grazing. And that day I didn't even bother to zip up the saddlebag after pulling out my plastic bag containing Sheila's brown bread and butter, and a pot of marmite. I sat on the sand in the sun, ate some of my lunch, read a little Yeats and looked for Ballyduff on my map. I was now preoccupied with Mollie's shoes, having seen how thin they were when I picked out her hooves that morning. A front shoe was cracked in half and slightly loose. I had to find a blacksmith soon and had been told I might find one in Ballyduff, about five miles away. Suddenly there was a commotion behind me.

Mollie had taken off at a gallop. She laboured up a sand dune, veered round at the top, slid down and continued up and down the dunes in circles, skidding in the soft sand, while bits and pieces flew out of the open saddlebag. I stared at her open-mouthed. It wasn't high spirits (very unlikely with phlegmatic Mollie), I could see that she was really scared. It took a few moments for me to realise what had happened. Out of the corner of her eye she had caught sight of a white plastic bag protruding from the unzipped saddlebag. Mollie had always had something of a phobia about plastic bags and had tried to escape this menace but it continued to pursue her, threatening her left flank, whatever evasive action she took. "Whoa Mollie, it's alright!" She galloped past me but on her next circuit I managed to grab her rope. She was still very frightened, breathing hard with dilated nostrils and wide eyes. The breeze fluttered the plastic, still sticking out of the saddlebag, and she tried to take off again, dragging me with her.

I managed to hold on and block her view of the offending piece of plastic while I calmed her down and zipped up the bag.

This behaviour came as a complete surprise. It wasn't the first time I'd left the saddlebag open and Mollie was always totally placid while I rummaged around there. Indeed it had always impressed me that she was willing to stand quietly while I heaved the bags onto her back, often missing the first time (they hadn't got any lighter) and banging her flanks as I struggled. In an instant this had all changed. It was a long time before Mollie's breathing returned to normal, and I repacked my picnic stuff in slow motion, talking to her quietly as I did so.

I had hoped to ford the River Cashen at the end of the beach but the tide was in and I didn't want to subject Mollie to any more unpleasantness. Following a track along the river I passed some salmon fishermen, bright in their yellow oilskins, hauling in their nets. No luck today, they told me. At Ballyduff's general store I bought my lunch, including an apple for Mollie, and some more packets of soup. I always tried to carry enough food for one night of wild camping since I never knew where I would end up. To my great relief, the shopkeeper knew where the blacksmith lived, though it was three miles away. "Just keep straight along that road. You can't miss it."

"Oh dear no, I don't shoe horses any more," said Michael. "I stopped seven years ago on account of my thumb, see." He showed me the scar. "No strength in my left hand. I'd do you the favour, mind, but you'd have to bring your own shoes. You can get them in Lerrig, and there's a farrier nearby who can nail them on. Just a minute, I'll measure her hooves for you... size 5½ you'll need, and don't forget to buy 26 nails."

My route was now dictated by my quest for a blacksmith, and my comfort by Mollie's new phobia. I stopped for the night near Causeway, en route to Lerrig, camping in a garden, and next morning covered the saddlebags with plastic to protect them from the rain. But Mollie was having none of it. She wouldn't let me come near her. I had to remove the plastic and just hope the rain would hold off; which it did, despite slabs of slate-grey cloud looking near enough to touch.

Lerrig was nothing more than a shop, but what a wonderful shop! It was multi-roomed and sold everything: carrots and apples, cabbages and hay, sweaters and stockings, hardware and horseshoes. With Mollie so jumpy I was nervous about leaving her, and before tying her up I checked the area for lurking plastic bags.

'I want a set of horse shoes, size 5½ please. Oh, and 26 nails.'

"I'll give you two extra, just in case," said the very friendly shopkeeper. "A farrier? There's one not far from here." He came out to admire Mollie and show me the way. "If you go a mile along that road you'll see the smithy on the right. He still does horses."

As well as shoes I bought a tether chain. More weight to carry but it eliminated the danger of the rope getting round Mollie's leg. If I needed to tether her again during the day I didn't want a repeat of the Cliffs of Moher scene. As I'd learned with Johnny so many years ago, the weight of a chain keeps it on the ground and under hoof. Much safer.

The new shoes and chain weighed down the saddlebag causing it to slip to one side. I felt that lop-sided luggage must be uncomfortable for Mollie and was forever pulling it back into position, only to watch it slowly slide down again. It wasn't worth re-balancing the bags when I was so near the blacksmith. After two miles I knocked at a door to ask directions from an admiring woman in hair rollers. The forge was only a few more doors down. "I hope he's there." So did I, but he wasn't. At least I could get no reply when I hammered on the door. Two apologetic black mongrels cringed in the garden, their wagging tails clamped between their legs. My knocks roused a neighbour from the caravan next door who came to help. He prowled around the house trying doors and said the smith was probably asleep. "He's fond of the. . ." And he raised an imaginary drink to his mouth.

I sulked back to the horseshoe shop, hauling the slipping bags up and cursing Mollie for needing footwear. I remembered a dream I'd had years ago about riding a pony to the blacksmith. "I'm taking him to get new shoes," I called out to a friend. Whereupon the pony turned around and said "But I don't want shoes, I want slippers!"

The shop manager was sympathetic and told me I'd certainly get the shoes done in Tralee. "There's a blacksmith in Station Road, right in the centre of town. Ask for Paddy." I'd hoped to avoid Tralee. Despite the romantic association with the 'Rose of Tralee' I'd been warned that "it's no more than a dirty ugly old town!" Irish songs are about people, not places. The 'Rose of Tralee' isn't about Tralee, it's about Mary, a kitchen maid who was 'lovely and fair as the rose in the summer' and who died of a broken heart when her lover, the son of her employer, was sent away by his irate mother and married someone else. It was he (William Mulchinock) who wrote the song at her graveside. (Or so they say. He must have been a fast worker.)

At least I now had a new song in my head and you can't sing and remain in a bad mood. Mollie, with no song in her head, kept hers and crept along thinking about plastic bags. The sun peered out from behind black clouds as I approached Ardfert. If I couldn't get a blacksmith, at least I could get history. Ardfert, with its cathedral and ruined friary, is one of the main tourist sights in flat and boring northwest Kerry. Having just ridden on to a new map, rich in promise of lakes and high mountains, I was impatient to reach Dingle.

I enjoyed the Ardfert ruins, despite my nervousness over leaving Mollie tethered to a gate covered with warning notices about fierce greyhounds. I'd asked permission and a woman had said darkly, "She'll be alright as long as the dogs don't see her." They didn't. The monastery was founded in the 6th century by St Brendan whom I'd adopted as my patron saint. He was a navigator, not a horseman, but maybe he did discover America and he certainly got around his own country and the outlying islands. There are St Brendan mementos everywhere, mostly in the scenic parts of Kerry. The saint received his education at Ardfert and became the best-selling writer of his times. The account of his voyages was translated into English, Welsh, Gaelic, Breton, Saxon, Flemish, Latin and French – pretty good going before the invention of the printing press. He had lots of adventures, including encountering a crystal mountain (an iceberg, maybe?) and once celebrating Easter Mass and lighting a fire on a domed island which turned out to be an indignant whale!

The roofless and glassless cathedral up the road reminded me of Tintern Abbey and other such British ruins. A symbol of the power of the Church in medieval times, it had a fine Romanesque doorway, splendid east windows, and some fancy crenulations.

The rain held off as I urged Mollie down the busy main road towards Tralee and the blacksmith – 10 miles away. As I approached the town a strong wind blew up and with the wind came flying plastic bags. It was a horrible ride, ugly and dangerous with Mollie frequently shying into the road into the path of the rush-hour traffic. I was soon lost in a complex of housing and industrial estates. No-one had heard of a Tralee blacksmith, and as I followed their vague directions to Station Road my heart sank as I realised it was indeed bang in the centre of town; I couldn't imagine that he would shoe horses in that location. If only these people had telephones! Station Road, when I finally got there, was narrow and jammed with cars but I could see blue flashes coming from a large open building that I rightly guessed to be the forge. I got off and waited for Paddy to come out to me, Mollie pulling back in fright at the sight and sound of the welding. "Haven't done horses for 20 years," he said, without a smile. "Whoever told you to come here?" I felt near to tears. "I reckon you won't find anyone in Dingle either. No call for it now, see!"

"But they told me in Clare that there would be plenty of farriers in Kerry."

"Did they now."

While we were talking, an elegantly dressed woman with what I guessed to be a German accent came up to marvel at Mollie and our achievements. "How far do you go each day?"

"About 20 miles, on average."

"Goodness, that's very impressive."

"No, it isn't," broke in Paddy the non-farrier. "In days back you'd take a pony 40 or 50 miles in a trap."

"But isn't it easier for a harness pony? Once it gets going there must be very little work involved. Poor Mollie's got to carry me and my luggage. Anyway, I couldn't do more than 20 miles or so. My bottom and knees get sore." I was feeling thoroughly fed up and not inclined to stand there chatting, holding a hungry pony. The woman spoke again.

"Do you need somewhere to spend the night?"

"Do I ever!"

"I run an independent hostel and we used to have our own pony so there's a field. It's only 20 minutes from here." I felt instantly cheered. At least I could have a dry night (the rain was not going to hold off forever) and make a few phone calls. There was a pony trekking centre near Tralee and they would certainly know of a blacksmith who still did horses.

The Dromtacker Hostel was a long 20 minutes away and the field a bit sparse. I led Mollie past a caravan to a grassy glade full of rusting machinery and washing. As I walked away I found her following me with pricked ears and a 'you can't mean *here*?' expression on her face. She'd been spoiled by last night's luxury. I pulled her tether rope across the opening, and added further deterrents to escape while the rain came down in torrents. I was glad to be inside, with the cheerful chatter of the hostellers and the shrieks of a horde of children, presumably belonging to the warden.

It was still raining hard the next morning, but at least there was a public phone at the hostel so I was able to phone William O'Connor. His pony trekking stable, El Rancho, was well known and I couldn't waste any more time looking for blacksmiths. He would advise me. I also wanted to learn about off-road routes through those tempting-looking mountains on the Dingle peninsula. If anyone knew about them, William would. Mrs O'Connor answered the phone. "I'm afraid my husband's away on a trek, but do come here for coffee and I'll see what I can do to help."

I found Ballyard on the map, just south of Tralee, and while waiting for the skies to brighten, I carefully encased the saddlebags in black, non-flapping plastic. I was determined to keep my kit dry. Earlier, Mollie had come up to me with a little whinny, clearly enthusiastic about the day ahead and the possibility of better grazing. I felt confident that her bag phobia would not be triggered by my inoffensive waterproofing, but nevertheless enlisted one of the other hostellers to help load her up.

I tied her to a tree, spoke soothing words and we approached with the saddlebags. She pulled back and the branch snapped. More soothing words, a thicker rope and a stouter tree. Again we approached, one holding each side of the saddlebags so that we could lay it gently on her back. She pulled back with all her strength – I could see the muscles in her shoulder and neck bulge with the effort – and something gave. From my position behind her I couldn't see her head but could hear a dreadful noise like a steam train leaving the station. Mollie's beautiful Peruvian head collar, designed to withstand recalcitrant Andean mules, had broken and the noseband was tight round her nostrils, suffocating her. Thank God I had her tied with a slip knot. I'd thought the head collar such a good design with the noseband tightening when the rope was pulled – I never dreamed that it could be broken. Indeed, only a few days earlier someone was telling me about horses breaking head collars and I said smugly "not my head collar". The person looked at me scornfully and said, "A horse can break anything!" Since the head collar was also the bridle I was in trouble, though I managed an improvised repair. Then of course I had to take off all that plastic that I'd so laboriously wrapped round the bags. Finally we were able to lift them onto Mollie's back, although it took ages. She was in a real state. Then all the children wanted pony rides which normally I wouldn't mind but it seemed foolhardy this morning. There was such a wailing when I said no, so I gave in, and although she was patient with them my heart was in my mouth.

It had taken an hour to get under way. Now the offending plastic was gone, Mollie was quiet enough, but it was still a horrid ride to Ballyard with lots of traffic and lots of plastic and I knew that Mollie considered the latter posed the greatest danger.

El Rancho was a beautiful place, and over coffee Anne O'Connor and I pored over William's brochures so I could see the routes he took with his pony-trekking clients around and across the peninsula. She didn't know the details, however; I would have to phone her husband for more information in one of his overnight places. She gave me the number. But she did know, definitely, that there was a farrier in Castlemaine, "over the mountains" by the name of O'Shea. And he did still shoe horses? For sure.

The road over the mountains was perfect, with a line of grass running down the centre and verges to provide a non-slip surface. Bluebells were still hanging on in sheltered glades under the beech trees, and a river tumbled down from the Slieve Mish Mountains to my right. As we climbed towards the highest point, the trees disappeared and I was surrounded by bare peaks and rain-washed rocks, with not a house in sight. Such a contrast to north Kerry and horrible Tralee. The sun came out when I reached the top of the hill, and I could see Macgillycuddy's Reeks to the south, where I had climbed Carrauntoohil, Ireland's highest mountain, on that family holiday all those years ago.

Only one car passed and the driver stopped to talk. He was flatteringly impressed at what I was doing and thought it was all a marvellous idea. "What'll you do with the pony when you finish the ride?"

"Oh, I'll find a way of taking her back to England. I couldn't possibly sell her now!"

What? I really had to get a grip on myself; of all impractical ideas this was the least thought out.

It was 7 o'clock when I reached Castlemaine so my plan was to locate the blacksmith and make an appointment for Mollie to be shod the next day. I found what I thought was the forge and asked a youth sitting on a tractor in the yard if this was the blacksmith's house. He jumped down and hid behind the vehicle. Taken aback, I asked the two eyes peeping behind the wheel, "Excuse me, sorry to frighten you, is this the blacksmith's?" Once I got closer I realised that the boy had Down's Syndrome. Then mum came out, saw me, and said, "Well, isn't this marvellous!" And marvellous it was for the next 15 hours. I have never been with a family where love was so evident, love turned both inwards to the family and out to anyone fortunate enough to come into their sphere. When Beth said of the silent boy, "Joe-Joe's our treasure," I knew this was the truth. There were four children and a bachelor uncle who got lonely living up the road by himself so now lived with the family, and Dinny the blacksmith who lost an eye on the job. I met the charming and mature daughter, but lost my heart to 12-year-old Anthony who was so polite and interested and just knew by instinct everything that needed doing.

Dinny had a quick look at Mollie's feet and, with relief, I handed over the shoes and nails which had been weighing down my saddlebag. "I'll do her first thing in the morning," he said.

There was no question of me finding accommodation elsewhere in Castlemaine. Mollie was tethered on some waste ground full of the usual rusting machinery, but with a good supply of grass and within snorting distance of the tent, and I was invited in for tea and biscuits in front of a cosy turf fire. I stayed chatting all evening, enveloped in the warmth of the family, all the stresses of the last few days disappearing.

When eventually my protestations that I really must go to bed were accepted, I was escorted to my tent by Anthony, clutching a hot water bottle in one hand and a mug of Bournevita in the other. I slept like a log and woke guiltily at 8.30 to the sound of metal hitting metal and a few minutes later Anthony was outside saying, "I'll take Mollie to the forge now. Mum has breakfast ready for you." On the kitchen table was a plate heaped with mushrooms, tomatoes, sausage, egg and bacon, and in case I was still hungry there was brown bread, toast and marmalade. By the time I'd staggered out to see how the shoeing was going, it was almost finished. Mollie's forefoot was resting on the tripod while Dinny filed away the overgrown hoof. The red-hot shoes had been burned into position so were unlikely to loosen during my next 400 miles. That's how long the previous set had lasted. I had paid IR£25 for those so had been to the bank in Tralee in preparation for this major expense. "How much do I owe you?" I asked.

"Six punts."

"Six punts! Are you sure?"

"Well I usually charge eight but. . ."

I paid eight. The next customer arrived, a jaunty brown pony pulling a cart, so I took a photo, said an almost tearful goodbye and set off towards Dingle.

Chapter 13

Mollie stepped out in her new shoes like a child in new wellingtons. For days I'd had her balancing along narrow grass verges to save her feet, but now she could trot briskly along the roads. And I was in the real Kerry at last! The showers couldn't dampen my euphoria; besides, they provided rainbows over Castlemaine Harbour. Beyond the silver bay were rows of mountains in different shades of grey against a rain-filled sky. It was the first of June. There were still bluebells beside the road and occasional primroses, but the fields were now full of yellow flag. Silly to hurry; I'd give Mollie a lunch break by the sea and have some of Beth's brown bread and the yoghurt I'd bought in the town.

After packing away my lunch I propped my elbows on the saddle and studied the map. I'd discussed possible off-road routes with William on the phone but was still undecided on where to go next. I considered retracing my steps towards Tralee to intercept his group as they returned to the stables. His knowledge of the peninsula would be such a help, and he could show me on the map the route he took between the high mountains above Lough Anascaul. Amid such beautiful scenery I longed to get away from roads and cars. However, my late start and the bad weather discouraged me – I'd have to hurry to meet the group and what was the point of going high if clouds hid the view? Probably I should just push on to the town of Dingle – the map showed all sorts of tempting back-roads. But tomorrow would be the start of the Whit Weekend and the town would be packed with holiday-makers. . . I'd continue west and decide tomorrow.

At Inch, 12 miles from Castlemaine, a dune-bordered finger of land projects into the sea. Between the dunes and the waves were three miles of hard sand – perfect for a gallop. No one else was around as we thudded through the surf and frolicked in the dunes. I felt a bit like a child playing on her own. Like hard times, fun times are best shared. Perhaps with a companion I would have gone right to Inch Point but I was content to stop after a couple of miles and walk Mollie quietly back. I needed to catch my breath, not she. She was superbly fit now after her regular 15 to 20 slow miles a day. I felt that we could travel forever.

If the scenery had been beautiful before Inch, it was stunning now. The road followed high indented cliffs flecked with cormorants and gulls. Blocks of white rain obscured parts of the mountains on the other side of the bay while the sun played on selected peaks bringing a blobby rainbow. I felt tears pricking my eyes. How perfect to ride past such beauty at two or three miles an hour, able to see every shifting pattern of light over the breaking surf. Normally I wouldn't sit and stare at a view for an hour – I'm too impatient – but on Mollie I could gaze all day while the scenery slowly changed. What could be better?

As I approached Anascaul the sun edged the clouds with silver and lit green fields beneath the brown dour-faced mountains. It seemed the loveliest town in Ireland. I would find a bed and breakfast place and celebrate Mollie's shoes and the Real Kerry. On the outskirts of town I saw a sign 'Evening Meals'. Why not have a binge? An Englishman emerged from the garden and said sorry, his wife was away and it was she who did the cooking. But he suggested a B&B and a pony-owning girl who could probably put Mollie up for the night. A little further on I was greeted by another Englishman. "Do you know about the old road over the mountains? It's lovely! Goes to Castle Gregory."

"Could I make it on horseback?"

"Should do. After all, it used to be a road. See you in the pub tonight!"

While looking for the pony owner I passed the South Pole Inn which seemed a particularly inappropriate name in verdant Anascaul. I learned later that it was built and named by the Antarctic explorer, Tom Crean. He was in the search party that found the bodies of Captain Scott and his companions. I wondered how often someone leaves that pub saying, "I am just going outside and may be some time."

There was scant information about Crean in Anascaul in 1984, but now there's a statue and a thriving Tom Crean Society in the town, with lectures, events and excursions commemorating this modest man. It is said that when he retired to Anascaul he 'put all of his medals away and never again spoke about his experiences in the Antarctic' although this is contradicted by the story that when his wife reprimanded him for cooking up eggs and bacon on a meatless Friday he responded: "If you had been where I have been some Fridays I would have eaten a slice off your arse." Crean had plenty to boast about. He spent more time in Antarctica than either Scott or Shackleton – and outlived them both. Two acts of extreme heroism stand out: having accompanied Captain Scott to within 180 miles of the South Pole he was sent back with two companions while the remaining team of five completed their ill-fated journey to the Pole. He wept with disappointment at not being chosen. When one man, Evans, fell sick on the return trek, Crean volunteered to walk alone to the supply hut to get help. Already weakened by the arduous

1,500-mile trek – pulling a sledge – that he'd just accomplished, and with only some chocolate and three biscuits to sustain him, he walked the 35 miles in 18 hours. His action saved the lives of the two men, and he was awarded the Albert Medal from King George V. Two years later he was on Shackleton's *Endurance* when it was crushed by the ice in Antarctica. Crean guided one of the lifeboats to Elephant Island and then made the 800-mile journey by small boat to South Georgia. Ironically the only time he reached the South Pole was when he came home to his pub.

U   U   U

Cathy was delighted to give Mollie her field for the night – her pony was elsewhere – and to have a short ride. She got off enviously, explaining that her pony was spoiled and very lazy. Mollie was lucky, after two nights of indifferent grazing in back yards she had a large field of short nutritious grass. I too was lucky. The Four Winds B&B just up the road had a vacancy. I didn't go to the pub; I can't even remember if I had an evening meal. I do remember luxuriating in a hot bath, chuckling with delight at the sight of a bed, and feeling guilty about my grubby, greasy, white-hairy saddlebags in such a lovely clean room. I washed some clothes and reorganised my luggage, looking out my Swiss Army knife and sewing kit so that I could repair the head collar. I like mending; it took an hour, but I was proud of the result. It would break if subjected to a hard pull, but perhaps that was no bad thing. Then I got out the maps and the brochures given to me by Anne O'Connor, and tried to work out the route of that old road over the mountains, which was only partially shown on my inadequate map. It was clear up to Lough Anascaul, and I could see its general direction over the col between two mountains and down to the broad river valley leading to Castle Gregory. William took his trekking groups along this route and had told me on the phone that the 'Valley of the Cows' was beautiful –

but that I'd never find my way in from the north. But I was now on the south side and felt sure that this track would be easy enough to follow. I'd been on tarred roads long enough, and had sufficient confidence now to do a little exploring. Besides, these mountains were the stuff of legends. Many, many years ago, around the time of Christ, there lived a small fierce Irishman called Cuchulainn. This Cuchulainn was apparently irresistible to women, which got him into all sorts of scraps. Near Anascaul he nearly met his match. His adversary was a giant, the woman who loved him was Scal Ni Mhurnain, and the weapons were boulders. The two warriors exchanged missiles for a week before Cuchulainn was hit. Scal, hearing his cry and thinking him dead, drowned herself in the lake at the foot of the mountains, hence An Scal.

Next morning I told my hosts of my plans. Kathleen immediately said, "Oh no, that's much too dangerous, you should go by the main road." I smiled patiently and explained that the whole point of riding a pony was to get off the roads and see the scenery denied to car drivers. "And I'm pretty experienced in mountains now, and I have a map and compass." Her husband joined us. "At least the weather's improving. The green road doesn't go all the way, you know. There's a cross-country stretch, I think you have to go northwest." Looking at the map and William's brochure, I agreed with him.

Mollie threw up her head when I came to the gate and started to walk towards me, her nostrils fluttering with her now familiar whicker. I told her we were going to have a special adventure today, gave her a thorough grooming and picked out her feet, admiring her new shoes, and took my final directions for the lane up to the lake. By the time we reached Lough Anascaul, rain clouds were whisking over the brown mountains and the lake shone grey in the dull light. A few cars were parked on the tarmac, their owners staring fixedly at the lake through carefully closed windows.

The enticing green road zigzagged up the hill between waterfalls and boulders left from Cuchlain's fight. Mollie, feeling grass beneath her feet instead of hard road, walked eagerly, head up, ears pricked. "This is what we came for, isn't it, Mollie girl?" I commented. My heart soared, although the old road was not without obstacles. Two stone walls blocked the track. The first was well built, and the most movable stones were to the right of an old stone pillar which presumably once supported a gate. The gap I made was narrow and when I led Mollie through, her saddlebag caught on the pillar. She surged forward nervously, ripping the canvas. I was annoyed with myself, having no suitable material with which to patch it and cursed my laziness for not making a wider gap. The next wall was easier, and soon we crossed a bridge over the tumbling river; the views, even in this dull weather, became dramatic. Grey slabs of rock beetled over the steep, boulder-strewn slopes, cut by cascading waterfalls, while the level ground was green with tussock grass and fluffy clumps of bog cotton. Behind me, and below, was the silvery lake and fading into the distance the green fields of Anascaul and blue-grey distant mountains. The path was clear and easy to follow, sometimes marshy, but not boggy, and we were soon near the col that marked the top of the Anascaul valley. In front of me was a broad, flattish area. I had been keeping an eye on the hoof-prints which periodically showed me I was not the first rider up the track that week, but was distracted by the fine views and it took a while for me to realise the prints had disappeared. Then the track ended.

The last section had been little more than a marsh between banks. Now the guiding banks had gone and I could see nothing but coarse clumps of grass separated by black muddy rivulets. Suddenly Mollie was floundering in bog. Her hind quarters went in above the hocks, she struggled free then sank again, this time up to her belly. Here she stayed, breathing heavily, head outstretched, chin resting on the ground. I had jumped off as she went down, and tried to undo the saddlebags, but my hands were shaking too much. From watching others on Willie's trek I knew Mollie would try again once she regained her breath. She did, but still to no avail. Desperately, I fumbled again to relieve her of the weight of the saddlebags, but couldn't reach the straps. I tugged hard on the lead rope and urged her to try again. Summoning all her strength she made a supreme effort, reaching up with her forelegs, her head thrust forward for balance and back legs thrashing until she succeeded in freeing herself. She stood panting on firm ground, her legs covered with brown slime and lumps of the stuff covering her head and neck.

I stroked Mollie's face and ears and apologised for getting her into this mess. I was still trembling but she was remarkably calm and soon started to graze. I needed to pause and try to work things out with my map and compass. The valley ahead lay to the northeast, so the Valley of the Cows must be the one on the left. That was northwest, and I thought I could see a faint path traversing the shoulder toward it. In any case I had to get away from the bog, so retraced my steps and to my great relief soon came across hoof prints going in the right direction. My joy was short-lived; after a short distance I lost them again. Leaving Mollie to graze I set off on foot to reconnoitre but after a few yards realised that she was following me anxiously. There was nowhere to tie her; we had to do our path-seeking together. Using the compass to steer us, I led Mollie northwest. I managed to keep high and reasonably dry, skirting round the worst bits of bog and safely crossing a small river, until we came to a viewpoint and the discovery that I'd made a needless detour. The valley that I had rejected as being in the wrong direction at the end of the track was indeed the correct one. The old road was clearly and temptingly visible far below us as it followed the squiggling river along the broad valley to Castle Gregory, though the route down was hidden from view.

But at least I knew where I was going; if I headed east across that flat grassy area I should pick up the path again. But it wasn't grass, it was bog.

Climbers and hikers dislike bog because of the discomfort of wet feet; there's little danger. But for a horse weighing a couple of hundredweight supported on pole-like legs, it's another matter. It was impossible to tell what was safe and what wasn't. Some wet areas looked lethal but afforded a firm footing, others looked almost dry and supported my weight but I would see Mollie go down. Time and again she sank above her hocks, struggling out before becoming more deeply bogged; but once she was again up to her belly, a pathetic legless figure with her chin resting on the ground and a look of defeat in her eyes. All I could do was urge her to make an effort, then watch helplessly as her struggles sank her deeper into the mire. I was as terrified that she'd pull a muscle as I was fearful that she would never get out. When she freed herself I hugged her in pride and gratitude and together we made our slow laborious way to the next viewpoint. When we reached it I shouted my relief. Not only were we out of the bogs, we were only about half a mile from the track. I could see it zigzagging up the far side of a deep canyon at the head of the valley, crossing the river near the top, then disappearing. I was perhaps 80 yards from where I'd lost the hoof-marked track.

Leaving Mollie tucking into the grass (it was now 5 o'clock and neither of us had had lunch) I started scouting out the best route and rearranging my night plans. I now doubted we'd get to Castle Gregory that day; better to camp in that lovely valley far below once we'd negotiated the switchbacks. There was plenty of grazing and we both deserved a good rest. But my musings were cut short. Between me and the track was the canyon, and I could see no way to reach the path running down its far side. Its steep sides were slick with rain, and grey rocks overhung the edge. To the north were more cliffs – not so steep – but deeper. The map showed an 800-foot drop to the valley; a person could probably make it down, I decided, but not a pony, and certainly not a laden pony. I felt close to despair. There was no choice but to cross that dreadful bog again to regain the high ground and retrace our steps. Returning to Mollie I told her without much conviction, to take heart, that it was nearly over. Taking the head collar I started to lead her back, but when she felt the soft ground beneath her feet, she made it clear that she would go no further. I mounted and urged her forward. We made reasonable progress, but with the extra weight she again went down, belly deep. This time she struggled free reasonably soon but one of her flailing hooves caught the back of my hand, which swelled alarmingly. I tried to get a grip on myself. Anxiety was making me careless; this was no place to risk a serious injury. But what could I do?

Then Mollie was down again. And this time she seemed ready to give up; she stayed immobile for what seemed like an eternity, breathing hard with the whites of her eyes showing. I knelt on the ground by her head, stroking her ears and talking, pleading and cajoling, I told her she must make one more effort, that we'd soon be all right. She turned her head and glanced back at the saddlebags. Of course! My earlier trembling had given way to a despairing calm and this time I was able to undo the buckles and remove the luggage. Mollie immediately renewed her struggle and managed to free herself. I knew then what I must do. There was no question of trying to reach the valley tonight – we were both nearly exhausted. I would set up my tent on the far side of the little river (the one that later plunged so frustratingly into the canyon) then try to persuade Mollie to join me. If only she could reach the river there was good grazing along the banks, and if I could find a ford, or a place where she could jump across, we'd be on the high heathery ground again with a clear route down to the valley.

Saddlebags are not designed to be carried and it took the last of my strength to heave them over the bogs and across stepping stones over the river. Dumping them on the firm ground on the opposite bank, I returned for Mollie. Without the bags surely I could lead her across that relatively short stretch of boggy ground. I'd worked out a moderately firm route but she resolutely refused to be led. When I got on her back she bravely took a step, sank, struggled out and stood firm. Nothing I could do, on or off, would move her. I took off the saddle and carried it across the bogs and the river. Then I set up the tent on the far bank. I needed time to think, but the only thought was that I *had* to get Mollie across the bog. She was standing on a little island of terra firma, and all around her was squelch.

Returning, I tried – whimpering in desperation – to lead her in every direction. I didn't care where she went as long as she got to solid ground. She stood firm with rolling eyes. My whimpers turned to sobs as I realised she was trembling. Overcome with remorse I pressed my forehead against her shoulder and wept. Mollie started nibbling at the scant grass. I took out her bit and went to the tent. I could see no way out. It was now 8 o'clock and with only three hours of daylight left I hardly had time to get help. And what sort of help could I get? Two wooden planks would do it – Mollie would walk along those to firm ground – or perhaps a roll of carpet. But they'd have to be carried up by hand; no tractor would get up to this place. And who would be willing to carry that sort of weight three or four miles and 800 feet up on a Saturday night? But I couldn't leave Mollie standing motionless all night, which she was apparently prepared to do. Horses keep warm by being constantly on the move. Black clouds were building up, rain was certain, and I was sure she'd catch a chill.

I did some fairly hard praying as I headed back to the Mollie Island. Having run out of options I just wanted some sort of divine solution. But when I reached the top of the hill my heart lurched in fear. She wasn't there. Had she tried to move and sunk into the bog again? But I couldn't see her white head. Then I raised my eyes and saw her calmly grazing on a firm grassy area on the far side of the marsh. She was safe! With a little cry of joy I floundered towards her and flung my arms round her neck. Now, at last, I could release all the desperate anxiety, guilt and loneliness of the last few hours in laughter and tears as I hugged and stroked her. We were all right. Together we had survived this dreadful day and tomorrow we would rest in Castle Gregory.

I spent the rest of the daylight hours devising a route from Mollie's grazing area to the firm ground where I had pitched my tent. The only potential problem seemed to be the river with marshy banks that separated her from this dry ground. From here I knew I that if I kept close to the cliffs I could stay on firm ground, and could now see where the path went, contouring the side of the cliff to cross the canyon where the river was shallow. We were so nearly there, the dangers were over and tomorrow we'd both be fresh. Mollie might baulk at crossing the river after her experiences of today, but if I left her untethered that night she would wander around keeping warm and regain her confidence. She could also make the most of the sparse grazing. I didn't think she'd go far.

The first drops of rain were falling as I climbed up the rise from the river to take a last look at my pony. She was standing watching me, ears pricked. "Good night Mollie!", I called out.

As soon as I reached the tent the rain came crashing down, beaten against the flysheet by strong winds. I had little appetite but made a cup of tea. My companionable radio refused to work. I couldn't concentrate on a book, so I got into my sleeping bag and worried about Mollie, the terrible day that she'd had and now no shelter from the storm. But she was used to rain, I told myself; she'd just turn her back to the wind and wait it out.

Waking at 6.30 I ate my breakfast apple, teeth chattering against the morning cold as I pulled on sodden socks and boots. I'd have a proper breakfast once I'd retrieved Mollie. Putting the core in my pocket as a Good Morning present, I crossed the stream on the stepping stones and started to negotiate the bogs, stopping to admire a handsome red fox which trotted calmly across the cliff tops in front of me. I wasn't surprised to find that Mollie had wandered from her evening grazing area. From the many hoof prints beside the river I gathered that she'd paced backwards and forwards looking for a safe place to cross. There was certainly better grazing on the high ground near the cliffs. I couldn't tell if she'd succeeded in crossing so I trudged in large circles, expecting any minute to spot her in a dip or over the next rise. But nothing. Calling her name as I walked, I reached the cliff edge and looked down.

In the green valley far below I could see, along with the greyish dots of sheep, something larger and whiter. Why surely that was Mollie! The clever pony must have made her way down that perilously steep hill. But was it her? It could have been sunlight glinting on wet rocks. I went back to the tent for my binoculars. Yes, it was Mollie alright... but she was lying down. Well of course she'd be tired after the hard day and the effort of climbing down the cliff. Horses often sleep stretched out like that in the early morning. I called and whistled, expecting her to lift her head. No movement.

Fear gripped my heart as I started down the hill, slithering on the wet rocks, and lowering myself backwards down the steepest bits, grabbing handfuls of tussock grass. I was muttering over and over again, "Let it be all right. Oh please God make it all right." Halfway down I paused to check again with the binoculars, but not after that. I didn't want to see any more, I just wanted to believe that it was indeed all right, despite the mounting evidence: the smooth line of crushed grass showing the slide of a heavy body and the position she was lying in. I knew then what I would find. Mollie was dead.

I stared at her body. This couldn't be true. No, it wasn't Mollie, surely it was another horse! Then I looked at the hooves and the irrefutable evidence of the new shoes.

I turned away and climbed back up the cliff, devoid of all feeling, mechanically picking the safest route to my tent. Methodically I began the familiar process of breaking camp, stuffing my sleeping bag into its sack, removing the tent poles and folding up the tent. As I put the tent pegs in my pocket, I felt something: a plastic bag containing an apple core. Only then did I start to cry.

Chapter 14

It doesn't hit you at first, grief. Just as the body protects you from fully feeling the pain of an accident, so the mind stays clear of an emotional shock. I felt unreal, as though I was watching a video of me calmly getting on with the things that had to be done. I finished packing up the tent, organised the saddlebags, and put the saddle and tack into a bin liner tied up with the reins. I carried the bags, one at a time, across the river, through the bogs and up to the cliff top, resolutely keeping my mind in the present. I dropped the bag with the saddle and tack down the cliff and watched it bounce out of sight. Then I climbed down with the strap of the saddlebags wound around my fingers, tightening with each rotation of the dangling bag. I was deliberately reckless, knowing that I'd be unable to release my fingers should I, or the bag, slip and gather momentum. The only thing that mattered was to steer my thoughts away from what I'd seen at the bottom of the cliff. For Mollie was not only dead, but horribly dead. The foxes had reached her first and started to feast on her soft body.

Dragging the saddlebags across the last flat stretch I propped them against a stone wall and returned for the grey bag containing the saddle. I was nearing the end of my strength. Someone would have to help me carry the two bags to the road.

I waded across the river and started walking down the track I'd seen from the cliffs. After about a mile I heard a whistle and saw a shepherd with his dog. As always when approaching a stranger, I mentally prepared my opening request, but all that came out was a sob. I couldn't talk about what had happened. The poor man was at a loss to know what to do. He put his hand on my sodden trousers. "But y're soaked to the skin!"

"No, no, it's my horse. . . I need help to get the bags. . ."

He couldn't understand me. "My horse is *dead*!" He still couldn't get it. Plenty of walkers come that way, but not horses. He looked perplexed and told me he was searching for a lamb, but he followed me to the bags and I pointed to Mollie. Then he understood. Or he understood the fact, not the emotion. What I needed most was cheering up. Leaving the bag containing the tack, we shouldered the saddlebags between us and he started a lively conversation, beginning "I'm after considering how old ye might be." After that subject was exhausted he went on to discuss my marital status, past and present, the problems of marriage, divorce in Ireland, bronchitis and how to cure it, lambs, sheep and sheep dogs. Did I earn a lot of money? Did I do manual work (looking at my broken nails and grime-engrained hands). It worked, I allowed myself to be distracted.

Eamonn and I carried the saddlebag between us. Sometimes we hugged it across our front; sometimes we humped it over our shoulders. We rested often. I had sunk into a dreamy state of deep fatigue, answering his cheerful questions automatically. Then we saw another figure high on the hill. "Noel! There's a tourist here with a dead horse! Are you going into the hills or are you going home?" Not surprisingly Noel was no quicker on the uptake than Eamonn had been. I could only understand one word of his answer. It began with F. "Never mind, let's just carry on!" I muttered. "Oh, don't you mind him. His bark's worse than his bite. "Noel, are you going into the hills. . .?" After what seemed like an age, Noel came down from the mountainside. A thin-faced, intelligent-looking young man of few words, he took stock of the problem, lifted up the bag and strode off down the path. We soon reached the road; Eamonn disappeared home (I didn't even have the chance to thank him) and Noel marched through the front door of the house opposite and dumped my bags without a word on the sofa.

The Hennessy family were watching Ronald Reagan on TV. All turned around with one movement and looked at me open-mouthed. Once my presence was explained I was given a chair by the fire. I peeled off my wet things, took off my sodden boots and socks, and sat like a zombie while Ronnie droned on in Ballyporeen. Tea arrived, then a meal (my first in 24 hours) and I began to feel better. In the late afternoon another son arrived and he and Noel discussed going back up the track to collect the saddle. I said I'd come but had a more pressing matter on my mind. "Can we bury the pony?" I asked. "I don't want to just leave her there. I can't just leave her there!" I started to cry again. The boys glanced at each other. "Don't worry, we'll deal with it. You stay with Mum."

Noel's mother, Kathleen, had invited me to spend the night and helped me move my stuff into the spare room. She was filled with admiration at my sleeping alone on the mountains.

"Dear Lord! I'm telling you, girlie, I wouldn't go there for all the tea in China!" She settled down for some story telling.

When her husband was alive they had lived along the track leading to the mountains. Indeed, she'd been born there in the little house whose ruins I'd seen at the junction of two rivers cascading down the cliffs. Everyone, she said, knew about the Thing that had haunted the valley about 80 years ago. It was like a huge barrel and it rolled around, up and down the hills and sometimes over the roofs of the houses, making a sound that was half-man, half-goat. Her father-in-law's cowman was once chased by the Thing and took refuge in the cowshed where he was trapped for three hours. In the end they asked the priest to perform an exorcism ceremony, and the Thing no longer bothered anyone in the house.

"Ooh Jesus, you'd never find me sleeping in those mountains. Here's another story. When I was a girl I went up the valley after our cows. And there was a large black bullock lying down. Huge, it was. Bigger than any of our animals and I didn't recognise it as belonging to any of the neighbours. I'd never seen it before. So I collected our own animals and I kept looking at this bullock and wondering about it, and I watched it get to its feet. I turned away for a minute and when I looked again it had disappeared. I never saw it again. I was that frightened; I ran all the way home."

Something had made Mollie try to descend the cliff. Or did she fall from the top? Did she lose her footing in the darkness or was she trying to escape from the storm? Was she looking for me or seeking better grazing in the valley? Or had something so frightened her that this sure-footed and sensible pony, born and bred in the Connemara mountains, the Mollie who'd always known what actions were safe and who just wouldn't allow me to do anything dangerous, had become reckless? I'll never know. I believe, though, that her death was quick. When I'd found her, her head collar was missing. Probably she had slipped and it had snagged on a rock and broken her neck.

Excusing myself, I got into bed, put the pillow over my head and sobbed.

Next morning I made some decisions. I would go back to England but leave my gear at the Hennessy's and try to hire another pony once I felt ready. The Hennessys encouraged this plan; they knew someone who could fix me up with a suitable animal. One of the boys gave me a lift into Tralee. It was Whit Monday and raining. The shops were closed and the place deserted except for clusters of young people looking for fun. I trailed dejectedly round, filling in time before the bus left. It was packed with cheerful youngsters, which increased my gloom.

Six hours to Dublin. It was too long, too much time for reflection. I tried to read but instead of the words I saw Mollie's outstretched body. I looked out of the window at the lovely translucent green of the evening fields and scowled at their beauty. A white horse was grazing near the road and my tears started again. I couldn't stop thinking about her; I recalled the shape of her ears as seen from the saddle, the pink diamond on her nose, her little moustache, her dark brown eyes with white eyelashes, her abundant mane and the feeling of the soft folds of skin between her front legs. I remembered the slap I used to give her bottom as I moved round her, grooming or saddling up, and of course her little gestures of affection.

The 'if only's' churned endlessly round in my mind. If only I'd been more careful in following the hoof prints; if only I'd turned back after the first bogging; if only I'd moved the tent to where Mollie was spending the night; if only I'd tethered her. Relentlessly I relived every moment, imagining the things I should have done, inventing dozens of plausible happy endings. But I had thought I had a happy ending when Mollie got clear of her island. After that elation how could fate deal me such a blow? In my worst imaginings, such an end had never occurred to me. If only...

"The horseman cannot hope to master his horse's fears until he is quite certain he has mastered his own."
From *Horse and Man: Aphorisms and Paradoxes*, 1939, by Alessandro Alvisi, Italian horse rider and Olympian.

Crossing the River Shannon

Above: "It was the first time I'd tried hitchhiking with a horse; it wasn't easy"
Below: Pierce and the "large orange crate on wheels"

"Only in Ireland!" I heard a tourist say.

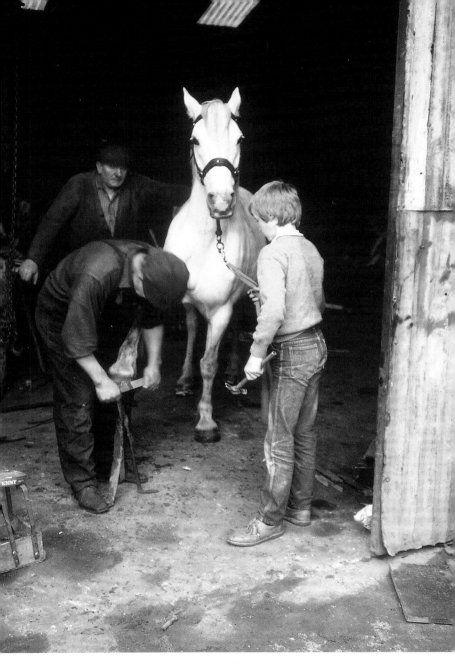

Dinny O'Shea puts the finishing touches to Mollie's new shoes

Above: The O'Shea family and the next customer
Below: "Goodnight Mollie!", I called

Peggy

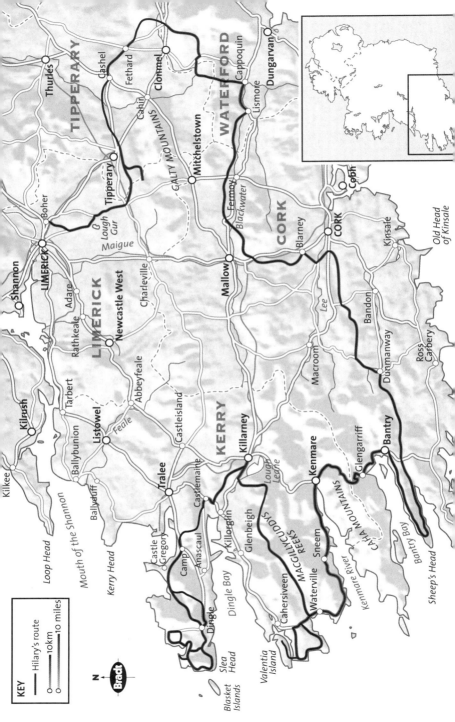

Chapter 15

Back in England I threw myself into work. It was the very early days of Bradt Guides, then known as Bradt Enterprises, and my loyal and hard-working assistant, Janet, had kept the whole thing going while I clip-clopped through Ireland picking up mail every week or so. Our 1984 catalogue lists the ten Bradt guides we'd published so far (and just five since going it alone four years ago) and a dozen or so imported guides, mostly from the USA, to pad out the list. My main income those days was from tour-leading (I crammed in three trips in 1984) and from the topographical maps I brought back from South America and for which I'd cornered the market. After Mollie's death – she wasn't insured – I had very little left in the bank.

I stubbornly hung on to that childhood dream, however. It had been too long in the planning, too persistent in my imagination to let go. One of the reasons I left all my gear with the Hennessys was to ensure that I returned. I knew that if I abandoned the ride now I would only look back on the adventure with sadness and – more importantly – I would never again feel the carefree enjoyment of off-road riding. I had not only lost my way on the Dingle Peninsula, I had lost my confidence.

In August I returned to Castle Gregory.

∪ ∪ ∪

"That's the house!" I said, relieved at recognising it after a gap of six weeks. It was the second good omen of the day, the first being the ease with which I'd hitched a lift to Castle Gregory from Tralee. I carried little luggage; most of the necessities for the next stage of my journey were stored at the Hennessys. Except a horse. And my courage.

A small white pony was grazing in the adjacent paddock and my heart quickened. Was it for me? But it wasn't even a pony. Looking more closely I saw long ears. Then Noel emerged from the house and I was immediately enfolded into the warmth of the family. Kathleen put the kettle on and showed me into the spare bedroom. My luggage was in the shed, a bit cobwebby, but intact. There was Mollie's saddle, and the saddlebags, and all the bits and pieces I needed to continue my trek. I had replaced the missing Peruvian head collar with a tough nylon one. Memories flooded back and I resolutely chased them away. Now was the time to look forward.

As soon as I dared, I raised the subject of a replacement horse or pony. Had someone heard about Mollie's death and offered me a mount? No, but Pedar would fix me up with something for sure. He was the local horse dealer and, incidentally, the owner of the animal in the field. It was a jennet (donkey mother, pony father) and was in disgrace. Pedar had sold it to a local man to pull a cart, but the animal was frightened by the white lines on the road (I can understand that; in 1984 they were a rarity) and had bolted. Before Pedar took it back, Noel was planning to use it for farm work but it was more interested in chasing sheep than helping to round them up, so had to be hobbled. He was a sturdy-looking animal so I asked if I could try riding him; I rather fancied travelling around Ireland on a jennet. But his appearance was deceptive. He turned out to be shaped like one of those toys you make out of a Styrofoam ball and matchsticks. There was nowhere to put the saddle on the spherical body, and when I mounted bareback I nearly fell off the other side.

I didn't want to impose on the Hennessy family any longer than necessary, so it was a matter of urgency to find a suitable mount. In those days few country people had a phone, so arranging to meet Pedar was a complicated process. First, one of the boys drove me to his house in Dingle, only to find that he wasn't in. But everyone is related here so his wife knew all about me. Her sister runs the B&B in Anascaul where I stayed the last night before my fateful ride over the mountains with Mollie. We arranged for Pedar to phone us at a nearby – nearish-by – hotel. This constituted a Night Out for Kathleen, who was dressed up to the nines including some rather startling purple shoes. When she opened the van she let out a wail. "Oh Jesus God, can you believe this?" Noel had used it to transport sheep, and the back of the vehicle bore evidence that they had enjoyed plenty of food and drink before setting out. "Oh Jesus, oh Sacred Heart, I'm telling you, girlie, I *scrubbed* that van out only last week, oh dear God…" At the hotel she made a beeline for the slot machine, and a few minutes later Pedar left a message that he'd be over next morning. Guinness and conversation flowed, Kathleen was eventually prised away from her gambling, and someone took us home in a cleaner vehicle.

Next morning, Sunday, I accompanied the family to Mass although my spiritual sustenance was limited to a walk in the misty sunshine to look for a phone box. I wanted to give my parents a progress report. The telephone operator's Sunday was clearly transformed by this break from the routine business of listening in to local calls. At first there was no reply, but he said, "Sure but I'll try again to show there's no hard feelings." When my sleepy-sounding mother finally answered, he let me chat for at least ten minutes – I'd paid for three – so the conversation must have been absorbing. Telecom operators in those days wielded considerable power. I was told a story about a businessman whose patience snapped at the telephonist's leisurely approach to her job and swore at her down the phone. It was probably a regular occurrence but this time he went too far and the operator cut him off. Not for a few minutes but for two months. His wife and daughter were able to make calls, but not him. Even when he tried to phone from friends' houses the operator's ever-listening ear discovered the deception and she unplugged him. Exactly two months after his oaths, he was re-instated.

When we got back to the house, there was Pedar banging some shoes onto a nondescript brown pony with a silly hairstyle. I looked at it in dismay. "It's awfully small!" I said doubtfully.

"She's perfect." (bang bang) "Carry you all day. Never gets tired." The pony couldn't have been more than 13.2 hands and I'm no midget.

"Don't you have anything else? Something bigger?" He shook his head. "What's her name?"

"Peggy. Pure Connemara," he added as an afterthought.

So I saddled up and trotted up and down the road and cantered in the field.

"She's got very low head carriage," I said snootily. This was putting it mildly; her neck was never above the horizontal.

Pedar stared at me. "D'you want a show pony or a worker? She'll do you fine. I drive her all day in my gig." Which explained the muscular neck, partially cropped mane to accommodate the collar, and brisk trot.

I really didn't like this pony. She was too small, too plain, and I couldn't forgive her for not being Mollie. But it didn't look as though I'd find anything else. Not for hire, anyway. We all went into the kitchen for cups of tea and business talk, but it was soon obvious that what Pedar thought was a fair rental fee and what I could afford to pay were very different. We argued back and forth for ages and failed to come to an agreement, so I suggested that I'd ride her the 13 miles to Dingle next day with the saddlebags, see if she was suitable, and we could discuss it further then.

After lunch I sat in the paddock and watched Peggy grazing, willing myself to like her. She had a thick neck, a sausage-shaped body and working-class tufts of hair on her fetlocks. Certainly no show pony. But perhaps I'd been unfair to call her a nondescript brown; she was actually the colour of a freshly-pulled pint of Guinness, with touches of foamy beige including a mealy muzzle like an Exmoor pony, and blonde streaks in her mane. But after Mollie, who drew admiring glances from everyone, Peggy was a definite comedown. I decided to go on a longer ride that afternoon, before encumbering her with saddlebags, so took a grassy track towards the mountains. When she felt soft turf beneath her hooves, instead of tarmac, Peggy stopped dead in surprise. Oh brave new world! Without her accustomed blinkers she could see mountains and sky – except that if she wanted to look at something above her she tilted her head sideways to peep under the imaginary blinkers while keeping her neck resolutely horizontal. It was very endearing and made me laugh out loud. Her brown ears were so sharply pricked that they almost met in the middle, and I was happy to enjoy her nice fast walk without trying anything more ambitious. Perhaps she wasn't so bad.

ᘉ   ᘉ   ᘉ

My evening with the Hennessys was everything I love about Ireland, full of laughter and conviviality. When I stayed there after Mollie's death I was too numbed by grief to appreciate the family properly. Kathleen was my favourite, not just for her turn of phrase and stories, but for what she had achieved. Having been brought up in a remote stone cottage at the foot of the cliffs in the Valley of the Cows, she had raised eight children, all of whom were doing well, some spectacularly so. She told me that two were in New York, one working as a Vogue fashion model, and that a daughter was in charge of customer relations in a posh hotel in the United Arab Emirates. Yet Sylvester, the oldest boy, said he remembered going barefoot to the village school where all ages were taught together in the one-room schoolhouse. Kathleen had visited the New York son and daughter, but didn't feel she could go again, despite their entreaties and promise of an air ticket because "Imagine the state of the house when I get back. Those two boys would burn the bottoms out of all the pans! Oh Lord, I couldn't risk it."

While the family chatted, I worked with needle and thread, mending the saddlebags and adapting the tack to Peggy's diminutive size. I shortened the girth and the belly strap that kept the saddlebags in place, and checked that the little straps that I'd used to attach Mollie's snaffle bit to the head collar were undamaged and would work on the replacement nylon head collar. It was not as glamorous as Mollie's but virtually indestructible.

Peggy still managed to get rid of it during the night. I'd left the head collar on to avoid a repeat of my early experience with Mollie when she wanted as little to do with me as possible and I'd spent two hours trying to catch her. However, a family search found the head collar trampled into the grass and Peggy was cooperative – she thought she was going home. She submitted to all the pushing and shoving and tightening of girths and straps that loading the saddlebags entailed, and when I led her round experimentally she didn't seem bothered by all the extra encumbrance. Probably not much different from her accustomed harness.

And it was certainly less effort to load a smaller pony – heaving the bags onto Mollie's back used to take all my strength. The size advantage was reinforced when I mounted. Much easier.

ひ　　ひ　　ひ

My route to Dingle was unadventurous. I had no intention of trying a cross-country route, even though the map showed some possibilities. Indeed, I wondered if I would ever feel brave enough to leave the tarmac again. Mollie's death in the trackless, boggy interior had given my confidence a severe shaking. Yesterday, during my ride along that track towards those fateful mountains, fear had bubbled up inside me. To be responsible for the health and safety of a trusting animal is such a big thing. Peggy had her own issues with cross-country work, so set off happily in the direction of Dingle and home. This was when I realised that she was exceptionally sociable – and probably also in season. She neighed seductively at every horse we passed, and hopefully into empty landscape when there was no equine in sight.

The road to Dingle was as scenic as I could have wished for. Peggy walked cheerfully past the bulk of Stradbally Mountain, and up the hill towards Conor Pass, Ireland's highest motorable road. Not that there were many motors on it that day. The narrow lane is cut into the hillside, and the challenges facing the drivers were evident in their tense expressions as they inched past me. For my part, it was wonderful. I just sat there admiring the scenery, while Peggy did all the work. The craggy, rock-strewn mountains harboured little lakes in their valleys and wisps of cloud on the peaks. Shaggy black-faced sheep grazed on the coarse grass and hooded crows circled above. At the top of the pass I dismounted to let Peggy get her breath back and graze while I ate the picnic lunch that Kathleen had provided. A local man came over to admire Peggy. "That's

Pedar's pony isn't it?" I explained about my ride – and Mollie – and he wished me luck.

I knew where I was headed in Dingle. The youth hostel had a campsite and a paddock for Peggy. My tiny tent was dwarfed by the nearby luxury canvas houses and it seemed strange to have a toilet/shower block at my disposal. With Mollie I had usually found a river to wash in or brought water to heat in the tent. Then, nervously, I went to see Pedar. I knew I wanted to hire Peggy; he was right, she was fine for the job. We just had to settle on a price that I could afford. Pedar was expecting me – he had just got back from helping the Hennessy boys with some sheep dipping – and said he needed a pint of Guinness before we could talk. But of course, once in the pub, I realised that we couldn't talk business without the other customers hanging on every word, so I chatted to them about my plans. "Ah yes," said one of them, "I saw a person yesterday riding through town on a horse all covered in luggage. But t'was a man." No it wasn't, it was me. I remembered the stares as I self-consciously rode past the shops. Glancing in the reflecting windows I could see a mound of beige-coloured luggage topped by a blue, shapeless lump with a little brown head sticking out of one end, a tail out of the other, and a set of twinkling legs underneath. I decided, now the weather was getting warmer, I'd better wear my tightest T-shirt. When we'd all finished our drinks I told Pedar I'd come to his house the next day to conclude our discussion.

Back in the tent, with the cheery sound of happy campers all around me, I sank into despondency. I was mourning the loss of Mollie both as my best equine friend and the most expensive item I'd ever bought. Could Peggy ever replace her in my affections and how was I going to afford to hire her anyway? Having set out on the Mollie trek with only very vague plans, I now had a rough route in mind, and the idea that my target should be a thousand miles in total. I would feel I had achieved something then. I'd worked out that Mollie and I had done about 450 miles in a month, but the first week was spent on an organised trek without luggage so we covered more ground; I reckoned I'd need to hire Peggy for at least six weeks, so Pedar's weekly fee was looking prohibitive.

Next day was my birthday, and it didn't start well. At 2am a group of French arrived from the pub in high spirits and settled into the tent next to mine with much shouting and laughing. I got so fed up I yelled at them to be quiet. It worked for only a few minutes.

Tired and still cross in the morning, I went back to Pedar's house and, with no-one listening to the conversation, came to an agreement quite quickly. Rather than a weekly charge he agreed that I could keep Peggy as long as I wanted – within reason. What a relief! "And you don't have to bring her back to Dingle. Leave her with Ted O'Connell near Limerick and I'll pick her up."

So I packed up the tent and went to give Peggy the 2lbs of carrots I'd generously bought her as a birthday present (someone might as well receive a present today). I found her standing outside the paddock near the collapsed gate. She took one look at me and my carrots and galloped off across someone's immaculate lawn. When I approached she trotted off again, taking a short cut across the porch steps where she very nearly fell, before being headed off and caught by the hostel warden, a pleasant young Australian who was accustomed to horses. Poor Peggy, she thought she'd come home to her boyfriend and familiar surroundings. No wonder she didn't want to have anything to do with me. I led her self-consciously to the campsite and took an age to get all the gear in place, watched by a growing crowd of campers. I gave pony rides to a couple of kids, then mounted with a flourish – and fell off the other side in front of the odious French group.

I headed west out of Dingle, down a lane sheltered by high hedges sculpted by the wind and past gardens boastfully sporting palm trees, to Ventry Strand. I wanted to give Peggy her first beach experience. The narrow, mauvish-coloured stretch of sand is backed by grass-covered dunes and cut by a stream. Walkers cross by the little footbridge but I wanted to test Peggy's competence at fording rivers. Mollie used to take this request in her stride, even quite deep rivers. But she had no fear of water, and regularly swam in the sea. Peggy's experience was quite different. She stopped, wide-eyed in astonishment at the edge of the beach, with much snorting, and it took quite a while to persuade her that it was safe to set hoof on it. She tiptoed warily along the firm sand (it was low tide) as though crossing a minefield, shying at the menacing lumps of seaweed. My suggestion that she approach the surf was too much for any sensible pony – here was water advancing at a gallop. No wonder she fled! Gradually her snorting became more subdued, and by the time we'd reached the river she'd managed a rather wobbly canter, I'd just avoided falling off, and she'd paddled in an un-wavy bit of shallow water. But she had no intention of wading across the river. Considering it was the first time she'd been to the seaside (despite living in a seaside town), I told her she'd been very brave and allowed her to return the way we'd come.

∪   ∪   ∪

I was heading for Slea Head on the westernmost part of the Dingle Peninsula. The road wraps itself around Mount Eagle, hugging the rocky coast where slanting grey shards of rock pierce the sky. Perilous waters, these. An old shipwreck still lay half-submerged by the cliff, a reminder that two ships from the Spanish Armada met their end here in 1588: the *Santa Maria de la Rosa* and the *San Juan*. Slea Head has always been one of Dingle's main tourist attractions so even in 1984 there were plenty of cars sharing the route with me. A sign advertising 'Beehive Huts' caught my eye and, having read about these stone structures, I decided to dismount and take a look. The Irish name is *clochán*, but 'beehive' perfectly describes their shape: squat little domes of roughly shaped stone, corbelled at the top so they needed no mortar. They could date from the 12th century, so I was told, and may have been dwellings although they seemed better suited to the hens that were living there. When I got back to Peggy, an elderly woman and her grandchildren were staring at all the luggage. I explained what I was doing. She found the idea that one could ride around Ireland almost impossible to comprehend. "But where do you sleep? Dear Lord, do you? Outside? Oh Jesus! What do you eat? Oh dear God…"

A track led tantalisingly to the most westerly mainland point in Europe, Dunmore Head, but it looked boggy and I was too nervous to try it. Instead I clip-clopped my way toward Dunquin, where the cliff rises sheer and black above the road and the local houses are built from the same dark stone. By the evening the clouds had cleared and the low sun lit the cliffs and turned the sea from grey to turquoise. I'd been keeping Great Blasket Island in sight but now the hazy silhouettes of other islands came into view, the perfect pyramids of Tearaght and the endearing profile of The Sleeping Giant, his hand resting on his pot belly and his mouth open above his crinkly beard.

At Dunquin I asked directions to the youth hostel. Yes, they had a bed but the warden didn't know where I could put Peggy. I'd spotted a likely-looking field next door, so went to ask at the adjacent house. A young boy answered my knock and I heard him go to the next room and relay my question in a language I didn't recognise. I was invited through to where a large family was eating dinner. In one fluid movement his mother had cleared a place, pulled up a chair, poured some tea and plonked two sausages on a plate. I felt quite dazed as I munched and slurped. "Didn't you know that Dingle is a Gaeltacht region?"

Eileen explained what that meant: Irish is spoken in the home in many households and the government provides a subsidy to encourage its use. Only the two boys were hers; there was a niece over from America and two girls – cousins – here from Cork to perfect their Irish. The whole room glowed with family warmth and goodwill. My English inhibitions melted and I heard myself say that it was my birthday. They all sang 'Happy Birthday' in Irish and added the greeting 'May you live to be 100'. My birthday was turning out very well indeed. Reluctantly, I said I must go since Peggy was tied up outside the hostel (had I known then that this was the last time I could safely leave her tied, I might have stayed longer). Father said she could go in the big field and Patrick, the young boy, took me there. When I saw it was huge and full of good grass I decided to stay two nights and visit Great Blasket Island which lay four miles off Slea Head.

This was a good decision. Great Blasket is gorgeous and just right for a day's walking. Until 1953 when the whole island was evacuated, there used to be a population of hardy fisherfolk, all of whom seem to have written books which have become classics in the Irish language. No, that's an exaggeration, but the three best-known ones have been translated into English: *An Old Woman's Reflections* by Peig Sayers, *Twenty Years A-Growing* by Maurice O'Sullivan (or Muiris Ó Súilleabháin if you prefer) and *The Islandman* by Tomás Ó Criomhthain. O'Sullivan's title comes from the traditional division of man's fourscore years: twenty a-growing, twenty a-blossoming, twenty a-stooping and twenty declining.

A sea mist all but obscured the island when I boarded the ferry, and on arrival the other passengers made a beeline for the café. I headed up the rough path to the northern end, climbing steadily in the mist and uneasily aware of a silhouetted figure keeping his distance behind me. At the highest point, just under a thousand feet up, the sun broke through the mist and gradually revealed the glorious view. With the aid of my map I could identify Valentia Island to the south, across Dingle Bay, and the blue mountain range of MacGillycuddy's Reeks to the east. I hoped to reach both places within the next couple of weeks.

The stalker turned out to be a pleasant German who was planning to camp on the island, and we ate a companionable chocolate bar together before I headed briskly back to catch the ferry. Numerous rabbits were sunning themselves outside their burrows, and I identified a lone curlew and oystercatchers on the shore. Green headlands speckled with white sheep were broken by scooped-out sandy bays. Too bad there was not enough time for a swim.

Back in the youth hostel, after checking on Peggy, I wrote this limerick in the youth hostel guestbook:

From England to Ireland, I travelled by ferry
And rode on a pony from Galway to Kerry.
Asked a lady from Arkansas
"Say, aren't you saddle-sore?"
And the pony and I both said "Very!"

Peggy had had a good rest and was eager to get going, though our planned destinations differed. She was still hoping to go home, whereas my route continued round Slea Head to Ballyferriter. I had bought some spray-on insect repellent in Dingle and with the warm, still weather bringing out a mass of flies, I wanted to protect her face from this irritation. After loading her up, I tied her to the fence post and, cupping my hand over her eye to protect it, I let out a jet of spray. I don't know what it was that frightened her so much – the noise of the aerosol, or some previous bad experience? – but she pulled back with such force that the concrete post broke. Concrete! She was unbelievably strong. Fortunately the new head collar proved almost indestructible. Later, I needed to tie her up again while I bought provisions from a village shop, but this time I tied her to a telegraph pole. Horses never forget; now that being tied was linked in her mind with danger, she once again pulled back with all her strength. I could see her muscles bulging with the effort. This time nothing broke, so I hoped she would think twice about doing it again.

Soon after we'd set out, Peggy was thrilled to see two horses ahead of her. We caught them up and I was less thrilled when the man accompanying them asked if I was going to Ballyferriter and when I said yes, he said, "Good, I'm tired, they can go with you," and turned them loose on the road. I refused to go along with his plan. The thought of being in charge of two loose horses on a busy narrow road for four miles and then waiting around in town with them for a tired (and no doubt thirsty) farmer, didn't appeal to me. He exploded into a stream of curses. "Go on, trot up the road!" he commanded. I walked and the loose horses investigated someone's drive. More oaths. So I trotted and they trotted behind until I slowed near a track leading into the mountains. Obviously familiar territory to the horses, which cantered away with the farmer, still cursing, at the rear. I was very relieved to see them go. Peggy, however, never got over her disappointment. She neighed hopefully every five minutes or so throughout the day, and scanned the countryside for her new friends. Poor Peggy. I had taken her away from her home and companions, and I was learning that she was the most sociable pony I'd ever met. If she were a person she would have been a party-going extrovert and a chatterbox. Depriving her of equine company made me feel permanently guilty.

U   U   U

My goal that day was the Gallarus Oratory, an early Christian chapel reputed to be the most interesting tourist site in Dingle. I asked directions from a fellow tidying the graveyard in the local church.

"Well, you see that – er – d'ye see it? In the valley?"

"See what?"

"Well do you see it?"

I tried to follow his directions but went the wrong way, heading for the wrong 'it'. When I finally got there I had to agree that Gallarus was, indeed, remarkable. Often described as being the shape of an inverted boat, it is constructed on a rectangular base from individually cut stones, carefully laid to create inward-curving walls which meet at the top. A doorway facing due west gives entrance to its dry interior, and it was not hard to imagine services taking place here all those years ago. Estimates vary as to when it was built, but it was somewhere between the 8th and 12th century. It has never been restored and is still watertight. The corbelled roof reminded me of Mayan architecture, so maybe St Brendan did get to the Americas as is often speculated. I paid only a quick visit since I was preoccupied with the vision of Peggy galloping away, towing a gate behind her, and as a reward for her staying tied I led her down the road feeling that a bottom/back rest would do us both good. Several cars passed, the occupants staring more than usual. Eventually I glanced round and saw that Peggy was walking briskly along with pricked ears, while her saddle and luggage dangled beneath her belly. Mollie used to stop when that happened, but Peggy seems to accept it as part of the day's measure of discomfort. Everything had to be taken off in the road, while queues of cars on their way to the Oratory waited for me to finish.

I dropped down to the coast, passed through the village of Ballydavid, and got permission from a farmer to camp in his field. It was a beautiful spot, with plenty of grass for Peggy and for me a view over Smerwick harbour to Dún an Óir. This was the scene of one of England's most shameful episodes in its seemingly endless attempts to subdue the Irish. In the 16th century, Henry VIII decided it was time to establish control of Ireland, which had deteriorated, in the monarch's eyes, to a country of chieftains who 'maketh war and peace for himself without any licence of the King'. His scheme of 'surrender and regrant', whereby chiefs surrendered their land to the Crown but received it back if they agreed to be ruled by English law, was not well received, especially since conversion to Protestantism was part of the deal. The Irish rebelled. When Elizabeth came to the throne she was determined to finish the job and sent her Lord Deputy of Ireland, General Arthur Grey, to deal with the rebels. These were not all Irish. In 1580 Pope Gregory XIII financed an invading force of 600 Italian, Spanish and Basque men who sailed into Smerwick harbour to come to the aid of the Irish rebels, of whom only 17 managed to join them on the tip of the Dingle Peninsula. The geography of the place made Lord Grey's job relatively easy, and his men laid siege to Dún an Óir, attacking from both the sea and land.

The 'Papists' were hopelessly outnumbered and outweaponed, and had to contend not only with Grey's 4,000 soldiers but his thirst for revenge: he'd earlier lost 800 troops in an unsuccessful battle in Co Wicklow. Inevitably the Catholics eventually surrendered. Had they known what was to happen to them, they would have fought on. When the three Irish leaders, including a priest, refused to accept the religious supremacy of the Queen, Grey ordered his blacksmith to break the bones in their hands and feet and, for good measure, to cut off the priest's finger and thumb which had touched the Sacrament of the Eucharist. They were hanged 24 hours later. After formally surrendering their weapons and ensigns, the foreigners were all put to death.

I knew none of this bloody history as I sat outside the tent writing my diary and watching the sun slide below the headland. Peggy, meanwhile, was staring longingly through the bars of the gate, looking like an Amnesty International poster. She wanted to go home.

U   U   U

My circuit of the Dingle Peninsula was almost complete. I had achieved my purpose of doing some gentle sightseeing while getting used to Peggy and – more importantly – she to me. She learned faster than I did, conveying her needs and wishes as eloquently as a pony can. I was just very slow on the uptake. One day, instead of her usual brisk walk she dawdled along with her nose to the ground, smelling the tarmac and every now and then stopping to scrape it with her hoof. I couldn't think what was the matter and got quite cross with her. Then she spied a woman crossing her front garden carrying a bucket of water. Peggy raised her head and gave a little whinny. Of course! "Would you mind giving my pony a drink?" I asked. The woman obligingly fetched a fresh bucket of cold water, and Peggy drank gratefully. She taught me always to give her a decent lunch break, too. If I neglected her needs by selfishly tying her up outside a pub, she would trail along afterwards with her head even lower than usual, stopping pointedly when in the vicinity of green grass. She knew better than to try to graze without permission; it was one thing I was strict about.

I had one last bit of sightseeing to achieve before returning to the Dingle youth hostel. Plonked in the northern end of the peninsula is Brandon Mountain, at 3,127 feet the highest peak on Dingle. Indeed, if it were not for MacGillycuddy's Reeks it would be the highest in Ireland, and I had read about the old Saint's Road up to St Brendan's Oratory, the ruins of a beehive-shaped chapel on the summit. It would be a lovely ride and the weather was clear. I had a great affection for St Brendan the Navigator who exemplified serendipitous travel. Having spent a busy time as a priest in the 6th century founding monasteries, he arrived in western Kerry to prepare for his great voyage into the unknown. It is said that he had a vision of the Promised Land while meditating on the mountain named after him. He built a coracle from wattle and hide, filled it with monks, and set forth from Brandon Bay. The voyage lasted seven years. He and his fellow passengers met psalm-singing birds, sea monsters a-plenty, a hermit clad only in hair who had survived for 60 years being fed by an otter, and even encountered a very cold and wet Judas Iscariot sitting on a rock in the ocean on day-release from Hell. He may also have reached America.

When I got to the trail, however, my nerve gave out – I just didn't dare leave the road. I knew I had to get my confidence back, and fortuitously I had a solution. My German friend, Susanne, was arriving in Dingle in a couple of days and would travel with me for a fortnight. It's always easier to be brave in company.

Chapter 16

Knowing my anxious-mother state I should never have offered to loan Peggy. Over breakfast I had struck up a conversation with a pretty young Swedish girl who had asked about my trip and expressed the right amount of admiration and sympathy over Mollie. She owned her own horse in Sweden, she said, and had been trying to hire ponies to go out unaccompanied, but no trekking stable would permit it. "You can take Peggy if you like," I heard myself saying. "I'm having a rest day tomorrow and it'll do her good to be ridden without the luggage." The girl was thrilled and I felt cosily magnanimous.

Peggy was sharing a large field with several sleek and sour heavy horses which pulled the caravans then popular in the area. I'd always been impressed at the courage both of the company trusting their horses to the care of inexperienced visitors, and by the tourists themselves who often knew almost nothing about horses. I arrived in time to watch a Frenchman retreating backwards towards the gate pursued by an evil-looking chestnut mare. One of Peggy's most endearing characteristics was that she'd walk up to me in the morning with a look of anticipation on her face, so handing the Frenchman Peggy's rope, I walked purposefully towards his horse, took its head collar, gave it some of Peggy's bread and led it to its temporary owner who was suitably impressed and grateful. I smiled a gracious we-horse-owners-know-all smile and Peggy pulled her rope out of my slack smug fingers and trotted off to rejoin her friends.

The Swedish girl, her boyfriend and Peggy left at around 11 o'clock and I set out with my picnic to walk round the cliffs of the chunky peninsula south of Dingle. It was another perfect day; very hot and rather hazy, and I relished the thought of being able to explore without Peggy-anxiety. The grassy path to the lighthouse took me close by the edge of deeply indented cliffs, the fluted brown-grey rocks dropping sheer to a dark-blue sea. Now the nesting season was over, there were fewer seabirds than I'd seen with Mollie, but herring gulls swirled below me along with the occasional black-backed gull. Ireland must have some of the finest cliff scenery in the world, but even more exciting than the landscape were the dozens of mushrooms I could see glinting in the grass in the nearby meadows. I react to a field of mushrooms as a fox does to a barn full of chickens. The joy of the grab takes over from mere need and I end up with far more than I can possibly eat. The plastic bag I carried back with me contained enough to feed the entire hostel.

Near the entrance to the harbour is a cave known as Nancy Brown's Parlour. It's one of those unexceptional Irish places that become fascinating once you know the legend associated with it. Within the cave, so they say, is a secret passage leading to the house of James Louis Rice who had made his home fit for a queen. His expected guest? Marie Antoinette. Plans were afoot to rescue her from the French Revolution and hide her in Dingle. This extraordinary story becomes plausible when you learn that James Louis's father ran a profitable wine business, his ships regularly plying the ocean between France and Ireland, and that his son was sent to school on the continent. Catholics were deemed unfit for secondary education in British-ruled Ireland. When young James left college he entered the service of the Emperor of Austria, eventually becoming his close confidante, and joined the Irish Brigade, an exiled band of Irishmen who fought alongside the French. When revolution erupted and the French royal family were imprisoned in Paris, James hatched a plan to use one of the wine ships to spirit Marie Antoinette to Ireland and to safety. They say that it was only the queen's last-minute refusal to leave her family that prevented the success of this course of action. Who Nancy Brown was, no one could tell me.

υ   υ   υ

"No sign of those kids with your pony!" said the warden cheerfully when he saw me. I couldn't believe it; it was nearly 7.30. I looked in my dorm for the saddle but it wasn't there. Nor was Peggy in the field. I was distraught, convinced that something terrible had happened: Peggy had been hit by a car, or had bolted or got caught up in barbed wire. Perhaps the girl or boy had had an accident. Why had I been so stupid as to lend Peggy to a couple I didn't know? She wasn't even my pony to lend! Then, at 8 o'clock, a hosteller on a bicycle reported having seen them about two miles away, and I burst into tears of relief.

Later I felt quite guilty about my anger at the two repentant teenagers. After all, they pointed out, we never agreed that they should go out for only a couple of hours. That was just my assumption.

"But you know what happened to my last pony," I said, my voice trembling. "Couldn't you imagine how worried I'd be?" I managed to introduce a semblance of sincerity into my voice when I said I was glad they'd had a good time.

"And Peggy had a good time too. She loved it!"

I hoped that was true.

υ   υ   υ

The plan to have Susanne join me had been hatched the previous October at Frankfurt Book Fair. Our friendship went back ten years to when Susanne worked on the German translation of the first Bradt guide, and each year we would have dinner together in Frankfurt and catch up on news. In 1983, naturally, I told her excitedly about my plan to do a long-distance ride through Ireland the following year. Susanne looked wistful. "You know what I remember most about my childhood? There was a riding stable nearby, and every minute I went there and cried because we had no money for riding lessons."

"Maybe you could join me for some of the time?"

"But now I'm not so excited about riding. I went with my first boyfriend on a horse and it galloped away and I fell down."

Nevertheless, we were both enthusiastic about doing a trip together so when I bought Mollie in May I wrote to Susanne and described my lovely strong pony who could easily carry extra luggage, and suggested that she join me for a few weeks. We could take it in turns to walk and ride which, at Mollie's slow pace, would not be strenuous. Back in England after Mollie's death I phoned her to discuss the revised plan and agreed that she should come anyway, and if I hadn't found a replacement pony, we'd just have a holiday in Kerry.

Dingle seemed the perfect place to introduce Susanne to Ireland and begin the second part of my journey. A small town with a harbour full of brightly painted boats, green hills beyond and immunity to the effects of tourism, Dingle is the focus for visiting this part of Kerry: 'A troupe of winding streets dancing down a steep slope of rock and gorse' is how my effervescent guidebook described it. I wondered how the locals could remain so friendly when they were in the minority in every pub and shop. Few visitors seemed prepared to risk leaving the main tourist sights, however. During my two-day sortie around the end of the peninsula I'd met only a couple of other foreigners, an Englishman struggling on a bicycle from which panniers and bags hung like clusters of grapes, and an American in a hired car trying to match each stone at Gallarus Oratory to those in his guide book.

Susanne had brought champagne from the Duty Free shop in Shannon. We sat outside with our mushroom soup and mugs full of bubbly and caught up on the news. Afterwards I took her to meet Peggy. "She's got a mouth like my grandmother," she commented.

The following day was another scorcher. Peggy had a well-deserved rest and we went to the beach, had a swim, and collected more mushrooms from the meadows overlooking Dingle harbour. And I speculated about sea monsters living contentedly in the bay, having read an extraordinary 17th-century newspaper report:

> A Wonderful Fish or Beast was lately killed, by James Steward, as it came of its own accord to Him out of the sea to the Shore, where he was alone on Horseback at the Harbour's Mouth of Dingle-Icoush, which had two heads and Ten horns, and upon Eight of the said Horns about 800 buttons or the resemblance of Little Coronets; and in each of them a set of Teeth, the said Body was bigger than a Horse and was 19 Foot Long Horns and all, the great Head thereof Carried only the said ten Horns and two very large Eyes. And the little Head thereof carried a wonderful strange mouth and two Tongues in it.

On first reading, this creature sounds utterly improbable, but then you consider 'about 800 buttons or the resemblance of Little Coronets' on its ten 'horns' and you think, yes, suckers on tentacles – it must have been a giant squid or kraken!

ʊ ʊ ʊ

In the evening Susanne had her first riding lesson. Peggy almost smirked when she realised what was atop her. She'd walk along quietly, a responsible look on her face, butter wouldn't melt in her granny mouth, then as soon as my back was turned she'd plunge her head down to eat, pulling the reins out of Susanne's hands. I had to keep her on a short lead rein. By supper time she was behaving better and Susanne had managed a short trot.

The two of us studied the map and a little booklet describing local walks. "You have to meet the Hennessys, so we need to go over the Conor Pass again, but I'd love to see if we can do it away from the cars." On my first day with Peggy I'd looked longingly at a green road (or boreen) that led southeast from the pass in the direction of Dingle. Now, with two of us, we could try it. Our little walks book showed a route up a minor road which joined this green road. From the description it seemed that there were no locked gates or impassable areas.

Peggy eyed me suspiciously when I went to collect her from the field. Up until now she'd walked towards me with pricked ears. This time she waited for me to come to her. At the hostel I looked properly at Susanne's luggage for the first time. She'd brought a shiny plastic blue-and-white striped duffle bag with a drawstring at one end.

"Why didn't you bring a rucksack?" I asked crossly.

Susanne stared at me. "Because you told me not. You said my luggage must be waterproof, and soft for fixing to the saddle."

Yes, I suppose those had been my instructions but I hadn't thought it through. How was I to attach this bag when there was hardly an inch of Peggy showing under the existing load? The duffle looked more like a laundry bag to me and needed an attachment at each end if I was to fasten it properly to the saddle. We didn't even have any cord with us. I fixed it to the rest of the luggage as best I could, and with Susanne walking beside me, we left Dingle, still bathed in hot sunshine, and headed for the mountains.

The little lane was bordered by flowering fuchsia hedges, their red-and-purple bells trembling above our heads, and led gently uphill toward the gap in the mountains.

Towards the end of the morning we crossed the Garfinny River, stopping to admire Ireland's oldest surviving bridge. This is thought to date from medieval times, and is beautifully constructed without mortar, using the weight of the stones themselves to retain the arch. Lord Grey may have taken his troops across this bridge on his way to Smerwick Harbour, according to a recently erected sign.

Shortly thereafter we turned west to meet our green road. It climbed up sharply, giving us a marvellous view across Dingle Bay to the hazy mountains of the Iveragh Peninsula. As we ate our picnic lunch in a sheltered sunny spot I was full of warm feelings of companionship. I like travelling alone but it was awfully good to be with a friend while I was still getting my courage back.

The track continued half-heartedly then petered out on a bleak hilltop. I could see where we were supposed to go; the Conor Pass car park was clearly visible, as was the grassy green road that had tempted me a week ago, but it was on the other side of a small river valley. 'Judge when to cross for yourself' said my little book. Easy enough on foot but too rocky and boggy for the pony. I began to feel anxious. Leaving Susanne reluctantly holding Peggy, I went ahead to check out possible routes. Two months earlier I wouldn't have hesitated to take a pony down this marshy path but now the sight and squelching sound of bog – even relatively firm bog like this – brought back hideous memories and a surge of adrenalin.

I returned to Susanne. Peggy was walking restlessly in circles, pawing the ground and snatching at tufts of bog grass. "She's a crazy horse!"

said Susanne. "She didn't like you going away so she started to eat the earth." Sure enough Peggy's mouth was muddy. I suggested that this time Susanne should look for a safe route while I stayed with Peggy. A track led down to the river; although marshy and rutted it seemed firm enough and there was an easy river crossing, but it ended in a bog where turf-cutters had recently been busy. I asked her to beckon me over if there was a safe way round the turf-cutting area. Peggy was bent on demonstrating the inadequacy of her lunch. She dug at the soft soil with her forefeet and grabbed mouthfuls of dirt. "It's no good," I told her. "You're stuck with me and this is how it is."

Through the binoculars I could watch Susanne carefully checking possible routes round the bog, and then two figures caught my eye: tourists walking along the skyline, evidently on firm ground. Susanne waved and I led Peggy down the squelchy track, my heart lurching in fright each time she sank above her hooves. However, after such a long spell of dry weather, the ground was basically firm and Susanne's route gave us no trouble. By the time we reached the road my confidence was at least partially restored. It was so much easier and safer with two of us.

Peggy's relief at feeling the tarmac beneath her feet was short-lived. Buoyed by our cross-country success, I suggested that we try another short cut to a road running parallel to ours across a watery valley. This time it didn't work. First I had to deal with the wire-netting fence at the head of the steep gravel track down to the valley, un-twiddling about a dozen bits of wire to let us through and then twiddling them all up again. The track ended abruptly at a ruined farm, and beyond were clumps of gorse (the dwarf variety, also known as Irish furze, and hellishly prickly) and boulders. I led Peggy who stopped at intervals with a mulish expression on her face. Susanne went on ahead and I saw her halt at a long, perfectly maintained wire fence that continued into a bog-fringed lake. There was no way round.

We went our separate ways back to the road, Susanne taking a laborious cross-country route to intersect the road lower down while Peggy walked briskly back the way we'd come with little 'I told you so' snorts, and grudgingly climbed the hill towards the road. She always objected to steep hills. Believing herself equal to any car when it came to roadwork, she considered rough terrain an unfair test for a harness pony. She approached hills like an inexperienced mountain climber, racing up for a dozen or so yards, then stopping to get her breath back. I tried to educate her into the proper mountaineer's plod but she wasn't interested, preferring to think up excuses for calling a halt. She was working on another delaying tactic: stopping to evacuate her bowels. Fair enough, I thought, I wouldn't want to continue walking under those circumstances, so I let her pause. She soon learned that by squeezing her droppings out one at a time ('horse-apples' Susanne called them) she could stop as often as she wanted. By the end of the trek she'd so perfected the technique I feared she'd do herself an internal injury by straining so hard.

Susanne was wading through waist-high shrubbery towards our meeting place. Her short cut had turned out, as most short cuts do, to be longer than my route and much more arduous. She'd had enough for the first day, and I'd had enough of her wretched stripy bag which caused the saddlebags to slip to one side (I was still not prepared to admit that she had brought exactly the luggage I'd specified). We agreed that she should hitchhike to the Hennessys and I'd meet her there. I described it as best I could since, in common with most rural Irish houses, there was no name or number on the gate. She passed me, waving, after 20 minutes or so, and I arrived to find her sitting outside the bungalow. Peggy's former friend, the jennet, hopped along by the fence on its hobbled legs, squeaking its greeting, but Peggy was more interested in grass so we turned her loose into the field and went in to see the family.

ʊ   ʊ   ʊ

The Hennessys were in fine fettle. Kathleen repeated for Susanne's benefit the ghost story of the giant barrel thing that had rolled around Mollie's valley, trapping people in their houses until a priest performed an exorcism. And she added another:

"One night I went to check on the boys before going to bed. As I was leaving their room I heard this noise. It was a wailing, like a woman crying, but with no pause or breath. I looked out of the window. Dark as dungeons, it was, and this cry was getting nearer. I'm telling you it was like no man nor beast. It made my blood run cold. I ran in to wake Sylvester. He was 12 at the time. You remember that night, don't you Vesta? The wailing noise came closer and closer then faded away."

Fascinating! This was the banshee wailer which is supposed to presage death. The origin of the word is interesting. *Bean sídhe* in Irish is literally 'fairy woman' but the meaning goes much deeper. Underground, in fact, to the Tuatha Dé Danaan people of Irish mythology who became invisible and took up residence in the 'fairy mounds' that can still be seen in Ireland.

After the ghost stories I told of my wanderings with Peggy before Susanne's arrival and mentioned the foul-mouthed man with two horses. "We know him!" Noel exclaimed. "You could only be talking about one fellow. Remember that time he came here, Mum?" They rocked with laughter and Kathleen continued.

"I was working in the kitchen one day and there was a knock at the back door. There was that farmer, looking all wet and sad. 'Could you give me a little piece of bread?' he asked, all humble. 'I've been out in the hills all day and haven't a bite to eat!' Well of course I invited him in and put the kettle on for tea and started boiling some eggs. Then he went to the door and shouted, 'It's OK boys, the kettle's on and she's boiling eggs,' and eight men appeared!"

The family spluttered with laughter. "Do you remember the shoe business?" Kathleen was too convulsed at the memory to continue. Sylvester took up the story.

"You see he damaged his shoe. Tore the sole away and it couldn't be mended. So he found a shop in Limerick that had the very same pair in the window. He went in and said, 'I've got a friend outside in the car and poor man he's only got one leg. He can't come in himself but he takes the same size as me so can I just try them?' Then he said, 'He'll only need one. Can I take it out so he can try it?' And of course that was the last the shop saw of him!"

Story time was cut short by the failing light. We had to set up camp in Peggy's field. My tiny tent was designed for a single person or couples as chummy as well-ripened peas in a pod. To give ourselves a little more room we pitched only the fly and hoped the weather would stay dry. It looked as though the cloudless days we'd enjoyed since my return to Ireland would last forever, but the weatherman had predicted thunderstorms.

It didn't rain and we both slept well so one minor anxiety about our trip together could be dispensed with, although mostly we planned to use hostels and B&Bs. Kathleen's story-telling continued over breakfast. I wanted to hear about life in Ireland in the old days. "When I was a girl they were mostly arranged marriages. It was important for the girl to have a fortune. She couldn't make a good marriage if she couldn't bring some money to the husband's household, so most girls left school at 14 and went to America to work as servants. They came back with their fortune and married a boy their parents had chosen. Only the eldest son stayed on the farm. The others had to find work somewhere else. Often they went to England. So a girl with a good fortune could marry a farmer and live with the husband's parents. Young people didn't have their own house in those days."

I reflected that times hadn't changed much; most of the households I'd visited had the eldest son working on the farm and living with his parents. If none of the sons had married they usually continued to live at home.

ʊ   ʊ   ʊ

I was concerned at the state of Peggy's shoes. The set that Pedar had provided were half-worn when he put them on, and now they were very thin and her hooves overgrown. Pedar had rather airily told me you could buy horseshoes in the pub in Dingle, but I'd never pursued that option. Noel said there was a blacksmith on the road towards the village of Camp, so we decided to pay him a visit after our planned frolic on the beach.

The beach was a seven-mile stretch of sand facing Brandon Bay. After doing seaside stuff our plan was that I would gallop away along the length of the strand to Rough Point at the tip of the finger of land that poked north into the Atlantic, and then head inland to Camp while Susanne returned to the road to hitchhike to the blacksmith where we'd meet. Peggy walked gingerly onto the sand, snorting in anxiety, but she was braver than her first time on Ventry Strand. I noticed with approval that her head carriage was becoming almost normal and she no longer peeped under those imaginary blinkers. Finding a spot away from the staring families, we removed the saddlebags and took it in turn to ride. I had a gallop and Susanne had a jog trot while I watched anxiously, expecting Peggy to take off at any moment. Peggy behaved impeccably. Susanne walked further along the beach with her, turned, and to my alarm I saw Peggy break into a canter with Susanne bouncing and wobbling, but

MY NAME IS PATRICK MORTIMER
I ERECTED THIS GROTTO
TO OUR LADY OF LOURDES
FOR BEEN CURED
ON THE 31 JULY 1980
AND ALSO FOR MY SON JOHN

ALL THANKS TO ALMIGHTY GOD
AND OUR BLESSED LADY

Ireland in 1984

Above: Roadside shrine
Below: Traditional Irish cottages like this have now been replaced by modern bungalows

Above: "A nondescript brown pony"
Below: Ready for the road: Kathleen with Peggy

Above: Peggy firmly vetoed my suggestion that we might swim
Below: Dingle Harbour

Slea Head with Great Blasket Island in the background

staying aboard. She pulled up wreathed in smiles. "That was fantastic! Why are you looking so worried? I galloped!"

We changed into our swimsuits and took it in turns to have a dip while Peggy pranced around excitedly digging holes in the sand with her forefoot. I thought it was time that she learned the delights of sea bathing. Swimming with Mollie had been one of the highlights of the group trek I'd taken with Willy Leahy before setting off on my own. Peggy reluctantly agreed to go as far as the surf, and even to let the waves break over her legs, but spun round every time I urged her to go deeper. I nearly fell off, and agreed that she'd been very brave and had done enough for the day.

Our plan for going our separate ways was a failure. Susanne's luggage, too awkward for her to carry with her, was insecurely attached to the saddle and prevented me from galloping. Indeed, it prevented me from riding at all since I couldn't get it properly balanced and the saddlebags constantly slipped to one side, or the stripy bag fell off. I was not happy. It took a couple of hours to lead Peggy along the beach to the forge where I found Susanne in no better humour. After waiting for an hour for a lift she'd been picked up by a man who 'wouldn't keep his hands with him'. Then, having located the blacksmith she was told that he didn't shoe horses these days. The same old story.

Susanne and I were hardly speaking. She, sensibly, was keeping silent until I was in a better mood, and I was still – quite unreasonably – furious over being denied a gallop because of her bag. I also had not forgiven her for that morning's comment that Peggy was stupid. "Stupid! She's the most intelligent pony I've ever known! That's the problem." Peggy had refused to be caught when we'd packed up the tent and were ready to leave. Over the last week she had learned that the day didn't end with her returning home to Dingle and her equine friends, and that she was expected to cope with all sorts of unreasonable challenges and spend each night in unfamiliar surroundings. No wonder her enthusiasm for the job was dwindling.

We all needed something to eat. Opposite the forge was an elegant gateway behind a triangle of very green lawn grass. Tying Peggy with the long rope to a side gate so she could get full benefit of this excellent grazing, Susanne and I settled down to our picnic and the map. Killarney was the next destination but the priority was to get Peggy shod and I knew where to go. My favourite family in Ireland lived the other side of the peninsula at Castlemaine. Dinny O'Shea had shod Mollie just before her accident and I wanted the family to meet Peggy. Our one-walk-one-ride method of travelling was not really working; Susanne had blisters from the previous day and there seemed little we could do to solve the luggage problem. We had to rethink our plans.

Our discussion was abruptly halted by a commotion from Peggy, who was plunging around with her head tucked into her chest. I knew immediately what had happened: her tether rope had caught round her back leg. I'd seen Mollie go through the same struggle by the Cliffs of Moher. Would I never learn? By the time I'd picked myself up (I'd been knocked down by the suddenly tightened rope) Peggy was standing motionless, trussed like a fowl, her head pulled sideways against her shoulder, waiting for help. She remained still while I fumbled with the buckle of her head collar and once she was out of her predicament she started eating again as though nothing had happened. However, I was mortified to find she'd sustained a nasty rope burn on the fleshy upper part of her hind leg. Pedar had told me that Peggy was not accustomed to being tethered. It was something else she would need to be taught.

We both made much of Peggy. Susanne commented how sensible she had been to stop struggling and wait for help, even though the position she had to wait in must have been painfully uncomfortable, and I immediately forgave her the earlier thoughtless remark. "Yes, ponies are much more sensible than horses. Thank goodness."

The yellowish-grey clouds that had been building up during the day broke in the predicted thunderstorm as we continued east. Cringing under our waterproofs, the idea of camping near the top of the pass no longer appealed and we started looking out for B&B signs. Usually they seem to grow like grass by the road but we'd hit an arid patch. Susanne went into a small post office to buy stamps and ask about accommodation. "You won't find one around here," said the post mistress cheerfully. We did find one around there, however, once we'd turned up the mountain road. The woman looked doubtfully at Peggy. "Sure you could tie her out there but what would the pet lamb think?" The pet lamb was a large and woolly sheep tethered by a leg on a grassy slope. The woman directed us to the proprietor of a restaurant who provided accommodation for caravan horses. Leaving Susanne to haul the luggage to our room, I trotted bareback up the road under a yellow sky and soon Peggy was happily sniffing at caravan-horse droppings in a large and pricey field. Later we had a large and pricey – and outstanding – meal at the restaurant, feeling guilty at the extravagance but, after all, Susanne was on holiday and we'd all had a tough day.

Chapter 17

We struggled with the errant bag one more time as we crossed the peninsula via the Caherconree mountain road between Camp and Aughils. The thunderstorm had only taken the edge off the heat and it was still very warm. Taking it in turns to ride, we ambled past cultivated land and a scattering of houses shaded by trees until the abrupt line where mountain and moorland took over. The heather was just starting to come into flower, and splashes of mauve punctuated the green bracken and grass up the hillsides. As we climbed to the top of the pass there were only sheep to observe our passing. No cars. We could have been hundreds of miles from the nearest town. Near the summit are the remains of an Iron-Age fort which was supposedly occupied by Cú Roí Mac Dairi, a giant who had the handy knack of rotating his fortress by remote control after sundown so that wherever he was in the world – and he was a great traveller – his enemies could never find the entrance. Unfortunately he hadn't taken into account the treachery of his wife, who poured milk into the river to indicate that he was at home, so he finally met a sticky end.

Our plan was that we would split up once we reached the main road that runs along the southern part of the peninsula. Susanne would hitch to Killarney and do touristy stuff for two days and I would follow after my visit to the blacksmith. First we had to phone the Aghadoe hostel, one of Ireland's most popular, to make sure they had room and check that there was somewhere for Peggy. Here, at least, was a hostel with a phone, but finding a phone box was a challenge. Eventually I was directed to a private house where, for some reason, they had a coin box in the conservatory. "Tomorrow, did you say? If you get here by 5 o'clock you should get a bunk." I explained about Peggy. "There's a big lawn in front of the house where I suppose you can tether her. But I don't want her eating the flowers." I assured him that Peggy's botanical interest was limited to grass, and that I would be make sure I arrived in Killarney in good time.

I left Susanne sitting rather forlornly beside a pile of luggage on the side of the road, and trotted briskly to Castlemaine, stopping to have a sandwich and ice cream at an outdoor café. I was still wary about leaving Peggy tied up because of her propensity for demolishing fences.

♘   ♘   ♘

A warm welcome awaited me when I reached the O'Sheas' in the early evening. The family had heard about Mollie's death and Beth told me that 12-year-old Anthony had taken it very hard. "I'm sure we could have done something to help, to prevent it happening," he'd said. As before, within moments of arriving I was sitting in front of a huge meal while Peggy had her old shoes taken off and her feet pared down. Then the family went off to watch one of the sons play football and Peggy and I were shown to Uncle Denny's acre where he had lived before moving in with his brother. It was still quite early so I leaned against a haystack in the sun and watched Peggy learn about tethers.

The single-stake hobble with which I had tethered Mollie was never entirely satisfactory. Although Mollie eventually got the hang of it, the radius between the stake and Mollie's munching mouth was too small. Rethinking the geometry of it, I realised that by tethering the pony from a back leg we got the additional length of Peggy's body so more grazing area. There was also the advantage that when the chain tightened it would be behind her. And the weight of the chain kept it on the ground so she wouldn't get tangled up as she had with the rope.

It worked perfectly. It took Peggy a while to learn that she could move around safely with this thing on her leg, and she was certainly quite cross about it, but by dusk she was grazing with her hind leg outstretched, at the end of her tether literally and metaphorically. I then turned her loose – the field was enclosed so this was just a preliminary lesson.

The haystack was probably not the best choice of back rest; I spent the next couple of days picking ticks off myself. I had set the tent up but never slept in it; Denny's neighbour Mary came across and invited me for a cup of tea, and we found so much to talk about that I ended up going to bed in her caravan at 2 o'clock. Our conversation began with Mary asking if I had any children. Normally in Ireland I'm reticent about my former marital status since I knew that divorce was illegal, but I explained that my childless state was by choice. "Oh yes, divorce is very straightforward in England," I said when she questioned me further. "After we'd been separated for two years it was by mutual consent." Mary, haltingly, told me her story.

Her husband had left her for another woman when their daughter was small. She felt utterly isolated, knowing no other single mothers and without her own transport. There was no bus service into Tralee where she might have met other women in a similar situation. Then the local priest preached a sermon on the wickedness of broken marriages. "I felt that terrible. Everyone in the village knew that he was pointing his finger at me." With immense courage she went to see the priest and explained her circumstances. "And you know what? Next Sunday he preached about the wickedness of husbands who desert their wives!" This may have made living in a small town a little easier, but Mary's house legally belonged to her husband so she couldn't sell it without his permission. She was stuck. And yet she still didn't believe in divorce. She wasn't alone in this. When Ireland held a referendum in 1986, the proposal to remove the ban on divorce was rejected by a large majority. It wasn't until 1994 that the electorate accepted a change in the law.

By the time I'd got the tent packed up next morning, Peggy was wearing new shoes and a smug expression. Then Mary's little daughter had her first-ever pony ride and loved it, and Anthony got on and showed that he could ride much better than me, even holding the puppy in front of him on the saddle. I loaded up the saddlebags, everyone waved goodbye, and Peggy and I set off in the sunshine for Killarney. I was soon able to leave the main road and follow narrow back-lanes which were lined with purple loosestrife, foxgloves, knapweed and all the smells of summer.

I ate Beth's picnic by a river so that Peggy could have drink. At least she was not as fussy as Mollie who considered an offer of water from my yellow plastic bucket as attempted poisoning, but she still preferred to watch me slide down a muddy, nettle-clad bank to a stream, then refuse the water that I brought back. If I could find a pony-accessible river like this one I always took Peggy there. She was often thirsty in this hot weather.

A little way downstream was a boy fishing. He walked up for a chat and to boast that he had caught an 8lb salmon in that same stretch of the river. "You English? I've got friends staying from Belfast. Come from the Falls Road area." I made appreciative noises. "I go up there whenever I can. We have a grand time." I asked politely what he liked so much about Belfast. "We go and throw stones at the soldiers." He went on to tell me of a gruesome shooting his friends had witnessed and I tried not to feel personally to blame for Northern Ireland.

At Aghadoe Heights at the top of the pass above Lough Leane, I saw why Killarney is so popular with visitors. Spread out in front of me was the lake, blue as the ocean, encircled by forested headlands and backed by MacGillycuddy's Reeks, a mountain range impressive by any standard, but wonderful in this setting. If this was good, when I saw the youth hostel my mouth must have dropped open. Aghadoe House was, and still is, an elegant manor built in pinkish sandstone in the 1820s and formerly the home of Lord Headley. "In most countries if a man steals land from the natives they put him in prison. In Britain they make him a lord," explained the warden later. It was burned down in the 1920s, along with so many gracious houses belonging to the English aristocracy, but restored to its original splendour, and has been part of the Irish Youth Hostel Association, An Óige, since 1957. I arrived before it was open and sat on the spacious lawn with a dozen or so cyclists and walkers who stared in disbelief at me, my pony and my saddlebags.

ʊ   ʊ   ʊ

While we waited, Susanne arrived having had a hugely enjoyable day. "I decided to hitchhike from the hostel to Killarney to see what the town was like. I was picked up by this lovely old priest and he said he had nothing much to do today and that he wanted to show me his country. So he took me to all sorts of interesting places, but best of all when he dropped me off at the hostel he said, 'This was the loveliest day of my life!'"

"How about yesterday?" I asked. "I felt guilty leaving you on the side of the road with all that luggage. How long did you wait?"

"Oh not too long. But I had a bit of a problem with this man. He talked a lot with his very thick Irish accent, and I couldn't understand him very well. But then he said there was a lake nearby and wouldn't I like to see it? Perhaps a little swim because it was so hot? I thought he was acting a bit strange, so I said no. Then he said something like 'just a moment to cool off my chopper in the water' and I didn't like this at all so I told him to take me immediately to the hostel. Which he did, very apologetic."

I tethered Peggy by her back leg, twisting my corkscrew picket into the soft ground of the lawn. I'd thanked the warden profusely for this privilege. "Just keep her away from my car," he said warningly. He'd already noticed her interest. Peggy loved cars; they reminded her of the good old days when she pulled a gig. The hostel was crowded with very noisy groups of very young people, all filling the capacious kitchen with smoke from their burnt sausages and frizzled bacon. We felt quite matronly, but at least we got a bunk each; latecomers were being turned away or put on mattresses on the floor. I kept popping out to check on Peggy who was still coming to terms with her tether. One time I found she'd pulled the picket up and was making faces at herself in the warden's wing mirror. I moved her to a firmer bit of lawn, well away from temptation.

That evening I discovered I'd reached a landmark: 100 miles since first mounting Peggy in Castle Gregory. Each day I measured our mileage on the map with a length of thread, marked out in miles to the inch, which I kept tied to my diary. I still have it.

ひ   ひ   ひ

We planned to stay a couple of days at the hostel and see the area properly. Susanne told me that the nicest place she'd been to with the priest was Muckross House and that she'd love to visit it again and see the inside. It was part of Killarney National Park, which is closed to vehicles, but the tourist office said that we could ride there. We needed to take Peggy out for the day since I didn't think I could leave her safely on the hostel lawn.

On our way to the park we called in on Donal O'Sullivan who ran a pony trekking centre. I wanted to make the most of the Iveragh Peninsula to the west of Killarney, and thought that he would be the best source of information for off-road routes.

"That's a grand pony for the job," said Donal, as Peggy neighed her greetings to his animals. "I'll get her some feed while we talk." He produced a bucket of special horse oats enriched with molasses which Peggy regarded with the utmost suspicion. It was possibly the first time she'd seen oats and I'd already discovered that she didn't have a sweet tooth. Sugar lumps were spurned and I hadn't been able to persuade her to eat apple cores, despite putting them in her mouth and holding it closed so she could appreciate the yummy flavour. As soon as she could, she'd spit them out. Brown bread was all this peasant would eat.

I tied her to a rail in the cowshed so she could enjoy her gourmet meal in peace while Donal and I spread out the map. "No, you won't be allowed to take the pony into the National Park," he said. "They've given me permission to take escorted groups but there are too many irresponsible tourist riders." That was a blow. What would we do with Peggy during the day? While we were considering our options there was a commotion in the cowshed and Peggy shot out backwards dragging the broken rail. That was the third bit of timber she'd broken in just over a week; I really *had* to cure her of this phobia. Despite seeing his property gradually demolished in front of his eyes, Donal offered to keep Peggy in the loosebox until the evening and then put her in a field for the night.

If oats were a possible first for Peggy, a stable almost certainly was. She stepped hesitantly into it and when I took her tack off and shut the loosebox door she put her nose over the top and looked so tragic I could hardly bring myself to leave. I felt even worse when I returned for my bag and was greeted with a 'Get me out of here!' neigh.

For the rest of the day Susanne and I behaved like ordinary tourists. We hired bicycles in Killarney which, I noted in my diary, had prostituted itself to tourism. 'It may once have been a charming town,' I wrote, 'and perhaps it regains its original character in the winter [it does], but in August we were not tempted to linger around the souvenir shops and rows of jaunting cars.'

Muckross House and its grounds, on the other hand, were unspoiled. We cycled along the narrow tracks – closed to motor traffic – and I could see for the first time why Killarney has excited visitors for so many years. No doubt the Victorians saw it at its best; Muckross House was built in 1843 in Tudor style as a sort of Irish Castle Howard, the owner, Henry Arthur Herbert, sparing no expense to make it equal to any other stately home in the Empire. He was successful. Titled visitors flocked there and left written tribute: 'There is no place which can compare with Killarney and I have seen much of the world' (Lord Castlerosse), 'I never in my life saw anything more beautiful. I might say so beautiful' (Lord Macaulay) and 'Within the circuit of a moderate day's walk [can be found] almost every possible variety of the wild, the majestic, the beautiful, the picturesque' (Lord Ritchie). Mr Herbert was an MP and his dedicated service to the Crown eventually ruined him. Queen Victoria paid a visit to Muckross in 1861 and the expense of keeping the royal party in the manner to which they were accustomed contributed to his bankruptcy. The Herbert family's association with Muckross, which had lasted two centuries, ended in 1899 when the house was sold.

The house is open year-round and I have enjoyed a recent winter visit as much as our tour of 1984. The Killarney inlaid furniture is an eye-opener, so beautiful and unique to this part of Ireland, and the huge antlers of an Irish elk, found in a local bog, are a reminder that evolution may sometimes lead to a dead end. The theory that this giant deer was made extinct by its impractical headgear seems entirely plausible. In the summer there's a folk museum and craft centre and the beautiful grounds with its lake views, fairy-tale woods with lumpy moss-covered boulders and a backdrop of mountains, can be enjoyed by all.

ᴗ   ᴗ   ᴗ

Over dinner Susanne and I planned the next section of the trek. Encouraged by the ease of hitchhiking, and gaining confidence in riding, Susanne felt that the one-walk-one-ride method was enjoyable for scenic stretches, but that she should hitch ahead on the main roads. I could then sharpen Peggy up with some trotting. We had already pared our luggage down so it all fitted in the saddlebags, leaving the unwanted stuff in storage at the youth hostel. We decided to keep our plans fluid, just focusing on one day at a time. Exploring away from the tarred roads was anyway going to be easier since the Killarney area was blessed with an inch-to-the-mile map that marked green roads and tracks. Our first goal would be the famous Gap of Dunloe, which I remembered from a family holiday in Killarney when I was a stroppy 15-year-old. Because it involved horses, it's the only bit of that holiday that I recall with any pleasure. No cars were allowed on the narrow road between the mountains. Visitors were plonked on horses – never mind if they'd never ridden before – and a little girl with a whip kept them at a brisk trot and denied the thirsty animals any water. At the end my mother had a half-crown-sized raw spot on her bottom, and never got on a horse again, whilst my father was so enthused by the experience that he signed up for riding lessons when we got home. The worst part of that holiday was the ascent of Carrantuohill, Ireland's highest mountain. The memories of loose scree and deep bog, swirling mist obscuring the views, and tears are still vivid. Even David, the spaniel, was miserable.

U   U   U

Back to the Gap of Dunloe. During the ice age a flow of rock, ice and glacial debris built up in the Black Valley, finding an outlet to the east of MacGillycuddy's Reeks and cut the deep gorge we now call the Gap of Dunloe. Three lakes were left in the wake of the receding ice, adding to the natural beauty of Ireland's most spectacular mountain pass which has been left almost untouched by the tourist industry. There's a collection of cafés and souvenir shops at the staging post known as Kate Kearney's Cottage but nothing on the mountain road itself except jaunting cars and self-willed horses with their ineffectual tourist riders. Only in the winter are cars allowed.

For nearly two centuries travellers have refreshed themselves at Kate Kearney's Cottage before setting off through the pass. Today they partake of coffee and cakes, but in Kate Kearney's time in the early part of the 19th century, it was a far more potent brew that was on offer. Kate Kearney's Mountain Dew was so 'fierce and wild, it required not less than seven times its own quantity of water to tame and subdue it'. The heady experience was no doubt helped by the fact that Kate herself was intoxicatingly beautiful. I wondered if it was Kate Kearney's Cottage that I remember from 1956. Probably not, because that little thatched cottage was notable, not for its refreshments, but for the toothless crone who hovered in the doorway. "I like to watch the motors," she told us.

I went to collect Peggy early the next morning. "She's very trusting," said Donal. "Walked right up to me when I came for her this morning." I was quite put out. I thought it was only me that she came to – when she felt like it. She was back in the stable and very relieved to be released from her prison. We trotted briskly to Aghadoe House, loaded up, and set off for the Gap of Dunloe.

Susanne and I had arranged to meet at Kate Kearney's Cottage, a distance of about five miles from the hostel. The luggage was now much lighter and Peggy sprightly after her day's rest, so we were soon sipping tea while Peggy neighed at the other horses and nuzzled for titbits. Some of the horse-hirers came over to talk to us. "Nice mare, who does she belong to?"

"She's mine. I bought her in Dingle." There was a reason behind this lie. Donal had warned us that the close-knit community of horse-hirers did not take kindly to outsiders. "So don't say Peggy's hired or they'll give you a bad time."

"Is that so? She's very quiet." (speculative look in her mouth) "Would you be selling her now?"

"Um, yes, but not for a long time."

"I'll buy her. I can pick her up in the truck when you finish your ride."

"Oh, she's not suitable. She coughs and there's something wrong with her leg. Besides, her previous owner wants to buy her back. Yes, he said he wants first refusal..." I floundered on but in the end had to accept the man's name and address. Even if Peggy had been mine, no way would I have submitted her to the drudgery of trotting up and down that same road each day.

U   U   U

It was another hot day. The sun shone on the rumps of drooping horses awaiting their tourist riders for the journey over the pass and back, but there were few visitors around when we set out along the white dirt road. Every now and then a jaunting car would trot by, but otherwise we had the pass to ourselves. The route deserves its reputation. The green and grey mountains crouched over the road, with their detritus carelessly dropped at their feet. Great rocks, the size of bungalows, had come to rest by the road, or were halted in their descent in gulleys or on ledges.

Sheep picked at the grass which remained green despite the drought, and the sun brought deep shadows across the valley.

We picnicked at a bridge where the road crosses the River Loe before it broadens into the first lake. It was a windless day, just a faint breeze wobbling the reflections in the lake. We were in no hurry to continue, but Peggy was in a tiresome mood; instead of grazing she paced up and down until I tethered her, which caused yells of anger from passing horse-hirers who assumed, reasonably enough, that we were irresponsible tourists with a loose horse. After the third lake the pass narrows, the road zigzagging up between steep black cliffs to Head of Gap with its views over the Black Valley and Purple Mountain, though in a few weeks' time this would be coloured with heather; the name derives from the purplish tinge of the rocks.

At the Black Valley there were decisions to be made. A youth hostel at the foot of the pass had looked inviting on the map but it was too soon to stop for the night. Every day we expected the perfect weather to break. We continued west along the valley, splitting up so that Susanne could take a short cut along a footpath marked on the map. I'd been tempted to ride it but a woman emerged from a cottage, peering at us in amazement, and advised us not to take Peggy. "'Tis awful rough."

Susanne was waiting for me where her footpath rejoined the road: "Hilary, you must look at the horses of that man over there. They're beautiful! He told me about them but I couldn't understand." (Susanne speaks excellent English but had a hard time, as I did, getting to grips with the Kerry accent.) I followed her directions down a grassy track and through a broken gate to a half-derelict cottage sitting damply under a high bank. An old man with a greasy peaked cap turned back to front and manure-coloured clothes was stacking turf. He greeted me enthusiastically. "It's my horses you'll be wanting is it? Let me show you."

He didn't need to show me, I'd already seen two of them as they grazed near the cottage. They would not have looked out of place in the show ring. There was a jet-black gelding that shone in the evening sun, and two chestnut mares as plump and glossy as conkers. But the one that had caught Susanne's eye was milk-white with a pink nose and hooves. "I look after 'em well," the old man said with satisfaction when I expressed my admiration.

I asked him about an enticing-looking footpath which the map showed as connecting our valley with the neighbouring one. It climbed to a pass and the closeness of the contour lines indicated a steep but not impossible drop down to the next valley. Could we safely take Peggy over? "Oh you'll get over there all right," he said rather too airily. "And you could camp anywhere in this valley. No-one lives there now. Plenty of good fields for your pony, or you could come in with me," he added, twinkling, his three teeth showing in a dark banana-shaped grin. "I'm all alone."

At the head of the valley, just before the pass, we found the most idyllic campsite of the whole trip. The track led us through several well-fenced fields empty of livestock but with plenty of lush grass watered by a small stream. We turned Peggy loose in the field that sloped down to the stream and set up our tent in the adjoining one. A large, flat-topped rock served as a table and the river, running into deep pools, as a bath. The water was almost tepid after its journey over sun-warmed rocks and the evening hot and still. I'm not one for leaping into every icy mountain stream with squeals of delight, but this was different. It was heavenly. We'd stocked up with food in Killarney so could indulge in tinned stew mixed with packet soup and midges, followed by yoghurt, fruit, and coffee. We climbed into our sleeping bags well-fed, clean, and in love with Ireland.

ひ   ひ   ひ

When I went to check on Peggy first thing the next morning, I found her lying down, dozing in the sun. I'd never seen her so relaxed, and was happy to leave her in peace while I checked out the pass on foot. The way up was marked with white-painted posts, which took a rough but dry route. I followed it to the highest point where the view was breathtaking: my nemesis all those years ago, Carrantuohill, loomed above me on the right, the clouds already gathering on its summit to confuse any climbers. In front was the green Caragh River valley disappearing into the haze and bordered on each side by steep mountains. I desperately wanted to go over this pass but without putting Peggy at any risk. The route down was certainly steep: I followed the white posts through bracken and boulders. It was these boulders that worried me; Peggy would have to pick her way very carefully. Yet she was a sensible pony and I'd seen horses and mules cope with worse in the Andes during the decade that I worked as a trek leader.

Susanne had the tent packed up when I returned. I reported on the situation. "As I see it we have three choices: we go back and round by the road; you go over the pass on your own and I'll meet you tonight; or we all go over if Peggy is sensible." We looked at the map. Going round would add a further 11 miles. We looked at Peggy, well-fed and content and oh so sensible, and decided we'd give it a go. If she made heavy weather of the ascent then we'd turn back; the descent into the next valley would be much harder. Peggy was in an exceptionally obliging mood, following us willingly as we led her along the track and up the rocky slope to the pass. She jumped up steep places and placed her hooves carefully between the rocks. She would be all right; I gave her a rest at the top and made a fuss of her before we started down the other side. It was not easy.

Peggy soon lost her enthusiasm and stopped every few minutes to force out a horse-apple. I couldn't blame her; the route indicated by the white posts was fine for walkers, taking them boulder-hopping down the mountain, but we had to try to find alternative Peggy-routes where she wouldn't slip on the rocks on her new shoes. Our progress was very slow. Susanne had to go ahead and find the best route and then return to be ready to drive Peggy forward if she did her mulish act and refused to be led. At least we had a good supply of brown bread as a reward for particularly accomplished slides and jumps.

We dropped 700 feet in less than half a mile and looking back at the steep rock-strewn hillside from the safety of the track at the bottom, it seemed incredible that Peggy had made such a descent. Our praise was effusive, but our relief premature. The marked path led to a stile over a well-made wire fence. There was no way round; we were stuck. Peggy grazed while we considered our situation. When we'd met the track at the foot of the hill we'd turned right, since the other way would have taken us to the wrong side of the valley. Scanning our route through binoculars from the top of the pass I had noted that this track apparently ended at a farmhouse, but perhaps it continued and joined the road we could see beyond the house. A few fields away a shepherd was busy with his sheep. I had no difficulty deciding which of us should go over and ask directions. I watched through binoculars as Susanne climbed the stile and made her way towards him. I could see her gestures and hear two voices but no words. I could tell that the meeting was not going well. Susanne turned and started back up the hill followed by angry-shepherd sounds. She arrived considerably shaken. "He said if he catches anyone tampering with his fence he'll shoot the person and the horse," she reported.

We nervously followed the track ending at the farmhouse, keeping an eye on the shepherd bellowing at his sheepdog below us and expecting any minute to feel a bullet in our backs. We were summoning the courage to open the farmyard gate when a man suddenly appeared. "It's him!" whispered Susanne in a frightened voice. But he was smiling broadly as he opened the gate. "Maybe it's his brother." Not a close brother at any rate since he was quite exceptionally friendly, racing on ahead to open the gates and chattering the while about ponies and tourists and the drought.

We'd made the right choice. A good track led us across the valley to the road. We stopped for lunch by the river and unloaded Peggy so she could have a much-deserved rest and feed before continuing west along Bridia Valley towards Glencar.

When we reached a sign for the Mountain Hut, an independent hostel, we were tempted to stop. But it was only 3 o'clock on a warm afternoon; it was too early and too lovely to call it a day. A woman came towards us carrying a heavy shopping bag. She lived at the house the other side of the wire fence and its stile (with, we learned later, her son the angry shepherd). "We don't have a car right now," she said. "I get transport at the end of the road." What transport could she get? I wondered. I was sure there were no buses. After walking the three miles from her house to the road she probably had to wait for a friend to drive by. She was glad to put the bag down and chat. Full of admiration that Peggy had come over the pass, she then said, "But why didn't you take the higher route near the lake? It would have brought you out behind the house, and there are no rocks!"

Chapter 18

Susanne was disgusted. "I think these awful Germans must be part of a disadvantaged youth programme. I'm glad there's no room!" It was Peggy who made the decision to stop at the Climbers' Inn. She raised her head, pricked her ears and let out a long, echoing neigh. All the windows shot open, heads poked out and the German equivalent of "Good grief!" accompanied the sound of footsteps clattering down the stairs. After we'd politely answered questions (in English, Susanne refused to reveal that she was German) and learned that there was no room at the inn, we fled to a nearby B&B. It was all shiny Wonderboard and fresh paint, run by an implausibly young couple who seem surprised to find themselves in charge of a guesthouse. We suspected that it was a wedding present from Dad. A plaster statuette of Jesus had pride of place in the lounge, gazing anxiously at his bleeding heart as though thinking 'How will I explain it to Mum? It'll never wash out!'

I thought a pub called The Climbers' Inn would be full of tourists in knee breeches, hairy socks and boots, but when we returned for a drink in the evening we found we were the only visitors. I had also thought that a pub in the heart of Kerry would be self-consciously Irish, but it was wholly delightful. There were very few women; most of the customers were old men with gnarled faces, reminiscent of a German woodcut, and cloth caps. We were delighted to recognise our smiling friend from the valley, the antidote to the 'I'll shoot the person and the horse' farmer. We learned that he was no relation to his neighbour ("His mother's awful hard on him," he explained, when we hesitatingly told our story about the gun) and that his name was Jimmy. He was so thrilled to have not one, but two ladies talking to him, that he became almost incoherent. His blue eyes wandered independently round the room and his grin got wider and wider showing a scant but serviceable number of teeth. We mischievously asked him if he was married. "Dear God no, oh Lord no, who'd have me? All I can hope for now is an old'un; I can keep her warm in the winter." Delighted laughter all round. Jimmy had a friend called John, very old and tiny and completely toothless, and took great pains to include him in the conversation and explain everything. More and more men joined us, complaining that women were in short supply since no one wanted to live in their isolated valley. One of the younger ones looked wistfully at Susanne. "What about all those ladies in Germany? Could you send them over to marry us?"

One of the old men, Michael, produced an accordion and rather pensively started playing. No-one took much notice. Jimmy tried to persuade us to dance and I wished later that we had; an Irish bar is no place to be inhibited. It was by far our nicest pub evening. Nights out in Dingle and Killarney had produced a tourist menu of over-amplified popular songs and easily-resisted inducements to merriment.

ʊ   ʊ   ʊ

We were heading, eventually, to Waterville at the end of the Iveragh Peninsula, so were enthused when the manager of the inn, Jack Walsh, told us of an old 'butter road' going over the nearby mountains which would be far more interesting than the road shown on our map. In the olden days men used to carry firkins of butter along these lanes to the ports; in this case presumably Waterville. A firkin held 56lbs of butter. Needless to say the old road was just off our very good inch-to-the-mile map covering the Killarney district (sod's law: all interesting places are on the edge of, or just off, the map) but we thought we could see an alternative access through forestry land. "Well, you might as well try," he said, so we did. First we needed to stock up with provisions and so I tied Peggy to a metal post by a petrol pump and shop. "Fill her up, please," I was going to say if someone came out. That plan was pre-empted when she did her 'Guinness for strength' act, but instead of the post breaking, the heavy-duty metal clip at the end of her extra-strong nylon lead rope snapped clean in half. I looked at the two pieces in amazement and speculated on the pounds of pull needed to break a metal clip. With that strength, I told her, she could jolly well carry me and my luggage and like it.

From Glencar we went briefly north, crossing the River Caragh at Blackstones Bridge, and passing through splendidly dramatic scenery of lake and mountain, before plunging into the pine forest to follow a track which continued encouragingly into open, rather desolate country very similar to Dartmoor. We could see a farm at the end and what looked like a path contouring round the mountains beyond, so were incredulous when the farmer and his family said they knew of no old road over the hills. We'd come at least six miles along that track and were less than a mile, as Pegasus flies, from the road to Waterville. Never liking to take no for an answer, I left Susanne and Peggy gloomily nibbling at their lunch under gathering clouds and climbed to the top of the nearby hill to see if it really was impassable. It was. Boggy with clumps of tussock grass interlaced with squelchy sheep tracks. Although I could see the

Waterville road from the top, there was no sign of the butter road which should have been just below me.

So we had to go back the way we had come. These days, when good walking maps of Ireland are readily available and long-distance trails clearly marked, it's hard to convey the frustration of exploring the country with half-inch-to-the-mile maps and no system of bridle paths. I would have so loved to get off the roads on to reliable, obstacle-free tracks, but it was always a hit-or-miss experience.

When we reached the forest we succumbed to temptation and followed an inviting-looking path lined with foxgloves and heather, which ought, we thought, to meet our road and cut off a five-mile loop. It did, but the last hundred yards were across a small footbridge over a stream with steep boggy banks followed by a stile over a high wire fence. I felt close to tears. At least Susanne could continue; I had to go back. We arranged to meet in an hour and a half, which meant Peggy and I had to get a move on. At first she was happy to canter back along the path, but once on the road and asked to trot she did everything she could think of to indicate that we should stop for the night. She ostentatiously sought out grass verges for her poor tired feet, turned into fields that offered good grazing, spooked along shying at imaginary horrors and stopped to force out horse-apples. We passed a field where a lovely black pony with a head like a chess piece trotted along the fence to greet us. Peggy gave it a 'woe is me, I'm so lonely and ill-treated' neigh and it obligingly jumped out to join her, whereupon she squealed and kicked. Really, horses behave so unreasonably at times. I was not pleased to find myself with a loose pony frisking about on the road, but fortunately it belonged to the house adjacent to the field and its owner cheerfully retrieved it when he heard our hoof beats on the drive.

When I reached our meeting place at a settlement enticingly named Knocknagapple, there was no sign of Susanne. I eventually found her talking to a farmer. He hadn't heard of the butter road either but, to Peggy's obvious relief, said we could camp in his field. She made a great demonstration of chomping ravenously around the tent while I wrote my diary, ramming home her complaint about how hungry and tired she had been. She ran away with a horse's equivalent of a snarl when I went to pat her. With her interest in cars she should have been ecstatic; the farmer's son collected dead cars the way other boys collect stamps and the field was full of them. While we were sorting out our stuff a flock of sheep burst through, over and under the gate. There were many lambs looking bigger than their mothers in their thick woolly coats, but still suckling energetically. I watched a pair of gigantic twins go one on each side of a little shorn ewe who was lifted right off the ground by their efforts.

The trouble with lush grassy fields is midges. After more than two weeks of sunshine, the skies were overcast and happy dancing insects sought out our bare arms. So we were pleased to accept the offer to cook our supper in the kitchen, sneak a look at the Los Angeles Olympic Games on TV, and chat to the family. The daughter told us she worked in a bar-cum-draper. What? Oh bars were very rarely just bars in Ireland, she said, they were hardware shops, grocers, drapers… The shop assistant had to be able to pull a pint or cut a yard.

The farmer told us this story: A friend was complaining that a dog was savaging his sheep. "It's your own dog," said his neighbour.

"Impossible, I lock him in the shed each night."

"OK, just watch that shed tonight."

The farmer set up watch and saw his sheepdog jump out of the shed's open window, kill a sheep, wash itself off in the river and jump back into the shed. It sounded far-fetched, but Noel Hennessy had told me a similar tale. He'd seen his own dog disappear up the hill after a sheep, creep by with blood on its muzzle and slink off for a swim in the river before re-appearing with a 'just a little business to attend to' expression on its face.

U U U

I could tell from looking at the map that the road to Waterville would be beautiful, following the River Inny through low hills and forests. But it would be a long day for Peggy, 20 miles, though easy going with some promising-looking stretches of the old road shown on the map. Everyone knew that it existed; no-one knew how much was usable now. Peggy and I had gone 17 miles that day, very little of it in the right direction.

Shortly after dawn the next morning I heard a grunting sound and looked out of the tent to see Peggy rolling energetically in the dewy grass before getting to her feet to start grazing. She knew the morning routine now, and wanted to fill her stomach before we packed up the tent. The clouds of the previous night had cleared, and the low sun outlined Peggy in gold and picked out a silver blanket of dew-covered spiders' webs covering the meadow. In this sort of weather, camping was sublime.

Once underway, our first bit of excitement was a sheep dip. A very cheerful affair for everyone but the sheep. The children sat on the wall of the corral in the sun, border collies crouched by the tightly packed flock and brawny men threw the sheep in one by one, pushing their heads under the frothy brown liquid. Emboldened by being two onlookers, not one, we stayed and chatted for a while. When I was on my own I'd passed sheep shearers without daring to stop; the cheerful togetherness of the men was too intimidating. American tourists, of course, step right in and get their legs pulled. I'd heard descriptions of what Paddy or Michael had told the video cameras about quaint Irish customs.

The grassy banks and stone walls were speckled and striped with flowers: foxgloves were still in bloom, as was purple loosestrife, knapweed and scabious. Blackberries were ripening on the roadside brambles and early hazel nuts promised a good autumn harvest. In contrast to England, where the grass verges and hedges are savagely cut back as soon as they reach their flowery best, I saw very little verge-cutting in Ireland. Too many lanes, probably. Later in the trek I met a huge hedge-trimming machine jammed along a grassy track. I was standing with Peggy in a gateway waiting for it to pass and peeping nervously round the overgrown hedge at the large man striding towards me with blazing eyes. I was sure he was going to tell me I was on private land. "Is this a main road?" he demanded.

"Well, er, no…," I faltered, waiting for the abuse.

"Then I'm lost!"

The road climbed up to the pass then dropped down to the long valley full of conifers and horseflies. Poor Peggy was driven mad by the flies but I daren't frighten her again by using the aerosol. We picked bracken fronds and fanned her head and neck as we hurried on to an attractive bridge across the river. Here we found our first stretch of butter road. At first it was a surfaced road serving a few houses, then a track, then a ghost of a track discernible by the banks that bordered a gorse-covered meadow. Then we came to a dead end: a stone wall. Not again! We were just about to turn back when an exceptionally handsome young farmer with a full set of teeth materialised out of nowhere. Sizing up the situation he removed the top stones from the wall, Peggy obligingly jumped over, we simpered our thanks and rejoined the road again, positively triumphant at having achieved a scant three-mile section of ancient road.

After that it was a question of following the river valley, crisscrossing the Inny over picturesque old bridges. The scenery became calmer, the hills lower, and the farms more prosperous-looking. Peggy kept herself amused by following close behind the person on foot and shoving her with her nose.

A gate stood open into a grassy field by the river, and I thought we could all do with a snack. We'd had an early lunch with scant grazing for Peggy. I took out her bit and let her munch away while we ate our biscuits. A very old man hobbled over, leaning on a stick, followed slowly by a very old dog. He chatted about the weather, the possibility of the drought ending that night, and what a nice pony we had. "Um. . . are we on your land?" I asked.

"That you are. I was wondering about my bull…"

We decided it was time we moved on.

υ   υ   υ

Susanne found a good spot for hitchhiking, and Peggy and I continued in a dreamy state, lulled by the straight road and lack of decisions. The day was cool and breezy with fluffy clouds in a blue sky. The haze of the last week had gone, leaving clear views of the layers of hills beside and behind us: green, then grey, then a distant blue. Reaching Waterville I found Susanne sitting on a wall a couple of miles from the town. With rain forecast we had decided to treat ourselves to a night indoors and we guessed that this popular town – a traditional stop on the Ring of Kerry circuit – would be full of tourist facilities. In the centre, yes, but not on the outskirts. We had a long search before we found a B&B for ourselves and a spacious field for Peggy.

Then – and now – Waterville was a typical Irish seaside town, though one with the added attraction of a large lake, Lough Currane, behind it. Rows of cheerfully painted terraced houses face a pebble beach, and there are neon signs announcing the attractions, and strolling couples down at the waterfront. A statue of Charlie Chaplin commemorates this famous visitor. Once upon a time, though, it had some even more important visitors: the boat that arrived in the harbour carried Noah's son and granddaughter

plus another 49 women and two men. Some say that they set sail before
the Flood, and others that in a fit of pique Noah excluded his son Bith
from the ark and that Bith's daughter, Cessair, learned from supernatural
sources that Ireland was free from serpents, monsters and the like (yes, I
know that puts paid to the St Patrick legend – and most other legends)
so would be a safe refuge from the Flood. Safe it may have been, and
paradise for a while since the women were divided up among the three
men, but things soon went wrong; Bith and another man died, and
the remaining one, Fintan, fled and turned himself into a one-eyed
salmon which served him well when Ireland was under water. Later,
he metamorphosed into an eagle and eventually back into a human,
becoming Fintan the Wise. But I've never quite got to grips with Irish
mythology; another source tells me that at the time of the Great Flood,
Ireland was inhabited by giants and monsters (the fomoire), so would
hardly be the secure haven sought by Cessair. Perhaps her supernatural
source got it wrong. Fintan the one-eyed salmon would have fitted right
in with this crowd, some of whom had one eye, some one leg, some a
goat's head and so on.

A new incarnation of the Flood began the next day. We woke to rain
lashing against our window and Susanne, shocked at this introduction,
after 16 days of almost unbroken sunshine, to Ireland's traditional climate,
said she was not doing any more riding. Not until the rain stopped,
anyway. We spread the map over the remains of our full Irish breakfast,
and worked out what to do with her remaining time. Only a few days
were left before she had to catch her plane back to Munich. Valentia
Island was the obvious choice. It was only about 15 miles from Waterville
and linked to the mainland by a bridge. "If you start now you'll get there
in time to find us somewhere to stay," I said pragmatically. But first we
went together to collect Peggy.

Perhaps the fomoire had got at Peggy during the night and whispered insurrection in her ear. To my astonishment, instead of walking up to me when I went into the field she trotted away and it was soon obvious that she had no intention of being caught. "Stupid horse," muttered Susanne, heading back to the B&B. Leaving Peggy eating busily, one ear cocked in my direction, I knocked on the door of the farmhouse and explained my problem to the farmer. "Like that is it? I can give you a bucket of horse nuts. That should do it." Indeed, Peggy's greed got the better of her and I was able to catch hold of her head collar. But instead of the lovely calm pony I had got used to, she was overwrought. She wouldn't let me touch her neck and started to pull back as soon as I tried to tie her to the gate so I could return the bucket. "What is it, Peggy old girl?" I asked. She and I had got to know each other pretty well during the previous three weeks and I generally knew what she was trying to communicate, but I couldn't tell if something had frightened her during the night or whether she was just being naughty.

The rain was coming in wind-driven spasms and Susanne was disenchanted with horse management and anxious to get going. Peggy was just anxious. She pranced and danced down Waterville's main street, shying at everything and making a scene about the rain. I discovered that she was even worse than Mollie in this respect, trying to face away from the wind and tensing her body against the watery lashes and exhibiting such misery that I forgot my own discomfort. My original plans to short-cut along the beach came to nothing because in her current mood I daren't ask Peggy to ford the mouth of the River Inny, so I had a long stretch of main road with plenty of traffic. Earlier in the ride Peggy had demonstrated that she had a thing about bridges and would make a fuss about crossing even wide ones. On reaching the Inny Bridge she stopped dead and stared in terror at the water on each side of the metal railings, before retreating backwards at a run in front of startled coach drivers and their passengers.

After the bridge I was able to get off the main road but she was no calmer. Shying violently at some imaginary horror she slipped and went down on her knees. With visions of Black Beauty and 'broken knees' I jumped off, sick with foreboding, expecting to see blood. But she was unhurt. I led her for a while after that and she started to quieten down.

Abandoning my plan for a scenic ride round the coast, I took the most direct route to Valentia across the peninsula in improving weather. The relentless grey of the sky started to break up allowing occasional glimpses of blue. Selecting a suitably succulent grass verge, I gave Peggy her lunch and made some damp sandwiches using the saddle as a table. My jacket, hung over a fence post, started to dry. As I led Peggy down the road a woman padded out of her cottage in bedroom slippers to have a chat. "Would you be walking all the way?" I explained that both Peggy and I needed a rest at times. "Would you like some milk? Mary, go get the lady some milk! She won't mind a mug, she's one of us." I was flattered. Not trusting her rather elegant daughter to get it right, mum trotted indoors and returned with a bottle. "It'll do you good. Fresh from the cow today."

We continued to Valentia in better spirits, broken only by a terrifying tree stump which had Peggy dancing all over the road again. Peggy frequently shied at large rocks and tree stumps. Strange that, after so many thousands of years of domestication, horses still have that instinctive fear of the crouching predator. Nor was she too keen on the long bridge across to the island, bouncing sideways in front of the traffic and staring popeyed at the sea. She continued with caution, flicking her ears back to listen to my mindless commentary, and poised to flee if the ocean rose up to attack her.

It was three miles from the bridge to Chapeltown on the southernmost of the island's two parallel roads. After a couple of miles a man in a van stopped. "Are you Hilary?" I looked at him in astonishment. "I've been asked to show you my field. You can keep the pony there. But first you'll need to go to the hostel with your bags, so just ask for Joe at the petrol pump when you're ready." There are a lot of advantages in having an advance envoy to sort out one's lodgings.

I arrived at the Ring Lyne bar and hostel at 5.30 to an uproarious welcome. Among the revellers who spilled out of the pub to look at Peggy was a very large, very drunk man.

"Is it a horse or a mare?"

"A mare."

"I mean, is it a female animal?"

"It is."

"Are you sure?"

"Look underneath if you don't believe me."

He went ponderously over and peered between Peggy's hind legs. "'Tis a gelding."

"First gelding I've seen with teats," I said sourly, tiring of the conversation. Suddenly he was in the saddle and yelling "Giddy up!". I held the reins firmly and persuaded him that Peggy was tired and deserved a rest. He was too portly and inebriated to get his leg over the saddlebags and had to be helped down by his sniggering friends.

Finally Peggy was de-bagged and unsaddled and I trotted her bareback the mile to Joe's petrol pump and his field; eight acres of lovely lush grass. Peggy needed a proper rest, so I asked Joe if she could stay for a couple of days. She'd have company too, a donkey with hooves that had never been trimmed; they curled up like Turkish slippers.

When I arrived back at the Ring Lyne, Susanne had returned from her sightseeing full of enthusiasm for Knightstown at the far end of the island. Although our hostel had pleasant, two-bunk rooms and a large sitting room, Chapeltown wasn't exactly the hub of Valentia. Perhaps we should move on tomorrow. We ate dinner in the pub and discussed the future. Susanne had to leave Ireland in three days' time and we both, at some point, had to pick up our extra luggage from Killarney. The present stormy wet weather would continue for the next two or three days, so the forecast said, so we might as well stay another day in Valentia then hitch into Killarney and give Peggy a proper holiday.

ʊ   ʊ   ʊ

We had a convivial evening in the pub and learned about the island from the publican. The inappropriately Spanish-sounding name was, it turned out, a corruption of Bheil-Inse. Oilean-Bheil-Inse means 'the island beside the flat land at the river mouth'. Islanders divided their memories into two halves: BB and AB; Before Bridge and After Bridge. The bridge was built in 1977, bringing undoubted benefits to Valentia along with an inevitable loss of island identity. Mr O'Sullivan gave us graphic descriptions of seriously ill people having to be taken by boat from Knightstown and then by rough road to hospital in Tralee. He described how horses and cattle used to cross on the same boat, or sometimes be swum across the narrow strait, and speculated on the possibility of getting Peggy across that way. It all depended on whether his son could come up with a suitable vessel. Fortunately for Peggy he didn't. "We don't see much of our young people now they can motor into Cahersiveen. They'll even go to Killarney or Tralee for a night out! I remember in the forties we had 'ballrooms of romance' where boy met girl. Everyone loved dancing in those days, but the evening would be over by 11." Before that there were country 'stages', wooden platforms by the road where people could dance.

The islanders are proud of Valentia's role in history. The island was the eastern terminus of the first transatlantic telegraph cable; the other end was in Newfoundland and the first ever telegram to North America was transmitted in 1858. Not content with this pioneering effort, the basic principles of television – translating light into its electrical counterpart (don't ask me to explain) – was discovered in 1873 by a telegrapher called Mr Hay. There must have been long boring hours when no telegrams were sent and a chap had nothing better to do than invent television.

And there's more. You can see the stone which played a part, in 1862, in the calculations of the longitude of the earth and hence the size of this planet. No, I don't understand that either, but here it is:

> The Great European Arc of Longitude was measured by triangulation from this spot to a point in the Ural Mountains in Russia and certain astronomical observation were made at the two ends. From such arcs as this, measured both east and west, and north and south, the size and figures of the earth have been determined.

If you want to go further back than the 19th century, there are also some well-preserved dinosaur footprints.

We didn't find all those sights during our walk around the island, but we saw some holy ones at St Brendan's Well where roughly hewn stone crosses vied for attention with some rather charming plastic saints and virgins. The wind was so strong we had a struggle to remain upright and our walk along the cliffs above the dramatic sea was a test of balance, strength and the waterproof qualities of our clothing. On the way back I visited Peggy luxuriating in her spacious lodgings, and saw, to my annoyance, that she'd got rid of her much-hated head collar. After a search I found it, but wondered how I'd catch her when the time came.

Back in Knightstown we warmed up over tea and apple pie and got talking to a very charming, very British young man who tried to convince

us that he was German. It was only when we met his mother that we
conceded he was telling the truth. He had been educated at an English
public school and now lived in London. The family had rented a yacht
for a week but Mutti's battles with seasickness and the family rules of
yachtsmanship had caused her to skip the Valentia section and go by
car with Bernhard. "Why don't you stay in our hotel? And have dinner
with us?" An excellent idea. They collected our luggage from Chapeltown
and we moved into a damp, decaying but beautiful old hotel overlooking
the harbour, which agreed to store my luggage while I popped back to
Killarney for a night.

That dinner, in The Gallery Kitchen, surrounded by impressive
sculptures, was one of the best I've ever had. It was run by an elegant
English woman who did most of the cooking. Her artist partner sculpted
during the winter and in the summer: "I nail his tiny feet to the floor
and make him cook steaks which he's awfully good at." We also found
exceptional singing at the pub round the corner. We were charmed by
Valentia: the dramatic cliff walks above a frothing sea, the narrow lanes,
congenial people, pleasant small town, and lack of popular tourist facilities.

U   U   U

We decided to leave separately the next morning. I wanted to head off
early in order to get to the post office in Killarney, pick up my mail, post
off some non-essential luggage, and be back in the hostel in time to claim
a bunk. Susanne, however, had got so involved in the romance of the
decaying hotel that looked out over a stormy waterfront that she chose
to do a French Lieutenant's Woman act on the pier while I was ferried
across to the mainland by a grumpy boatman – his only passenger.

I walked two miles to the main road carrying my plastic bag of
essentials for the night and stood damply watching cars approach

through curtains of rain, then whizz past ignoring my outstretched thumb. Sometimes the drivers glanced in my direction before staring resolutely ahead. I couldn't blame them for not wanting to have the interior of their car soaked by a hitchhiker of indeterminate gender. The wind blew in from the sea and there seemed no hope of a reprieve from the weather. I recalled a conversation between a farmhand and his Anglo-Irish employer after a stormy night:

"It rained thunder and lightning and lotions all night, and didn't the rain have the wheat threshed and the oats made into porridge."

"Well, you must pray for fine weather, Michael."

"What use is prayer when the wind is from the west?"

The Irishman's way with words is well known and is one of the pleasures of talking with rural people and, of course, reading Irish literature. I'd heard an erudite discussion on the subject of television. Perhaps, as one speaker suggested, the Irish are freer with their imaginative use of English because it was a language they had been forced to adopt. Or that having been a nation with no middle class they are not restrained by 'proper' English usage. Whatever the reason, when asking directions I'd rather hear 'Take the road out of town and 'tis all a fall of ground' than a more useful but less poetic British version. Information here was also agreeably coloured by the desire to please:

"How far is it to the youth hostel?"

"Three miles."

"No, make it two, Michael, the poor girl looks tired!"

Then there's the desire to impress:

"The farmyard's a dangerous place, Sir!"

"Why so?"

"When coming home last night with my gallon I met a rat. There wasn't hundreds of them, there was thousands of them. They was filing past me like sheep in the road."

"How many rats did you see, Pat?"

"Two, sir."

That same farmhand complained about his employer's dog:

"That bull bitch is a dangerous animal, Sir. Sure her bare teeth were against my naked sinews."

"Did she tear your trousers, Pat?"

"No, Sir."

The builder who eventually picked me up was concerned about Modern Youth. "I'm telling you, an educated Irishman is useless! He's soft; doesn't want to get his hands dirty!" In the good old days, he told me, there was no problem finding hard workers in the building trade "We didn't have strikes in those days." The conversation turned, as it often did, to The Troubles. "'Tis a desperate shame. It's hooligans and criminals that join the IRA." He liked England, having worked for Morris Motors in Birmingham in the fifties and he preferred to work for the 'English gentry' in Ireland. "They don't bother you. They have someone else to look after the work. The Germans, now, they're on the job the whole time watching what you do. They're that exact."

The youth hostel, when I finally arrived, was full of inexact young Germans burning sausages in the kitchen. There were no bunks left so I was allocated a mattress on the floor. Susanne, always a successful hitchhiker, had arrived before me and achieved a bed. We cooked the special goodies I'd bought in Killarney and retreated to the characterless pub down the road for a farewell drink.

Susanne left for Shannon airport early next morning.

Chapter 19

For two chilly hours I waited for a lift back to Valentia. I tried looking pathetic, cheerful and interesting in turns. I bought a newspaper but gave up reading it because I couldn't hold it and put my thumb out. I took out my book, but thought it made me look too resigned to my situation; hitchhikers need to look eager. Salvation finally came with a young German couple who not only picked me up but had no particular plan in mind and decided, without any urging from me, that Valentia would be as good a place as any to visit. I bought them a picnic lunch and we drove round the Ring of Kerry being tourists and stopping to look at trestle tables covered in 'antiques' and bric-a-brac, and photographing donkeys posing with baby goats in their pannier baskets; once again I blessed my fortune that I was not touring Ireland the conventional way. I had, of course, told the couple all about my ride and Peggy and was pleased but a little anxious when they suggested we stop at her field to say hello. I hoped she would show appropriate delight at my return but suspected she'd walk away with one of her sour looks.

To begin with, I couldn't find her. Eight acres is a lot of land, but after climbing over a couple of walls (the gateways were too muddy to use) I saw her grazing with a herd of cows. She liked cows – they were company. When I called to her she put up her head and watched our approach carefully, then gave me that most intimate and moving of horse greetings, a whicker. To my uninitiated German friends this minimal vibrating of the nostrils was unremarkable, but I was deeply touched by such a demonstration of affection.

Most of the following morning was spent walking around the muddy fields trying to cajole Peggy into taking up her responsibilities again. She made it quite clear that she liked me as a person, but as a boss I left much to be desired. One look at my too-ingratiating smile as I walked towards her with one hand (holding the head collar) behind my back, told her that her holiday was over, and she trotted away. Eventually I went to find Joe and a bucket of horse nuts. "We could be at this all day," he said after about half an hour as Peggy galloped by with her tail in the air, shaking her head. She was interested in the contents of the bucket, but backed off whenever I lifted my hand to her neck. Eventually I managed to grab a handful of mane and she was then all sweetness and patience while Joe fetched the head collar. Trotting bareback to the hostel I could feel the tension in Peggy's muscles. She was full of beans after her rest.

While in Killarney I had given some thought about how to cure her of pulling back when tied. Enough was enough, I had to be able to leave her safely now that I was alone. I'd bought a length of foam-rubber tubing and some strong rope.

Threading the rope through the tubing, I doubled it twice round her neck, made sure the knot couldn't slip, and tied the other end to a telegraph pole. Then I retreated to watch. Sure enough, Peggy started straining at the rope but nothing could break and the padding on the rope prevented any injury. She was looking thoughtful and both the telegraph pole and her neck were intact when I came out with the bags.

The wind had changed direction, the sky was clear and the visibility marvellous after the rain. Peggy bounced across the bridge sideways, snorting and staring at the sea, then settled down to co-operate on my chosen route around Bolus Head to the youth hostel at Ballinskelligs. From the top of the hill I could see Puffin Island and the Skellig Rocks. The sky and the sea were flecked with birds. Some 20,000 pairs of gannets nest on Little Skellig and there are also puffins, guillemots, petrels and fulmars. Great Skellig, or Skellig Michael, with its monastery tantalised me further but the sea was too rough for the boat trip. Instead I sat on the hill overlooking St Finan's Bay, eating my lunch to the sound of Peggy's rhythmic grazing, and stared at the view. The Irish playwright, John Synge, wrote about this place:

> …and, over all, the wonderfully tender and searching light that is seen only in Kerry. Looking down the drop of five or six hundred feet, the height is so great that the gannets flying close over the sea look like white butterflies, and the choughs like flies fluttering behind them. One wonders in these places, why anyone is left in Dublin, or London, or Paris, when it would be better, one would think to live in a tent or hut with that magnificent sea and sky, and to breathe this wonderful air, which is like wine in one's teeth.

Peggy slithered down the steep hill to Waterville beach which was crowded with happy families. A promising green road led off the far end, which would have cut off a loop in the road had a stone wall not blocked our progress only 50 yards from my destination. It was made by a macho farmer using gigantic boulders and, after I'd hauled down a couple and dropped one on my fingers, I decided it might be easier, after all, to retrace my steps. The same cowardice persuaded me not to attempt to circle Bolus Head by linking the two dead-end tracks shown on the map with a climb across the intervening saddle. I had to readjust to being on my own again and start being more courageous but that afternoon I had the excuse that I needed to ride directly to Ballinskelligs to get to the youth hostel soon after it opened. It was a tiny hostel – only 12 beds – and I wanted to make sure I got one of them.

A warm welcome awaited us. "That's the first time we've had someone arrive this way!" said the warden approvingly, summoning a friend with a camera. "You can put the pony in with Trigger." Peggy would like this plan: she'd neighed at Trigger, a Shetland pony standing waist deep (if ponies have a waist) in purple loosestrife, as we'd approached the hostel. Trigger's child owner took us up to the field and the Shetland trotted up to greet us: an absurd creature with tiny little legs and ambivalent feelings about having a visitor for the night.

When I went to check on Peggy early next morning I found her standing companionably with Trigger in a shed; he had obviously been a good host and shown her the facilities. I felt very guilty separating the new friends, especially when both neighed frantically until out of earshot. After that, Peggy perceived every cyclist as a horse and every child's scream as a neigh. She really was exceptional in her craving for company.

When not neighing, Peggy concentrated on anticipating my route so she could be assertive about her own preferences. Every crossroads was a tussle. We were heading back to Waterville, and this time I hoped to manage the shortcut along the beach; it would be well worth it, cutting off a long stretch of main road. Peggy galloped enthusiastically to the mouth of the River Inny but refused even to consider fording it. Secretly agreeing with her that it did look wide and deep, I gave in and resigned myself to four boring extra miles.

ᴜ ᴜ ᴜ

Waterville was celebrating August Bank Holiday with banners across the street and a very noisy funfair which unnerved us both. It often surprised me that while I was prancing down a busy street, usually sideways if there was something upsetting Peggy, the majority of shoppers would pretend not to notice. In South America or Africa, people would have put down their baggage and relaxed into a comfortable staring posture, but in Ireland the Anglo-Saxon 'it's rude to stare' ethic is strongly adhered to. Not, I learned afterwards, that my pony and I went unnoticed. During the Mollie days I talked to someone in a pub who'd seen me a few days earlier. "She rode through the town at nine in the morning," he said to his friend. "You can imagine what that did to Lahinch! The place was buzzing for days." Yet from the amount of attention I got at the time I might as well have been invisible. People in cars feel comfortable staring, however. I'd hear the screech of brakes as they nearly collided with another ogling driver. So perhaps I left Waterville buzzing as well as blaring as we headed for Lough Currane and, I hoped, a green road over the mountains which was marked on a very old large-scale map I'd been shown in Ballinskelligs.

Maybe that road had existed once, but I could find no sign of it now. However, the wooded shores of the lake were so beautiful it was no hardship to retrace my steps and resign myself to following the main Ring of Kerry road to Caherdaniel. I'd hoped to avoid this because the prospect of riding along Ireland's most famous scenic drive in Bank Holiday traffic didn't fill me with joy. But I needn't have worried. There were plenty of cars, yes, but with long gaps in between, and it deserves its popularity. The road circles the peninsula, high up the side of the mountain, with sheer cliffs on one side, and a drop down to the sea on the other. Each curve brings a new sea view. After the rain of the last couple of days it was now clear and calm, so the sea looked Mediterranean blue and the mountains a vivid green. At Coomakesta Pass, the highest point of the drive, the road makes a hairpin bend and I found a track over the shoulder where I could be alone to take a tea break and gaze at the view that was one of the loveliest of the whole trip. I could see back towards MacGillycuddy's Reeks and the tip of the Dingle peninsula and down to a little horseshoe-shaped harbour full of yachts, their sails very white in the late afternoon sun.

I had made up my mind to camp wild that night. I'd been pretty self-indulgent recently, with hostels, B&Bs and even (gasp!) a hotel. I was missing Susanne more than I liked to admit. I had always hated asking farmers for a field for Peggy and a place for my tent. Never mind that they were usually willing and hospitable, it seemed an imposition and I was unduly sensitive to the occasional rebuff. The absolute freedom I felt when camping far from any house or road was very precious. I thought I might have found the ideal place when I followed a beautiful green road running just above the harbour. It dead-ended at a deserted house, and although it was really too early to stop, it offered such tempting camping, with a stream nearby and lovely green grass, that I had nearly made up my mind to stay. However, a peep through the window showed that it wasn't deserted after all, just apparently unoccupied. And you never know in Ireland. You see a decaying, half-ruined house and inside there's a decaying, half-ruined person.

So because of my cowardice I ended up camping by a rubbish dump. Once Peggy and I had thought of stopping for the night, we couldn't get the idea out of our heads. To Peggy's despair I passed plenty of fields with good grass, but always with a house nearby, and I just didn't want to make the effort to ask permission. So when I followed the track that turned out to be the route to the rubbish dump for Derrynane National Park and found an unfenced, overgrown field, I thought that it would do.

We had gone 24 miles that day and I didn't feel like looking any further. The national park seemed to be mainly woods so we were running out of choices. And anyway, there was one big advantage to this site; a river ran past the bottom of the field beyond the wire fence, frisking over sun-warmed boulders and providing a perfect bath. I washed my clothes and hung them around on the bushes and gave Peggy a drink from my plastic bucket.

Now, I don't understand about the right sort of grass and the wrong sort of grass. To me, grass is grass, and if it's succulent and green, then it's gourmet grass. Not to Peggy, it wasn't. Maybe it was too overgrown and sour in its old age, or maybe the proximity of trees alters the flavour. I thought she would be thrilled by the ample grazing I was providing but, after I had debagged and unsaddled her, she investigated the field, ate a few mouthfuls, then came and stood by the luggage as if to say 'OK, I'm ready to go now'. While I set up the tent she paced up and down, stared at the distant horizon, then walked briskly down the grassy track leading through the woods to the 'gate' (a few strands of barbed wire) and stood hopeful of release. With hindsight I realise that she was eloquently telling me that dinner was inadequate and we should go somewhere else, but at that stage I still wasn't fluent in Peggy-speak. The only concession I made was not to tether her, though I put the hobble and chain on without attaching it to the stake. She didn't like the arrangement, but, as I explained to her, it was her own fault. I didn't want to spend another two hours trying to catch her the following morning.

I needn't have worried. I was woken at seven by Peggy strolling up and down outside the tent, clanking her chain like the Canterville Ghost. After some meandering we arrived at Derrynane House so I decided to make an unscheduled stop and learn about Daniel O'Connell who, I'm ashamed to say, I'd never even heard of until I came to Ireland. This was the man that Gladstone called 'the greatest popular leader the world has ever known' and the Irish knew as 'the Great Liberator'.

O'Connell was born in 1775 and largely brought up in Derrynane House by a rich uncle who undertook to educate the boy in France, since Catholics were denied secondary education in Ireland. He later studied law and became a successful barrister, often supporting Irish tenants in their appeals against eviction by ruthless landlords. Ireland, in those days of famine and oppression, experienced a constant seesaw of peasant rebellion followed by brutal oppression by their British overlords. O'Connell had seen enough bloodshed in the French Revolution, and declared that 'No political change whatsoever is worth the shedding of a single drop of human blood'. He set about to promote reform through legitimate channels, eventually standing for parliament (representing County Clare) in 1828 and winning by a landslide. As a Catholic he was barred from taking his seat. Such was his popular support, however, that the government, fearing civil war, passed the Catholic Relief Act in 1829. Thus O'Connell became the first Catholic Irishman to sit in parliament at Westminster where he became an advocate of Home Rule. It was while pursuing this objective that he was found guilty, in 1844, of 'creating discontent and disaffection among the Queen's subjects' and imprisoned. The House of Lords reversed the decision but during his incarceration his health deteriorated and he died in 1847 aged 72.

It has been written that 'Daniel O'Connell found the Irish peasants slaves. He left them men'. This is no exaggeration when you consider that in the late 18th century a Catholic was forbidden to purchase land, hold public office, engage in trade or commerce, enter the bar, carry a sword or own a horse worth more than £5.

From the outside, Derrynane House is an austere pair of grey rectangles, one upended and crenulated, but I found the museum inside interesting and enlightening. I was surprised to learn that this peace-loving man had killed a rival in a duel. Plagued by remorse he had thereafter worn a black glove and settled an annuity on his victim's daughter. The duelling pistols and glove are on display.

I was the only visitor, so when the nice girl at reception asked if there was anything else she could tell me I mentioned that I had a pony outside and could I possibly have permission to ride around the grounds, which I'd already discovered comprised 120 hectares of woodland and coast. Great excitement. Everyone went out to admire Peggy who was standing looking pensive, having, I think, given her padded neck rope the full test. I had a hard time undoing the knot. She never again pulled back when tied.

Derrynane House may be unimpressive architecturally but its location is nothing short of superb with its own stretch of yellow-sand beach, rocky inlets, and dunes. Alone on the beach, Peggy needed no urging into a gallop to the far end, then trotted back through the surf with her head up and ears pricked. As I patted her neck I thought proudly of how far she'd come, geographically and psychologically, from that first day in Castle Gregory when I had such doubts about her suitability for the job. I hadn't done so badly myself.

ʊ   ʊ   ʊ

Caherdaniel was my next stop, specifically to visit a horse-owning publican who knew about the old road over the mountains. The green road that I'd tried to find in Waterville originally ran to Kenmare, and Ted Butler told me I should be able to pick it up at intervals along my route. He helpfully marked it on my map, but maps and reality do not always coincide. I found the section out of Caherdaniel and gave Peggy a long lunch break on some green pasture. I knew she'd been deprived the previous night. While she chomped noisily I lay back feeling the sun on my face and listening to the sounds of nature. In my drowsy state the firkins that were carried along the butter road became giant fir cones strapped to the back of Irish peasants; or perhaps they were self-propelled like one of my favourite animals, the pangolin.

One thing was certain, those firkins hadn't trotted this route for many a day. Once Peggy and I reached the top of the hill I couldn't see any sign of the path. I was feeling braver than yesterday, so rather than retracing my steps I led Peggy slowly down through very difficult terrain: bogs (though not deep), mini-cliffs, boulders and dense clumps of gorse, towards the line of houses where I judged the road to be. I was no longer terrified of bogs – just nervous; I knew the very dry weather had rendered them much safer. Peggy never sank above her fetlocks. She was very obliging, only stopping occasionally to register her disapproval by forcing out a horse-apple. In return I was generous with her brown-bread rewards. I had to zigzag down the steep bits, retracing my steps periodically when I came to mini-cliffs. Once I was cursing her for stopping yet again, when I looked round and saw that the saddlebags had started to slip (always a problem when there was not my weight in the saddle). She was in a very awkward spot, but stood immobile until I'd undone all the straps and heaved them back into position, then pushed me with her nose and walked away. I left her to graze each time I checked the next section of the route and took down stone walls. Her longest wait was while I followed a well-worn cow path with increasing confidence as it wound its way through prickly gorse and low trees to a large field, beyond which I could see the road. When Peggy and I reached the field, however, I found we were separated from the road by a channel about five feet deep and full of water. Damn. I walked up and down it until I found a section that was less steep, with some stones providing firm footing at the bottom. Peggy courageously slid down the hill, jumped the ditch and then got into difficulties on the far bank, which was very soft mud. For an awful moment I thought she was going to get trapped in that ditch but she managed to struggle up the other side. I felt very shaken by this, but Peggy was quite calm and we were both delighted to feel tarmac beneath our feet again. I was so proud of Peggy and wished Susanne were here to join the praise. I was becoming quite soppy about her.

Peggy's delight at being on the road was short-lived since, fired with enthusiasm for butter roads, I followed an old man's advice and tried a short cut. To begin with it was a good track serving various houses, and when it dead-ended at the last house I asked directions. Despite the woman's specific instructions I went wrong and even in my new adventurous mood was so daunted by the endless expanse of bog and tussock grass that I turned back. The kind woman caught me up, out of breath and babe in arms, to show me the proper path which, she warned me, was very rough. It was even worse than before – the three Bs, bog, boulders and bloody gorse with some very deep holes in between.

The final descent was unnervingly steep and when I got to the bottom I found that we were separated from the road by a very sturdy barbed-wire fence. Going back was unthinkable, so I examined the fence carefully and saw that the end post could be pulled up to leave a rocky and steep gap which I hoped my brave little pony could jump through (to get back on a road she'd do anything). When I pulled the post out, a stray bit of barbed wire leaped out at my face, knocking my glasses off and impaling a nostril. I could feel blood running down my upper lip and looked without success for a tissue, while pretending to adjust the saddlebags in case one of the many cars decided to stop and help. I eventually found a tissue, Peggy jumped through the gap, and I let her stay on lovely safe tarmac for the rest of the day.

A Connemara Journey

∪   ∪   ∪

My diary entry for 8th August reads 'Awake at 6.30 with baaing sheep and lowing of cars' which reminds me how pleasant it was to camp away from all man-made sounds as well as how my brain was decaying. Knowing that Peggy deserved a proper field that night, and having spotted a desirable-looking white farmhouse across the valley surrounded by green fields, I had struck it lucky with a sweet old man offering me a camping spot by the river. It was a perfect place, sheltered from the wind and out of sight of the farmhouse, and with acres of lovely grass for Peggy. The farmer's son came down to ask me to share a cup of tea with them just as I was enjoying a thorough wash in the river. He tactfully withdrew, but reappeared after a decent interval to ask me to come for breakfast the next morning.

My early rising enabled me to be loaded and ready to go in record time. I left Peggy to finish her breakfast and tapped tentatively on the farmhouse door. Only Dad was up; John was still sleeping, having been to a dance the night before; a major undertaking with no car. The family's last vehicle was parked in our field and occupied by some happy hens. Our conversation was halting because of my difficulty in understanding the broad Kerry accent. We talked of horses. "When I see the horse I'm remembering my father. He was the last person in this family to use a horse. Rode everywhere – Sneem, Kenmare…"

"There and back?" (Kenmare is 20 miles away.)

"There and back."

Peggy was very jaunty that morning; ears pricked so sharply I feared she'd strain them as we trotted through Sneem. This slightly self-conscious village had recently won an award for its tidiness, and was indeed very much prettier than I was accustomed to in Ireland. There was a little church with a salmon weather vane (for this is a salmon fishing area) then a bridge over the River Sneem, and a row of brightly painted houses facing the village green. And when I say brightly painted, I mean all the colours of the rainbow: purple, maroon, orange, yellow, white, pink, turquoise, green.

In Ireland, house painting seems to be the only expression of individuality left to the owners of uniformly rectangular bungalows. Even these were mostly yellow, but in terraced houses you see orange with turquoise trim, yellow and red, and the very popular chartreuse which manages not to blend with Ireland's other 39 shades of green. Sneem, however, had given some thought to colour co-ordination and was indeed a most attractive village.

I managed to pick up another stretch of butter road here. It began, as usual, as a lane serving occasional houses, the grass verges overgrown with flowers including the orange montbretia lily which has run wild in south Kerry and west Cork. Inevitably, the road ended at the last house, but while I was debating with myself whether to turn back, a woman hobbled out to complain about Ireland. She had awful problems with arthritis, she told me. "The doctors here are rubbish, all they think about is getting their cheque from the county council… we've no proper welfare system here. In England, now, they look after their people…" And so it went on. Finally she drew herself up proudly saying, "I'm of English heritage myself." I managed to stop the flow long enough to ask if the road continued. "Yes, you'll have to open that gate. I'd do it for you but my feet, you see: when I last saw the doctor he said nothing could be done. I'll just have to live with it…"

Beyond the gate was a rocky but clearly defined track. Peggy was depressed at leaving the road but I was happy to lead her and pick blackberries which were now starting to ripen. After about half a mile we came to a gate beyond which the track joined a broad forestry road, though, irritatingly, the gateway was too narrow for Peggy plus saddlebags so I had to unload her. But at least it was unlocked and after a few miles of peaceful pine forests we emerged onto the main road and I soon saw the cheering little green 'Post' sign indicating a post office-cum-shop, along with a public phone. I needed some provisions. Dinner last night had been a creative combination of dried potato, milk powder and minestrone soup. While I was buying bread, cheese and yoghurt I spied a tourist outside taking photos of Peggy standing with her luggage underneath the 'Post' sign. I imagined the commentary back in America. "See here, isn't this quaint? They still use mail horses in the west of Ireland." The friendly shop attendant was also much taken by my means of transport. When another customer arrived he said: "I see you didn't bring your horse, Mary. 'Tis all the fashion, you know!"

A hysterical bull was bellowing hoarsely in the field outside. Since this was the beginning of the next stretch of butter road I decided to believe the fellow when he said it was blocked off. I could just as easily follow the main road for a bit. We stopped and ate lunch in a field a few miles further on. While I was musing to myself that the yarrow in these parts was the same colour as my blackberry yoghurt, a farmer arrived carrying some fearsome implement and said pleasantly that it was his bull yelling outside the post office. "I'm thinking he might make his way down here."

"Am I on your land?" I asked, anxiously.

"Yes, but you be finishing your sandwich."

We chatted about horses, bulls and the drought and he disappeared up the track, only to reappear silently just as I was having my afternoon pee.

U   U   U

We were fast approaching Kenmare, and since I wanted to camp well before that biggish town I took my courage in both hands and turned up a rather impressive drive. A woman answered my knock. "I'm sorry to bother you, but I'm touring Ireland on horseback…" She jerked her head back and said:

"Jim, there's a tourist here with a horse." Jim peered suspiciously over her shoulder.

"Are you alone?"

"Yes."

"Quite alone?"

"Yes."

"Do you promise there's no-one else with you?"

Farmers with suitable camping fields have a hard time round the Ring of Kerry. Too many hikers, bikers and campers try to take advantage of them. Once I'd persuaded the farmer that I really wasn't concealing 13 giggling teenagers in the bushes, he was all helpfulness and showed me a good flat field with adequate fences, though he asked me to tether Peggy while I went to town. I hitched into Kenmare with ease and had a hearty and healthy meal at a wholefood restaurant. It tasted damned good – it was the first proper meal I'd had for three days. I peered longingly in the restaurant window as I rode through Kenmare the next day. Then I looked *at* the restaurant window, saw my sack-of-potatoes reflection and straightened up for one of my public appearances. Not that anyone took much notice, though the high street was busy with shoppers.

I decided to modify my original plan to follow the coastline to the end of every peninsula. Beara, I decided, would have to be explored another time. I had plotted out a route over the mountains to Bantry Bay along irresistible unsurfaced roads. I just hoped they were usable, not more blocked-off ancient green roads or tracks which petered out into bogs.

Peggy seemed depressed. When we passed a pony in a field she hardly raised a neigh. In earlier days her yells of greeting said '*Hello!* How wonderful to see you!' Now her little whinny just said 'Hi'. And she no longer bothered to greet donkeys at all. Perhaps their inferior status had been brought home to her by an unfortunate fellow who lurched towards us dragging an enormous ball and chain. Irish donkey restraints were ever ingenious. I'd seen them hobbled front legs together, back leg to front leg, and anchored to a mobile log. If Peggy was gloomy, I was uneasy. I had a feeling of foreboding about my chosen route; it was too reminiscent of Mollie's last day. Even the weather was similar, with grey clouds gathering overhead. Peggy sensed my anxiety and crawled along with the greatest reluctance, jumping at every boulder and peering wide-eyed into every gateway. I passed a stony-faced woman and child who didn't return my greeting. When I knocked on a door to ask if the road really did run over the pass, it was a ghost house, the sound echoing through the empty rooms. Grass grew up between the flagstones by the neglected garden. I rode on, thinking of the early 19th-century traveller in Kerry who was told: "Now hear me, will you sir, for it's a lonesome way you're taking, and them mountains is the place for all manner of evil doings from the living and the dead…"

We reached the last house before the road narrowed and climbed, I hoped, towards the pass. I could see someone busy in the garden, so tied Peggy to the gate and went in to make my enquiries. Several snarling dogs rushed at me as I made my way down the path to the dwarfish figure. Heavens, a double amputee… better not stare. The legless man looked up at me as he weeded his potato bed. "Sure, but you can go over the mountains. 'Tis a road all the way." He looked a bit scornful at my doubts and rose to his feet. Perhaps I should have stared after all.

Chapter 20

After the last house, the road narrowed to the width of a car, and a ribbon of grass started to appear along the middle. If I had been reassured by the gardener that the road did, indeed, run over the pass to the next valley, Peggy was still filled with foreboding. She crept along looking for things to shy at, and sulking about the steep incline. Since I had considerately done the climb on my own feet I needed a rest at the top more than she. I took out her bit and let her have a leisurely lunch while I ate my bun and apple, and took my last look at Kerry. I could see most of the county: behind me stretched the Kenmare River and its bay, and MacGillycuddy's Reeks, while ahead was the deep tree-lined river valley backed by the hills that divide Kerry from Cork.

We descended without incident into the valley. The youth hostel by the river was tempting but it was on the main road, and anyway, it was too early to stop for the night. I was still on the large-scale map and had spotted another green road over the next range of mountains to Bantry Bay. I reckoned I deserved a B&B after five nights of camping. Peggy was not impressed at this decision. She slowed to a crawl and sought out promising-looking fields that, in her opinion, would do nicely for her accommodation.

I was in no hurry to stop; it was a most heavenly valley. The narrow road that followed the east bank of the River Sheen was bordered with flowering buddleia bushes where peacocks and red admirals jostled for space, and the clumps of brambles were so covered in ripe fruit I could snatch the blackberries as I passed. It felt like early autumn. The rowan trees were red with berries and I could sniff that late summer-holiday smell of bracken, gorse and heather. The blackthorn bushes, white with flowers when I started my trek with Mollie, were now heavy with green sloes, some already turning dusky blue, and green berries clustered round the holly stems. Holly is one of the remnants of the native forests that once covered the hillsides of southwest Ireland. The holly and oak trees were mostly felled in the 17th and 18th centuries for iron smelting but a few pockets remain, especially in west Cork. This roadside greenery was striped with white from silver birch trees and masses of ripening hazel nuts dangled in easy reach above my head. I'd never seen so many; at home the squirrels would have got them. "That's it," I said aloud. "There are no squirrels here!"

I was wrong. Later research revealed that, as in England, the native red squirrel was being replaced by greys which now outnumber them six to one. It is also thought that the red squirrel became extinct there in the 17th century but was reintroduced in the early 19th. They flourished unopposed until 1911 when Lord Buckingham had the unfortunate idea of giving a dozen grey squirrels as a wedding present to the daughter of the Earl of Granard at Castleforbes, County Longford.

> A wicker basket containing eight or twelve squirrels… was opened on the lawn after the wedding breakfast, whereupon the bushy-tailed creatures quickly leapt out and scampered off into the woods where they went forth and multiplied.

The ascent to the next pass was a much longer, tougher climb than the last one, and the landscape increasingly remote. And spectacular. Craggy mountains surrounded us on all sides, scooped and carved into gullies and cliffs, their green broken by patches of bracken, gorse and bog grass, while Kerry and the river valley faded into the haze behind us. Tarmac had mostly given way to gravel and grass and the feeling of being miles away from anywhere was exhilarating. When I paused to look at the map there was complete silence broken only by the distant bleating of sheep. The top of the pass was marked on the map as 'Priest's Leap', 1,895 feet, and I wondered about the origin of the name. It has a deliciously wicked ring to it – was the priest involved in an illicit liaison and leapt to his death rather than face his superiors? Or did a priest secretly go up to that place – by motorbike perhaps – and leap for the sheer fun of it?

Peggy wasn't about to do any leaping. She snailed up the steep hill with her ears back, finding every excuse she could think of to stop. I was leading her – or rather hauling her along – and got cross so took out the whip (this was normally tucked away out of sight, to be used only in emergencies) so she went to the other extreme and jogged, treading on my feet and pushing me in the back with her nose. Then she stepped on the reins and broke one of the straps that held the bit to the head collar. This made me crosser still. I tied the bit and reins to the saddlebags and went on leading her, both of us grumbling at each other, while I wondered how long it would take to reach the Glengarriff road. I could now see the inlet of sea at Bantry Bay behind another low range of hills and a patchwork of green fields. Our road, however, contoured along the side of the mountain, seemingly into infinity.

We were plodding along when I saw, to my great surprise, a car parked at the side of the road. At the same time I noticed to my dismay that I'd lost the bit and reins. Curses, I would have to tether Peggy and walk back and find them. Better make contact with the car driver first or he might think it all very strange. He'd taken his children up the pass for a picnic, and once I explained the problem he offered to drive me back to search for the missing tack while his kids looked after Peggy. A very fortuitous meeting since we found the reins on the far side of the pass – it would have taken an hour to walk back up there and down again. As we drove, Tom went straight to the point. "You single? Would you be thinking of marrying an Irish farmer, now?" He was divorced, so he said.

Reunited with our dependants, I thanked him and we went our separate ways. With that delay, and the fact that we'd been on the road for ten hours, I decided to listen to Peggy's ever more obvious hints and camp for the night. For a while we had been following a tumbling river, fed by little waterfalls, which had carved its passage deep into the valley on our right. No access there, but from time to time a small stream flowed across the road, and when I saw a patch of good grass by one of the streams and a flattish area for my tent, I stopped. The views were glorious and I could indulge myself with a B&B tomorrow. I sat outside until the sun went down, repairing the bridle and watching the red sun turn Peggy's Guinness-coloured sides to chestnut. Then as it slipped lower she became a dark silhouette outlined against the blue-green hills and glinting bay. When there was 'not enough daylight to cover the dark' I got into my sleeping bag for some cramped but cosy letter-writing by candlelight. Emerging from the tent for a final pee I found a newly risen yellow moon and the lights of Bantry and Glengarriff twinkling below. Beautiful!

I described the morning in a letter to my friend, Susie:

As I suspected, it wasn't a restful night, what with Peggy clanking her chain and blowing raspberries at me through the door and the sloping ground causing me to slide to the back of the tent. Then I was woken sharply at seven by what sounded like a full-blown cavalry charge complete with whooping Indians. Peering out, I found myself surrounded by a large herd of sheep which were being driven up the mountain by two very efficient sheepdogs urged on by a vocal shepherd. "I hope I didn't disturb you," he said politely when he spotted me and the tent.

Peggy was still tethered and had registered her disapproval at the arrangement by depositing the biggest pile of droppings she could manage as near to the tent and my luggage as possible. I released her to catch up on the grass-that's-greener-beyond-the-tether, lit my little stove to boil water for my tea, sliced some stale brown bread which collapsed into crumbs, decided the butter really was rancid so smeared on some honey and had breakfast listening to *Today* on my radio. Such is my morning routine when camping. Then pack up the tent, picking earwigs out of the interior and slugs off the bottom, and begin the time-consuming task of fitting everything into the saddlebags. Then it's time to get Peggy but I'm always bent double by this point. Camping gives me backache and packing luggage aggravates it till I'm like a stage arthritic. I manage to straighten up by the time I'm ready to load her, which is a good thing since I need all my height, and strength to heave the saddlebags into position. This is where Peggy's experience in harness really pays off – she stands stock-still as she's been taught to do while the harness is put on. The whole process from getting up to getting on takes at least 1½ hours. I suppose it's progress from the 2½ hours when I first started this trip.

We were nearer civilisation than I'd realised, and before long we joined a proper road that closely followed the very lovely River Coomhola whose dark mysterious waters slid past huge moss-covered boulders overhung by trees. At the main road I had to make a decision – should I turn right to Glengarriff or left to Bantry? Either would have a selection of B&Bs. I went left and had only gone a few yards when a car stopped and the driver came toward me saying, "We were just talking about you!" It was a couple from Marlow (three miles from my home) giving a lift to the German mother and son with whom Susanne and I had dined in Valentia. Having rejoined their hired yacht, they were hitching back to the island to pick up their car. Such a happy coincidence couldn't be ignored so it didn't take long for Bernhard and his mother to convince me to make this a rest day and join them and the rest of the family for dinner on the yacht that evening. So in a few miles, to Peggy's surprise and delight, we turned into a 'Farmhouse Accommodation' drive where our night-time requirements would be taken care of.

ひ   ひ   ひ

I had letters to post and mail to pick up in Glengarriff and quickly got a lift with a local man who knew the legend of the Priest's Leap. It was in 1612, he told me, when Father James Archer, fleeing from English soldiers, leapt with his horse from the top of the pass and landed just outside Bantry – a distance, as the horse flies, of at least ten miles. He told me there was a monument at the place where he landed showing the imprint of his horse's shoe. I never found this, but retracing the route recently I found a quatercentenary monument (a carved stone) marking the spot on the top of the pass, along with a metal cross.

This was my first mail pickup since arriving in Dingle three weeks ago, and I'd been anticipating it with increasing enthusiasm. In those days, with no mobile phones and very few call boxes, a traveller in Ireland was completely isolated. This was part of the pleasure but also added a touch of anxiety. This wasn't the place or time to receive bad news.

"How did you say you spelt your name?" The girl in the Glengarriff post office shuffled through the letters sitting in the B pigeonhole of the poste restante shelves and handed me a satisfyingly large number of envelopes. I retreated to a nearby café to read them and had one of my prosopagnosia moments. You don't know what this means? Nor did I at that time, I just knew that I had a problem recognising people. A shirtless man was sitting at a table as I came in and shouted, "Hey, hello, come over here!" So I said, "Hello!" in equal delight thinking him to be the farmer who had helped to retrieve Peggy's reins the previous day. So I bought him a cup of tea and was ever so chatty until the truth slowly dawned that he was not my farmer at all but one of the ferrymen touting for custom to take trippers to the nearby Garinish Island.

Glengarriff didn't impress me. There were coach-loads of tourists, every other house seemed to be a B&B or hotel, and when I finally found somewhere to get a bite to eat (I'd left the café in a hurry) I was served lumpy packet soup and plastic cheese between two slices of Wonderloaf by a surly girl who charged me more than I'd paid for a full meal in other places. This is what I wrote back in 1984, but having returned recently I must admit to having done Glengarriff an injustice. The row of multicoloured houses (and, yes, hotels and B&Bs) which make up its main street are varied in architecture, and sit in a deep glen backed by craggy mountains. With its location around an inlet at the head of Bantry Bay, it deserves its large number of visitors.

The name Bantry Bay had a familiar ring about it. I'm not sure if I actually remember the attempted French invasions from school history or whether I was confusing it with Botany Bay, but reading up about it provided me with further understanding of the Irish struggle for independence. This time it was the strangely named Wolfe Tone who was the local hero. Unlike the Catholic Daniel O'Connell, born 12 years later, Tone was born into a Protestant family in 1763. He also studied law, practising as a barrister in London where he found Whig allies to the cause of Home Rule in Ireland. With the French Revolution in full spate, rebellion was very much in the news. Even among liberal Whigs, however, there was little support for a break with Westminster, whilst Tone wanted an Irish parliament as well as full religious emancipation. To this end he founded the Society of the United Irishmen in 1791 and, abandoning hope of parliamentary reform, sought the help of France to achieve his aims through force of arms. Although not yet officially at war with Britain, Napoleon Bonaparte's France was happy to join forces against its traditional foe.

The French fleet that arrived in Bantry Bay in 1796 was impressive: 43 ships and over 14,000 men. With five per cent of the Irish population now members of the United Irishmen, it was reasonable to suppose that they would rise up against the British in support of the invaders. As it was, the December weather was against the French and after waiting several days for the gales to abate so they could make a landing, they returned to France – much to Wolfe Tone's disgust: 'We were close enough to toss a biscuit ashore.' Had it been a calm day, Irish history might have been very different.

After further attempts to generate an uprising with the help of the French, Wolfe Tone was captured and sentenced to death in 1798; he committed suicide before the hangman could carry out his duty. He is remembered for his attempt to unite the people of three religions, Protestants, Catholics and Presbyterians ('Dissenters') into one cohesive group of Irishmen, a necessary first step to achieving Home Rule:

> To subvert the tyranny of our execrable government, to break the connection
> with England, the never failing source of all our political evils, and to assert
> the independence of my country – these were my objects. To unite the whole
> people of Ireland, to abolish the memory of all past dissentions, and to

substitute the common name of Irishman, in the place of the denominations of Protestant, Catholic, and Dissenter – these were my means.

Bantry House owes its opulence to the failed French invasion. Its owner, Richard White, trained a militia to oppose the landing, and provided storage in Bantry House for munitions. He was awarded his baronetcy 'in recognition of his spirited conduct and important services' at that time and later became the first Earl of Bantry. The White family had every reason to be grateful for the turmoil in France – his son, the second earl, filled Bantry House with some very choice pieces of French furniture which were going for a song at the time. It is the stateliest of Irish stately homes, jaw-droppingly beautiful inside and with a formal garden and a hundred acres of woodland. Without Peggy to worry about, I could indulge in a proper visit and stroll around the grounds while filling up the time before I was due to meet the Schünemanns. Bernhard had suggested that I intercept his father and young friend (who weren't expecting me) as they docked the yacht at 6 o'clock, to be joined later by Bernhard and Margret.

A keen wind nagged me as I paced up and down the pier and watched fishermen unloading boxes of mussels. I saw no fish being landed, but many years ago a traveller (or maybe a Bantryman) had written that 'you could fall off the pier and they [the fish] would support your back'.

The Germans were embarrassed to find a lone woman watching their every move as they brought the boat in and tied up. They said afterwards that they assumed I was a highly critical expert. Bernhard and his mother arrived later than expected; they had not had an easy time getting lifts. "I have to teach Mother to be a better hitchhiker," said Bernhard. "She doesn't understand the proper etiquette. Like you can't turn down the radio or open windows or say 'in Germany it is other' when people talk about forestry practices." Margret took the teasing in great good humour and I was delighted to be sharing a meal with friends again, even such new ones.

◡   ◡   ◡

It was a grey morning when I left my rather pricey B&B. I'd been thoroughly spoiled by the non-commercial hospitality of most Irish farmers, so to be charged two Irish pounds for Peggy's accommodation shook me. Peggy would have told me it wasn't worth the price. She was standing waiting for me at the gate and neighed her greeting. This was not affection: she'd kicked over her bucket of water and raised a thirst, and had evidently been trying to explain her plight to a neighbouring farmer. "Whose pony is that?" he asked eyeing me suspiciously. "Who gave you permission to put it in this field?" Farmers were always on the lookout for tinkers who turn their horses into any field that happens to be handy.

My plans after Bantry were completely fluid. I had no idea where to go next so, while waiting for the Germans, had called in on the tourist office for their advice. The girl suggested a circuit round Sheep's Head, a long finger pointing into the sea which had only beauty to commend it so was seldom visited by tourists. That suited me fine. Soon I had to head inland to make my way to County Waterford where a friend was expecting me, and such a narrow peninsula would help satiate me with the ocean. But it was a grey sea I rode beside; a grey sea under a grey sky skulking low over the hills. A few gloomy cormorants were drying their wings on rocks, while I had my picnic overlooking the bay. Then in the afternoon the sun came out and transformed the colours to those of a child's painting: blue sky, green hills, yellow gorse, turquoise sea. Later, as we progressed along the narrow road known as the Goat's Path, the sea turned silver and the mountains of Kerry stood in dove-grey rows across the bay under a wallpaper-cream sky.

Peggy indicated that she was thirsty and since I could find no running water I knocked at a door. Three little red-haired children ran out in great excitement and were lifted into the saddle by Dad while Peggy drank long and deep from a blue washing-up bowl.

Fingers of cloud were tickling the surface of the ocean. With a sea mist on its way I hesitated briefly before deciding to continue to the end of the peninsula. It was easy to be seduced by the scenery – the changing sea and sky, lumpy hills and stunted vegetation: wind-sculpted trees, heather and bracken. Sheltered hollows protected tall trees and houses and by 7 o'clock I could no longer ignore Peggy's hints that it was time to stop for the night. I rode up the drive of a beautiful farm surrounded by green fields and said my piece to a startled-looking mother and son. No, they hadn't got any available field. Peggy was even more disgusted at this obvious lie than I was, and almost refused to leave. Actually I could well understand their desire to reserve their best pasture in time of drought. I thought perhaps I could camp wild but could find no running water. Then a loose horse trotted up and my heart sank; I'd never get rid of it. I implored Peggy not to neigh and amazingly she held her peace, and when I brandished my whip the visitor lost interest and wandered away.

The wild part of the peninsula ended as I crossed the neck of the mountains and started down towards the more populated, sheltered southern road. An old man standing by his gate peered at me. "Is that a mule?" He still kept a workhorse, he told me, but was unsympathetic to my plight. "No, I've no land." Could he suggest somewhere? "No. It's still early, you can go on someways." I went on 100 yards or so and finally met with success. A young farmer milking his cows had no objection to my camping in one of his fields and showed me where to put the tent. As

I was leading Peggy through the gate I heard a shout. The old man was standing silhouetted against the sky waving his arms negatively. To my acute embarrassment I realised they were father and son. Whatever Dad's objections had been, the young man brushed them aside and the old man came into the field all friendly for a chat and brought me some milk.

One of my fibre-glass tent poles had broken. The tent could still be pitched but its rear end didn't look right. Mine didn't feel right either after 21 miles. I sat down carefully outside the tent, sipping my milky coffee and watching a cheese-coloured moon rise over the evening clouds. Peggy was lying down. Rest for the weary travellers.

We did another 20 miles the next day, heading back east along the southern road, but my memory is of a sun-drenched stroll by the sea with languid curlews wandering along the shore and a heron flapping lazily overhead. When the road veered inland, baby rabbits dithered by the roadside, and a prurient pair of donkeys, distracted from their business by the sight of Peggy, followed along their side of the fence *in flagrante*. The bushes were heavy with blackberries. Frustrated by my hit-or-miss passing grabs, I dismounted and filled a plastic bag which I tied in front of the saddle. Then, spurred out of my lethargy by the thought of a blackberry lunch, I urged Peggy into a trot. Result: blackberry sludge. I dumped it, and Peggy, who like all animals hated to see food wasted, ate the sludge so her granny lips were covered in purple froth. Thereafter I had to compete with her in blackberry picking. She became quite skilful, plucking them delicately off the stem one by one.

It was Sunday. I passed a couple of villages with clusters of people gossiping outside the church, but otherwise the road was deserted. At Friendly Cove I took my last look at the sea which I had now followed, on and off, for over 700 miles, and headed east.

Above: Looking south from the Dingle Peninsula high point, with Susanne's
stripy bag adding to the luggage
Below: Peggy was often in demand for pony rides

Above: Ancient Ireland: the Gallarus Oratory, an early Christian chapel (Kerry) and Kinneigh Round Tower (Cork) are both about a thousand years old

Below: A deserted cottage on Great Blasket Island, evacuated in 1953

The Gap of Dunloe

Above: Kate Kearney's Cottage
Below: Approaching the Head of Gap

Descending the Black Valley

Top: At first Peggy was in an exceptionally obliging mood
Above: Enough!
Below: Peggy and Susanne look back at the route of our descent

Chapter 21

At Durrus I headed inland towards Dunmanway and a tilled landscape of patchwork fields. Almost immediately the atmosphere changed. The air felt softer without the sea breeze, and smelt of grass and cows instead of seaweed and bracken. I followed a river known as Four Mile Water, and while giving Peggy a long tea break on the juicy grass verge, I spied some promising white blobs in a cow pasture. Mushrooms! I collected far too many and, tying the bag carefully to the saddle, I continued to a farm, set in such improbably green fields they couldn't possibly say no to my camping request. The Crawleys wouldn't have said no if they lived in a desert. The lounge, where I sat with the family and their friends drinking tea and watching the Olympics on TV, radiated warmth, humour and friendship. A beautiful boy of about 18 stared at me with large brown eyes. "He's brain damaged, poor lad," explained the farmer. "Can't speak." Peggy had acres and acres of mushrooms to trample. I could hardly bear it; I already had far too many. Supper was mushroom soup followed by fried mushrooms on bread, with mushroom salad on the side.

I heard no Peggy sounds during the night and got up to look for her in some anxiety the next morning. She had five interconnected fields to choose from so of course I found her in the farthest one, lying down in the dewy mushroomy grass. During my search I'd made the unwelcome discovery that I was sharing the acreage with a large virile-looking bull as well as cows. I hoped the bull wouldn't get it into his head to show off to the ladies. They all crowded round to watch me pack up the tent, the steam rising from their lowered heads. I tried to avoid making any sudden movements; my Waterford friend had recently been tossed by a bull, cracking a vertebra, so I was doubly cautious. And frightened.

During this slow-motion performance Peggy had got bored and strolled over to the gate in the hope of finding someone more competent than me. Then, as I was pulling up the zip on the saddlebag, she sauntered back with a resigned expression and waited to be saddled. The bull and cows followed me to the gate with what I hoped was friendly curiosity and allowed me to leave with my vertebrae intact.

My choice of route was excellent; a narrow track took me over some very wild, rock-covered hills, bright with flowering heather, and down into a valley where the tower house of Castle Donovan dominated the scene. Built in 1560 by Donal O'Donovan, it was damaged by Oliver Cromwell's troops and is now gently crumbling into the landscape. "You've got a grand rigout there," called out an old man on a bicycle as I trotted past. I was heading for an independent hostel that had been recommended by one of my dorm-mates in Valentia.

ʊ   ʊ   ʊ

Dunmanway is not on any tourist route so the newly opened Shiplake hostel was half empty. It was a very special place, my favourite of all the hostels I stayed at, run by Mel and Vary Knivett, an English couple practising The Good Life. West Cork seemed particularly favoured for organic smallholdings, and I met several English and German families working the land. The Knivetts grew their own organic vegetables and made and sold dairy products with the help of the sweet-faced Jersey cow called Hazel. I liked Shiplake and its produce (especially the yoghurt and ice cream) so much that I decided it was time Peggy had a rest day and I went into Cork to collect my next batch of mail and buy a battery for my inoperable camera. There was only one other family staying in the hostel so I had the dormitory to myself, and after the Germans had finished cooking vegetarian spaghetti in the kitchen I could pick the caterpillars out of my organically grown cabbage and prepare my own cholesterol-rich meal. Mel himself had done all the renovating of what was once a derelict cottage, and had done a beautiful job. The bunks were comfortable, the loo – a long-drop above a grassy bank – serviceable, and the shower, open to the sky with steam-loving plants growing from cracks in the wall, delightful. Peggy was equally happy in her field with Hazel for company.

I should add at this point that since then Shiplake has been upgraded to become one of the most highly-praised independent hostels in Ireland, so you no longer have to traipse out into the night for a pee.

One of the Knivetts' English farmer friends was going to Cork the following day to get some cheese-starter, so I was able to cadge a lift. Having arranged to meet Paul at the creamery, I arrived in good time and watched the milk churns brought in by every possible means of transport – lorry, tractor, saloon car, donkey cart, pony cart. The milk was weighed and a chit signed. Paul turned up with his churns in the back of the car and soon we were driving along the little lanes towards Cork and talking about the joys and sorrows of self-sufficiency in Ireland. Lovely in the summer but hell in the winter (at least for a man living alone). I heard how one year Paul and his friends had scythed, threshed and winnowed the wheat by hand. "It was quite enjoyable but damned hard work and there was the constant anxiety of the weather breaking. Now I hire a combine harvester: a wonderful machine!"

We arranged a meeting time and place and I set out to see a bit of Cork and do my shopping. First, I picked up my mail; this was a mistake since the news I read dulled any desire for sightseeing. Captain Flint, the African grey parrot who'd lived with my family for 30 years, was dead. He'd been ill when I left England so I thought I was well prepared for his death but I wasn't. I walked through Cork with tears running incontinently down my face. I still miss him. It's worth a little diversion to talk about Flint; there are not many pets that are with you for three decades. He was born in the Gold Coast (now Ghana), purchased as a chick by a colleague of my father who was working in West Africa at the time. I was 12 when my mother drove us, grumbling children, to Waterloo to pick up 'a crate' that had been shipped from Africa. We stayed in the car reading until we heard shouts and laughter on the platform. Coming towards us was a porter swinging a large home-made cage. Inside was Captain Flint with his head thrust through the bars. He and the porter were competing as to who could whistle the loudest.

Flint was only shut in his cage at night. He had a perch outside the upper window and one on top of his cage. He used the increasingly tattered curtain as a ladder from one to the other, taking time out to swing wildly from the pelmet. However cold it was, the window had to be open in the morning so he could greet the milkman. Flint recognised the milk float long before we could see it, and hastened up the curtain to welcome the milkman with his whistles. His greeting was always returned. The dustmen produced the opposite effect. When he saw them coming he hurried down to the windowsill and wrapped himself in the curtain where he stayed motionless, with just his red tail showing, until the danger was over. He nearly had a nervous breakdown when milkman and dustmen arrived together.

Flint was a poor linguist. Despite our efforts he only learned one phrase – and that was one we accidentally taught him because he was always getting up to mischief. "What *are* you doing?" he would ask at intervals. He did do a perfect Greenwich Time Signal, however, and even now, when I hear the pips, I think of him.

ᑌ   ᑌ   ᑌ

There's a saddler in Cork so I bought Peggy a tasteful new lead rope and some Extra-tail fly-spray. Now we were inland, away from the sea breeze, I couldn't bear to see her so tortured by insects; she would just have to get accustomed to aerosol sprays, just as she'd finally accepted being tied. Her unsuccessful struggle against the rope that secured her by Derrynane House had done the trick. Poor Peggy, it was ironic that her fight against servitude to the English was extinguished outside the house of Daniel O'Connell.

There was a new arrival at the hostel. A very blonde, very young, very shy, very pink German with a bicycle. "I thought in Ireland there is many rain. But there is many sun!" After a teatime snack of full-cream milk, brown bread spread with cream and topped with bramble jelly, and ice cream, I went to saddle Peggy and give promised pony rides to the family before having a luggage-free canter. Then I found a very strong tree, tied Peggy round the neck with the padded rope, and gradually taught her, with the help of the Knivetts' best organic bread, that the aerosol spray was not going to kill her. She hated it to the end, but did learn not to struggle when I produced it.

After Shiplake I planned to follow as straight a line as possible to Blarney. I couldn't quite bring myself to avoid this famous attraction although I had no intention of kissing the Blarney Stone. After that I would take as scenic a route as possible across the southern part of Ireland to Lismore, County Waterford, to stay with my travel-writer friend Dervla Murphy. My odyssey thus became a journey. Now, when plotting the next part of the route, instead of my eye settling on the brown and blue bits of the map that indicated mountains and river valleys, and picking out the promising dotted lines of footpaths and tracks, I became, as they say, goal orientated.

Fortunately, serendipity is never far away in Ireland. Soon after settling down to lunch by a stream which offered a free supply of watercress to go with my cheese sandwich, I saw movement out of the corner of my eye. It was an otter. It came strolling along the mud and stones at the edge of the river, sniffing the air in a short-sighted sort of way, its dark coat in wet spikes and its blonde whiskers quivering. I tried to creep closer but it heard my approach and splashed hurriedly away.

A nearer goal than Blarney was the Kinneigh round tower which, I had read, was unique in that it is the only one built on a hexagonal base. During my travels with Mollie I had spotted the remains of round towers in Galway and Clare standing enigmatically on the skyline, but had never investigated them, although round towers are a speciality of Ireland. They were always attached to monasteries and most were built in the days of the Viking invasions, so dated from before the first millennium. No one can agree on their purpose. Certainly they were religious buildings, built by highly skilled monks, so may have simply been created for the glory of God, a finger pointing to heaven, and as bell towers (the Irish name *cloigtheach* means bell house). The four openings, or windows, at the top were usually aligned with the cardinal points of the compass, which would have had religious significance. Perhaps they were also safe-deposit places for monastic treasures. Some think they were used as places of refuge, which is why the door is generally not at ground level, so accessible only by rope ladder which could be hastily drawn up. Round towers would seem particularly uncomfortable hiding places, though. I imagined a brown spiral of monks sitting on the central staircase with the rope ladder coiled at their feet, waiting for the 'all clear'. Actually, looking at Kinneigh pointing insolently at the sky next to its church I was reminded of a remote tribe of Indians I once visited in Bolivia. They too had a church and a separate bell tower, built by the missionaries, but they worshipped the tower as a phallic symbol and sacrificed animals in front of it.

∪   ∪   ∪

"I wonder if you can let me have a field for my tent and my pony for the night?"

"That I can. And you come in now for a cup of tea." I was served tea in the sitting room where the TV, full of sound and fury, but pictureless, was the only secular decoration. There were seven religious paintings, along with china decorated with religious motifs and two statuettes of Jesus and Mary lit by a candle. "Sorry I haven't any white bread," said Mum as she brought me freshly baked 'brack' (brown bread), ham and tomatoes.

I was woken at 6 by a scraping noise. Peggy was scratching her back on a low-hanging branch with a look of ecstasy on her face. She ignored my greeting so, rebuffed, I went back to sleep. I was just boiling my water for breakfast when I was summoned to the house for 'a cup of tea'. I was no longer surprised, but no less delighted, when this turned out to be a full breakfast. I still marvel at the generosity of the Irish. Before saddling up I gave Peggy another back scratch, her favourite on the side of her withers. It made her mouth quiver like a dowager who's been told an off-colour joke, which always made me smile.

The rocky sheep pasture of coastal Cork had given way to wheat fields enclosed by hedges and the record harvest had brought a new bonus: spilt grain on the road. The radio warned drivers to take care, 'it's as dangerous as black ice', but next day I collected bagfuls for Peggy who kept her eyes peeled for the telltale golden splashes. I let her pause and hoover up the grain. "That's an economical way of travelling! Just needs an occasional change of water I see!" said a cyclist cheerily as he splashed through the smelly evidence while I struggled up from the river with a bucket. A car passed full of waving black-and-white figures, and a mile or so later one of the nuns ran out of a house and invited me in for tea. Peggy was thrilled: they were horse breeders and had loose boxes full of elegant animals. Not for riding, of course – no-one seemed to ride for pleasure in Ireland – but for showing in hand. There were other stables along our route. By the time we wearily reached a B&B near Blarney after a 21-mile day, Peggy's throat must have been sore from neighing. It was my favourite accommodation of the trip. Four laughing daughters greeted me delightedly and escorted Peggy to a rather threadbare field full of young calves which followed her around hopefully, looking for an udder.

Next morning, Mr O'Keefe drew me a careful map showing a short cut to the castle entrance. I don't quite know how I ended up in the castle grounds, but, after apologising for trespassing to a rather frightening woman on a bicycle, I found that the exit I was planning to slip through surreptitiously had a cattle grid and a narrow gate. There's no way you can surreptitiously unload and reload a nervous pony. Peggy was no better on private land than I am; she too hated trespassing.

Blarney is famous for the wrong reason, but this doesn't matter if the lure of kissing the stone draws more visitors than would normally be attracted to a very fine castle set in splendid grounds. The view from the top, of the 'Big House' set in formal gardens planted with beech, chestnut and cedar, is magnificent. Visitors who don't have an anxious pony tied up outside can spend some happy hours exploring the 60 acres of varied parkland, including a poison garden. If you've ever wondered what wolf's bane or mandrake look like, here you are. Paul from Shiplake, who had built his own home, had told me how much he admired the castle's 15th-century builders for its clean lines and carefully calculated strength: the walls are 12 feet thick at the base but then taper upwards. The Blarney Stone is under the battlements above an 80ft drop. Whoever thought up the idea that the gift of eloquence would only be bestowed if the kisser bent backwards to do his or her obsequious act had a shrewd eye on the commercial – not to mention erotic – possibilities. A strong and eloquent Irishman is required to ensure that tourists don't plunge to their deaths (though not even a doll could actually fit through the gap beside the stone) and the official photographer is the only one who may record the scene. To add to the excitement, a conspicuous sign near the stone gives the location of the nearest defibrillator. The origin of the kissing tradition is obscure, but the story goes that Queen Elizabeth I put considerable effort into trying to wean the Lord Blarney off 'dangerous Irish practices' (the mind boggles). When he countered with 'fair words and soft speech' – she expostulated, 'This is all Blarney. What he says he never means!'.

◡   ◡   ◡

I headed north towards the Blackwater River which runs from the hills of Kerry, through Lismore, to Waterford. I loved the inland scenery of little green fields bordered by unruly hedges or bracken-covered banks brightened by clumps of gorse, but missed the coast where the views and light were constantly changing. So it was on the quiet lanes of Co Cork that I first realised that I could read on horseback. A marvellous discovery, since I'd come to a particularly enjoyable bit in my book,

Good Behaviour by Molly Keane. To give my thighs a rest I sometimes read sitting sideways in the saddle. The Pony Club would be horrified.

A fine rain was falling in the late afternoon when I came to a deep wooded valley. Ahead of me were the Nagle Mountains; they looked gentle enough on the map – none of the closely crowded contours or dark browns that are so exciting to the adventurous map reader – but they still commanded respect so I decided to stop early for the night. Crossing a bridge over a river, I saw below me a grassy clearing in the pine forest with a newly constructed path leading to it. By the little silver gate was a sign announcing that this was a Mass rock. I went to have a look. Beyond the grassy clearing a narrow footbridge crossed the stream and the path led to the rock where Mass was celebrated in Penal times (the 17th and 18th centuries when Catholics were forbidden to practise their religion). A simple aluminium cross marked the rock, along with a plaque in Irish and English.

It was a perfect campsite. It had fresh running water, flat ground for the tent, and plenty of lovely green grass. I had to unload Peggy on the road and coax her up the flight of steps, through the narrow gate and down 12 steps to the clearing. There was no need to tether her in such an enclosed area, I just stretched her rope across the entrance to the path to discourage her from gazing over the gate and drawing attention to herself.

I still hadn't learned about The Wrong Sort of Grass, nor did I correctly interpret Peggy's strange behaviour that evening. Instead of settling down to graze, she showed an uncharacteristic interest in my activities. She hung around the campsite putting her nose into everything, chewing the tent and my jacket, and showing particular interest in my soup cooking on the stove. I was afraid she'd burn herself (or knock over the soup) so pushed her away. Undeterred, she came back and I found her standing with a guy rope in her mouth dangling its tent peg. Of course it was all very endearing and I didn't really have the heart to get cross. I even let her lick out my saucepan.

Next morning I was woken at 6.00am by Peggy stamping and snorting around the tent. My little room wobbled as she tripped over guy ropes and rubbed her chin along the flysheet. "For heaven's sake go *away!*" I shouted. She did. I dozed in blessed silence for another hour and then unzipped the flap and looked out. I couldn't see her. She must be behind the tent near the river. I dressed, crawled out and looked around in increasing disbelief. Peggy had gone. A wave of sheer panic swept over me as I recalled that morning in the mountains of the Dingle Peninsula when I first realised that Mollie was missing. Struggling to keep calm I considered the possibilities. Had she been stolen? It was possible, but unlikely in such a hidden spot and with my tent close by. I checked the area for hoof prints but the ground was too hard to see them. With her fear of bridges I was sure she wouldn't cross the narrow footbridge to the shrine. Then I noticed that the ground had been disturbed around the path leading to the gate; it looked as though she'd scrambled up the bank to get round the rope blocking her exit. There were definitely fresh prints on the path which was strewn with wood chippings; I'd smoothed it last night after pitching the tent to cover up the evidence of our visit. The gate was closed but she'd either jumped down onto the road or climbed up an equally steep bank through the pine trees to a large field above. I pulled myself up the bank to the field, praying that she'd be there. She wasn't.

I tried to think calmly. Before Mollie's death I might not have been too worried, but now I'd learned what horrible surprises can lie in wait for the unprepared. I was beside myself with anxiety. Suppose she was hit by a car? Or hurt in a dozen other ways? I thought she would probably head back to the stables where she'd enjoyed such good hospitality the day before, so started back along the road. It curved between high banks and

I could never see more than 100 yards ahead of me. This was ridiculous; I'd never find her this way. Perhaps I should flag down a passing car? But there was no traffic on this minor road and she'd had over an hour's head start. I returned to the campsite to collect my binoculars and on impulse crossed the footbridge and said a little prayer at the shrine. Then I climbed back to the field above the gate where I could get a good view with the binoculars over the surrounding countryside. A herd of cows was grazing in a field about half a mile away. And among the black-and-white animals was a brown one. I jogged across the wide upper field to the bramble-covered bank that bordered the cow pasture and climbed up. There were the cows and, stuffing herself with grass while watching me out of the corner of her eye, was Peggy. Then she walked towards me with a little whicker.

Just how or why Peggy came to be in that field I'll never know. The gate was open so she probably just walked in looking, as always, for company. But how did she find a field so far off the road she knew? If, as seemed equally possible, someone had come across her in the early morning and kindly put her in with the cows, why hadn't he shut the gate? I couldn't imagine who would be up at that hour anyway. Thinking the occupants of the house opposite the field might be my saviours, I knocked gently on the door to proffer my thanks. But the house was still asleep.

Adhering to the rule that gates should be left as you find them, I led Peggy out and of course was followed by a herd of cows. Perhaps on normal days they obligingly take themselves into the farmyard for milking, but today they all accompanied me down to the road while I ineffectually said, "Shoo". I had just tied up Peggy and collected a long stick to drive them back when the flustered farmer appeared on the scene. "I think I may owe you a big thankyou," I said between moos, but he just looked mystified when I explained about Peggy.

Each time I tied Peggy that day she whinnied when I returned. "Bitch!" I said, "Think I'll forgive you that easily?" It was a blustery day; the grey sky above the forestry pines was full of wind-blown crows as we climbed the heathery hill to the pass over the Nagle Mountains and dropped down through beech and holly to the Blackwater Valley. Just before the main road I passed a house with a B&B sign, a row of beehives and a 'honey for sale' notice. Mmm, honey! I tied Peggy to a gate and went in. Two women came towards me: they were mother and daughter and mother's left eye had disappeared beneath an enormous swelling. She was allergic to bee stings and had been stung on the eyelid a few hours earlier. She hastened to add that they were her husband's bees and he didn't even notice the stings. Yes, they could sell me some honey and how about a cup of tea? The daughter went out to offer words of comfort to Peggy while I gratefully munched on fruitcake and drank numerous cups of tea (my breakfast had understandably been a bit inadequate) and chatted about bees and England. I wasn't allowed to pay for the jar of honey I took away with me.

If I had been unnerved by Peggy's adventure, she was transformed. Thereafter, I couldn't leave her for more than a few minutes before I would hear her neigh, and have to go out to reassure her that I still loved her, and promise that I would never tell her to go away again. Endearing though this was, it did put a dampener on some of my pleasures. She had always had a puritan streak and disapproved of pubs, but now it was like being back in the days of prohibition. I would just be settling down to my glass of Guinness when I'd hear pitiful neighs and have to finish my drink by her side. She didn't even have the excuse that she was tied up so couldn't share the refreshment. One time when I was enjoying a drink in the evening, knowing she was safe in an adjoining field next to my tent, I was called back by heart-rending sobs. I mean neighs. This time I thought she must be greeting another horse nearby, but no, she wanted me. So I had to forgo a second glass of Guinness and return to the tent and write my diary by candlelight.

♘   ♘   ♘

I could have followed the River Blackwater to Lismore but that would have been along the main road. Besides, I wanted to visit friends of the Knivetts, organic-farming enthusiasts in Shanballymore, not far from Mallow. The map showed a track crossing the river at an encouragingly marked 'ford', but the boreen I took ended in a farm, not the river, and I was too cowardly to knock on the door and ask. I'd been horse-travelling for over two months now and had rarely met anything but kindness and hospitality from farmers; that my shyness should so irrationally persist infuriated me. I ended up adding another four or so miles to the day's total and was so irritated by my shortcomings I could hardly enjoy the views of the magnificent Blackwater with its deep wooded banks. Eventually, crossing by the Ballyhooly bridge, I was cheered by the impressive view of the castle overlooking the broad, gently flowing river. Before the bridge there was a ford here, and the castle was built in the 16th century as a defence against enemy incursions (the river otherwise providing an effective barrier).

The lanes leading to Shanballymore were peaceful, narrow and fly-ridden. I found an adequate picnic spot by the roadside and sprayed Peggy – much to her anguish – with Extra-tail. At least I had the sense not to tie her up while I did it, and to reward her with her favourite brown bread afterwards. Peggy was hungry after her adventurous night so, deciding to give her an extra-long lunch break, I settled down with my book. I soon became aware of someone clearing his throat. "Do you mind parking the horse a bit further down? There's a man here going to throw a bowl."

I gave him one of my blank looks and he pointed down the road, and sure enough there was a man, surrounded by onlookers, about to throw a metal ball down the road. And when I was out of the way he threw it; someone marked the spot it landed with chalk, and they continued on their way. Afterwards I read up about road bowling, a Cork tradition (they held the first World Championship the following year). The bowl is a cast-iron cannonball which, in the right hands, or hand, can achieve speeds of 165mph and a distance of 200 yards. The technique looked, to me, a bit like cricket, but is bowled underarm. The team that completes the agreed stretch of road in the fewest number of throws is the winner.

ᘉ   ᘉ   ᘉ

The Wenlocks and their organic-farming methods were well known, so I was able to get directions to their smallholding. After pitching my tent near the cabbages and tethering Peggy on the lawn, I drank goat's milk and talked with Chuck and Gilly about their efforts to keep at least one of the Irish county crafts alive. Two elderly brothers in the Waterford town of Tallow made willow baskets, a craft they learned from their father. When they retire there will be no-one to continue the tradition, so Chuck went there each week to learn the craft. Bundles of willow, some white and some brown, were hanging in the shed. The Wenlocks cut their own white willow but the brown (which is artificially coloured) had to be imported at great expense from England. The native Irish willow is weaker and shorter.

When I was staying at Lismore I visited Tallow and the two old basket-makers. One of the brothers showed me a baby's cradle that a man had brought in for repair. It had been his cradle when he was an infant, and now he wanted it for his firstborn. The old man remembered making it.

I had the uncomfortable feeling that, in terms of dominance, Peggy now had the upper hand. First her pathetic neighs were far more effective than broken fence posts in ensuring that she never stayed tied up and lonely for long, and she completely had my measure when it came to general competence. That day, as so often happened, the saddlebags slipped while I was leading her. And when, as so often happened, I didn't notice and pulled crossly at her rope when she stopped, she looked me straight in the eye with a bored know-all stare, then complacently stood while I grovelled my apologies and tugged at the straps. I had only two weeks to go before I needed to return her and she was doing everything in her power to make me change my mind. If only I could.

I made my way to Kilworth, a market town with a broad main street, a church, and stone walls shielding Peggy's view of the River Araglin, so we crossed it calmly before turning left towards Lismore. The lane was exceptionally beautiful, winding through deciduous woodland and conifer plantations, with occasional views of the river set in a deeply wooded valley. High hedges shielded large houses and cattle farms – altogether more prosperous-looking than west Cork – with some areas of heathery moorland for additional interest. I crossed the county border into Waterford, and in the early evening rode over the Blackwater River bridge, with its imposing view of Lismore castle, and clip-clopped over the cobblestones of Dervla's courtyard where she and her daughter Rachel were waiting for us.

Chapter 22

August 25th 1984

Dear Kate,

Sorry about the lack of news but there were far more interesting things to do at Dervla's than write letters. But now she and Rachel have gone off to Edinburgh and I've elected to stay on for a few days and house- and pet-sit. It's a responsible job: there are three cats, a flock of bantams, some bantam chicks that'll die in minutes if I don't keep their water filled, and – nicest of all – Orlando, a goat of indeterminate sex, who's suffering from unrequited love for Peggy. He's her host, since she's sharing his orchard, but she's horrid to him, ignoring his adoring eyes and even pretending to bite him. Orlando needs a lot of love. When explaining my duties Rachel said 'sometimes you just have to go out and tell Orlando you love him' and sure enough I sometimes hear him bleating by the gate and go out and stroke him until he's happy. It's lovely being in a house – a real house with a table and a bed and a kitchen and hot water and books and time to enjoy them.

   I got a lot of entertainment out of listening to Dervla and Rachel packing for Edinburgh. "Oh Rachel, that's <u>absurd</u>, you can't take <u>two</u> skirts", says Dervla, packing a briefcase with books. She took no other luggage apart from a small rucksack containing her 'fleabag'. The clothes she was wearing would be perfectly adequate for her appearance as one of the guests of honour at a Literary Event. Just after I'd seen them off I answered the phone and told an elegant-sounding Scottish voice that Dervla was away. "You mean she's left for the airport already?"

"No, she's hitchhiking to Dublin for the ferry."

While the Murphys were here I went riding, blackberrying and mushrooming with Rachel, and now I'm going out for rides on my own to explore the area. Peggy is really enjoying being a normal riding pony without being encumbered with luggage, and gallops and jumps with zest. One day we had a visit from Joe, the ex-tinker who I remember from my last visit when I couldn't understand a word he said. This time I had no problem. He was full of fascinating stories about animals and tinkers. "Know what to do when you see ashes from a tinkers' fire? Dig around and you'll find a horseshoe nail, or maybe a screw... It's the sign of which family was there." He also told me that foxes and badgers are sworn enemies. "A badger can kill a fox easy. Drive them out of the earth by urinating in it. The foxes won't stay then."

And talking of tinkers, Peggy has a mystery in her past. We passed a gypsy camp during one of my rides in the area: an untidy collection of caravans, washing and piebald horses. I thought Peggy would be thrilled by all the horses but she was truly terror-stricken. It took me ages to persuade her to pass, and all the time she made a rather dreadful roaring noise through closed nostrils as though the smell was more than her memory could endure. Strange. Rachel says her pony was equally frightened of them.

I'll end on a pompous note. Last time I was in Lismore I met several people who, when they learned I was here again, have invited me for meals and – this is the good bit – I've dined in a castle two nights running! Different castles, too.

I can't pretend that the Duchess of Devonshire had invited me to dine at Lismore Castle, her Irish home, but the agent was a good friend of

Dervla's. At one of these dinners a horsey woman had produced her address book with the assurance that her friends would love to see me and Peggy. Alarmingly, they all lived in houses of sufficient importance to be marked by name on my map. Which was more frightening, I pondered, a Waterford farmer or a 'horse Protestant'? I'd heard a few stories about farmers getting fed up with people camping on their land without permission. "Remember Michael and the Germans? He came across them in his field when he had the front-loader on his tractor. He picked up the tent and dumped them in the ditch while they were sleeping!"

On my last day at Lismore I spread the map on the table and worked out my route via these Big Houses, but left the first part unplanned. I wanted to ride over at least two more mountain ranges before descending to the Tipperary plain. The Knockmealdown Mountains, on Lismore's doorstep, would be the first whichever route I took, but then I had to decide between Galty and Comeragh. They both provided an excuse not to go directly to Limerick where I had to leave Peggy, now horribly close as the crow flies.

∪   ∪   ∪

Handing over the care of the Murphy animals to a neighbour, I rode out of the yard trying not to listen to Orlando's pitiful bleats as the love of his life clip-clopped away over the cobblestones. Of the two roads over the mountains I chose the one less travelled via the village of Cappoquin. The rain that had fallen during my first couple of days in Lismore had washed the air clean so the Knockmealdown Mountains were purple with heather, not blue with haze. On such a clear day the impressive neo-gothic Mount Melleray monastery, shining grey-white in the foothills against the dark pines, seemed too near to miss. I thought I remembered someone saying I should visit it, although the only information I could find was that it was built in 1832 by the Cistercians when they were kicked out of Melleray in Brittany. I didn't even know if it was open to the public. Once there, I couldn't find anything to visit except the toilets (and a modern chapel with some good stained glass) but there was some excellent grass and Peggy was hungry so I propped myself against a telegraph pole and had an early lunch. While I was eating, a man strode purposefully towards me. Oh God, was he going to tell me I was trespassing? No, he'd seen the pony and couldn't resist coming over for a chat... What a marvellous way of travelling. He told me Melleray Abbey was famous as a Scout centre: the Scouting headquarters of Ireland, in fact.

The lower flanks of the mountain were covered in conifers, but happily these gave way to heather and gorse as we climbed towards the pass. For the last few days when I'd found myself singing "It's a long way to Tipperary" I'd checked myself and said "It's not actually", so when I reached the county border at the top of the pass and saw 'Tipperary's golden vale' spread out in front of me I felt a real thrill, almost as though Tipperary were my destination. The corn had been harvested and the patchwork fields were not golden but all shades of green and stubble yellow. While I gazed at the view, someone else gazed at me. Why, I wondered, was a sheepdog living here alone, tied to a new and quite cosy-looking kennel? His desirable residence was a good two miles from the nearest house.

The road was unfenced and small sheep tracks ran through the heather in all directions. I couldn't resist attempting a cross-country route down to Newcastle and the River Tar. Peggy was cross at leaving the tarmac. She sulked along, snatching mouthfuls of long grass, but I was ecstatic at this heatherfest. We were waist-deep in purple and mauve bushes buzzing with bees and fluttering with butterflies. The going was rough but dry, and the view open enough that my direction was clear, though I had a few anxieties about the little streams that cut deep channels in the folds of the hills; would the banks be boggy or too steep? And if I did get across would I find a way out at the bottom of the mountains? Although I was now much more confident going across country, I hadn't completely shaken off my fears. Fortunately, sheep paths naturally follow the easiest route and we crossed the streams without difficulty and arrived at a farm track. This led to a gate opening onto a farmyard ankle-deep in slurry. Hysterical dogs barked inside the barns as I nervously made my way out through several more gates on to the road.

The road was little more than a track that, to my delight, turned into a genuine green road (completely covered in grass), running alongside a stream and bordered each side with bracken. I even knew where I was on the map. We emerged in the village of Newcastle and continued east for another few miles before I succumbed to Peggy's increasingly forlorn hints that it was time to stop for the night. My choice of farm was a happy one. The Moores were elderly, outgoing and very friendly. Peggy and the tent went in a large and, considering the drought, miraculously green field with Neddy the donkey, and I accepted the invitation to come to the house for tea. Bread, ham, salad and tomatoes were on offer, along with conversation and a spot of tourism. Mr and Mrs Moore were longing to show me the *lios* in a neighbour's field. After all the myths I'd read about these fairy mounds (or, more mundanely, hillforts) I welcomed the opportunity actually to see one. Archaeologists date them from the Bronze Age, around the 18th century BC. We climbed through a gap in the hedge and saw a symmetrical grass-covered circle surrounded by a depression that may have been a moat. No one knows anything about them, but Mr Moore said someone had excavated the ring and found many small cells; just large enough for a person to squat inside them. There was laughing speculation about small people – fairies. No one believed in them, of course, but when I said I wouldn't mind camping there Mrs Moore said, "Oh dear God, stop! Would you really?"

During our evening chat the Moores said I must visit Vicky, an Englishwoman who had set up as a harness-maker nearby, so after a two-boiled-eggs breakfast I set off for her cottage. She lived alone with no immediate neighbours but dogs, pigs and a mare and foal for company. "A Frenchman who owned this property asked a friend of mine to look after a stallion and some mares for three weeks. He never came back. So I said I'd take a two-year-old filly to break and – poor thing – she was already in foal." Vicky was sitting astride a saddler's bench stitching a browband. Her little workshed was full of tack: racing saddles (Vincent O'Brien commissioned work from her), bridles in for repair, and her favourite, sets of harness in black patent leather. It takes a week to make a saddle, and three weeks for a set of harness.

I left reluctantly and returned to the farm for a second cup of tea and a bottle of milk for the journey. Before going to see Vicky, I'd watched Mrs Moore milk their cow by hand. I envied the practiced ease with which she produced two jets of milk into the pail. I'd once tried this myself, and my aching fingers extracted about a cupful in 15 minutes. "Oh, cows are clever animals. They won't release their milk for someone they don't know. Watch that one, she kicks…"

My next social call – another Moore recommendation – was Pat Melody's bar and trekking centre in Ballymacarbry in the Nire valley. It was always worth talking to stable owners since they knew suitable riding places. Pat and his wife Carmel were as friendly as everyone in this little corner of Waterford. Peggy was given a lunch of horse nuts in the stable while I discussed local trekking over yet more coffee and a sandwich. Pat used to organise a two-day trek in the area but his route was mostly through forestry land and the gates are locked. The usual story.

"I'll open a gate for you," he said. "You can ride for miles in these woods…" and he gave me very specific directions. Then he looked at me speculatively. "You're going to miss the pony when you hand her back, aren't you?" I felt a lump in my throat just thinking about it.

"Would you like to buy her?" A half-formed plan has swept into my head. If Pat bought her, I could see her next time I visited Lismore.

"Sorry," said Pat, "she's too small."

Oh well… Pedar might not want to sell her anyway.

The gate that Pat opened gave me access to a lovely soft pine-needle-covered path that ran for some distance beside an indecisive stream. When I came to a farm and six slavering sheepdogs rushed out, I persuaded myself that Pat didn't actually mean me to go through the farmyard (which, I've since learned, adjoined the road), but to follow the small track that ran behind the buildings. The track meandered aimlessly through the plantations of spruce and pine and it was soon clear that it had no intention of going anywhere near the road. I was furious with myself for once again letting my cowardice contribute to being lost. I kept telling Peggy we'd go on to the next curve, then the next one, so after 45 minutes when I did decide to turn back I was easily tempted to try a path leading off the main track in roughly the right direction.

At least this path took me out into open ground, so I parked Peggy and climbed to a high point to get my bearings. There was no sign of a road, just mountains. Never mind, my compass seemed to think my chosen direction was the right one and my track led to a gate. I decided that if it were open I'd try to make my way across country. Peggy whinnied to me as I returned, but had to resign herself to more cross-country work since the gate was indeed open. The next stretch was moorland, densely covered with heather and sheep, and beyond that was a valley with cultivated fields so presumably with access to a road. I came to a wire mesh fence and followed it around to a place where it had been flattened down either by or for sheep. I covered the mesh with logs and Peggy stepped carefully over into more heather and long grass, with some patches of bog. Peggy pottered along slowly, pretending to look carefully at the ground for a safe foothold (which she was allowed to do) then grab a mouthful of grass (which she was not allowed to do). I saw a farmhouse in the distance and headed with difficulty that way but found, to my disgust, that a deep gully prevented us from reaching it. However, I had more luck with another gap in the fence and soon joined a boreen. To my pleased surprise I was able to follow it safely down the gully, across the river at the bottom, and out onto the road only a few miles above my planned route. Not bad for someone with no sense of direction.

Before long I passed a sign announcing 'Handicrafts, teas, etc.' And thought the 'tea, etc' was too good to miss so tied Peggy up and went inside. I was amazed when the girl looked up from her knitting machine and said, "Oh there you are. We were beginning to think you'd got lost." I was just about to say that she must be mixing me up with someone else when she said that Pat Melody had phoned and asked her to look out for me. He was soon on the scene with the news that he would, after all, like to buy Peggy. I told him I'd contact Pedar as soon as possible.

After tea, Peggy and I headed off into the evening and a pass through the Comeragh Mountains known as The Gap. I was rather excited at doing this – Pat had assured me it should be passable on horseback, though it's shown as a footpath on the map. At least, he said, I would have no problem finding my way since the route is marked with white stakes. It turned out to be one of the loveliest bits of the whole trek and came as an added bonus when I thought I'd finished with good scenery. Peggy and I climbed up through deep heather in full bloom, with the chequerboard fields of Tipperary below and a dramatic gashed and gullied mountain range in subtle greens, greys and heather-mauve to the side. The going was rough. I was considerate and led Peggy who was very tiresome, stopping at intervals and pretending to admire the view and then plunging her head down to snatch mouthfuls to eat. When we got to the top there was no sign of the 'hand of man' in any direction, just mountains, and the going was even more difficult, with some boggy stretches and deep bracken. Then in a V between the hills, there was the vale again, with just a green square lit by the sun like a partly cleaned oil painting.

It was quite late – about 6.30 – and rain clouds were building up behind me, so I decided to look for a suitable campsite. Peggy was telling me that if she didn't have her supper soon she'd die, and I wanted one more night in the wild before heading for civilisation. Soon I came to a flattish area with reasonable grass and a little stream, tethered Peggy to one of the white posts that had so helpfully marked our route, and got the tent set up just before it began to pour. I was worried about Peggy but she turned her back to the wind and waited it out stoically, while I cooked my soup to the pungent smell of burning daddy-longlegs. The heather was infested with them, and they kept flying into the tent and drowning themselves in the wax of my candle.

I woke the next morning to a beautiful sunny day – despite the weather forecast's insistence that it was going to rain – and let Peggy off the tether to fill her stomach further afield. I no longer needed to worry that she'd run away or that I'd be unable to catch her. My plan was to partially circumnavigate Slievenamon, which shows on the map as a brown fingerprint on the green lowlands. It's a strange mountain, an isolated 2,368-foot lump of sandstone with no neighbours. The name means 'Mount of the Women' and features in one of the many legends about Fionn mac Cumhaill (Finn McCool in English) who was Ireland's equivalent of King Arthur. He used to exercise his warriors on the hill (no doubt it muscled them up wonderfully) and when it became time to choose a wife, he thought it would be jolly to sit on top of Slievenamon and award his hand in marriage to the first maiden to reach him. But, sneaky fellow, he'd carried his choice up the mountain the night before, and produced her in triumph just as the first eager sweaty maiden reached the summit. This chosen bride was Gráinne, daughter of Cormac MacAirt, the High King of Ireland, and she did not share his delight. The legend says that she was repulsed by this man who was the same age as her father, and at her betrothal party fell in love with Diarmuid (Dermot), a man with an irresistible beauty spot, eloped with him and became the stuff of other legends.

Looking at the map it seemed that a half-circuit round the mountain would be feasible in the time available. It would have been had I not taken the wrong turning, and followed several dead-end tracks and tricky cross-country sections before emerging on the right road, but too late to show up at the first Big House where I had an invitation.

Peggy deserved a decent meal so I asked a farmer leaning over a gate if he had a field available. He wasn't sure, but finally decided the clover meadow would be fine and he'd put the old cow elsewhere. "But remember," he said, "clover's very rich. It could make your pony ill." Indeed, I knew that colic could be fatal. For a while I tethered Peggy within reach of some grass, but not the clover, but she looked so anguished at this arrangement that before I went to bed I released her and resigned myself to worrying about her all night. Before I could even get into serious anxiety mode, however, I heard a voice saying "Hello" and there was a woman with a tray piled with sandwiches and biscuits, along with a thermos of tea. "John asked me to look after you," she said. She squatted down outside the tent in the dark, while I rather self-consciously drank the tea and ate the sandwiches, and chatted. She was matron of Kilkenny Orthopaedic Hospital and has nursed in a variety of London hospitals so the conversation centred happily on joint experiences from my previous existence as an occupational therapist.

U U U

It was only six miles to Fethard, a lovely walled town with an ancient church. I felt like Mrs De Winter approaching Mandalay as, in the late morning, I rode up the long stately drive lined with chestnut and oak trees, and passed under two arches to arrive at the splendid 18th-century Grove House. But instead of Mrs Danvers waiting to greet me there was the delightful Rosemary. She was so welcoming to both me and Peggy that I felt perhaps I belonged in a Big House after all. I hadn't really planned to stay, but when I was shown to the spare bedroom I lost the desire to assert myself. Peggy joined some thoroughbreds in a spacious field; I wondered if she'd be ashamed of her working-class origins in such high society.

When Rosemary's husband, Harry, arrived, I soon realised he was one of those rare people, even in Ireland – a brilliant talker. Anecdotes about Irish life just poured out of him and I took to trailing around after him, notebook in hand, trying to record his best stories. "Mikey was helping me make some formal flowerbeds," he told me. "The plan was that I held the string taut so that Mikey could cut the turf in a straight line. This was fine until Rosemary called me into the house for a phone call. I let go of the string and when I returned I found that he had carefully cut round the resulting squiggles." I later met the delightful Mikey who told me that Peggy had "a grand set of legs".

In Ireland the average farm is 60 acres; 20 per cent of farmers own 80 per cent of the land. Grove House had 683 acres. "Yes, it's hard work running such a large farm. Sometimes I think we're crazy." He explained that he wasn't a direct descendant of the original owners but a cousin. And anyway, no one really expected the house to survive the burnings of 1922. The local villagers, however, asked the popular Captain Barton to return. "He should have hung a Union Jack from the window and gone away for a year or so," said Harry ruefully. But there was no concealing how much he loved the estate and had devised all sorts of ingenious ways of managing it.

Describing the economics of rearing bullocks, Harry said, "We're just a warehouse for grass." I'd noticed that each field had a broad solid jump incorporated into the fencing. "We use the horses as bicycles. Cows jump vertically, but horses learn first to jump wide. So we can check on the cattle and get a bit of jumping in at the same time."

Something I was steeling myself to do was phone Pedar to give him a progress report and ask if he might be willing to sell Peggy to Pat Melody. I'd convinced myself that this arrangement would be rather like having a child at boarding school – she might be lonely at first but would soon make friends and I could see her in the holidays. But Pedar said no, he needed her for transport.

It was September 1st. Each day, since Peggy and I had set out on our journey on July 15th, I had measured our mileage on the map with my length of thread and noted the figures in my diary. That night I added them all up and discovered that I had passed the thousand-mile mark.

Chapter 23

As I prepared to leave the next day, Rosemary was bringing horses in, ready for the blacksmith's monthly visit. I'd just finished picking out Peggy's hooves and had noticed how worn her shoes were. Rosemary came over to look, and agreed with me that although she could make it to Limerick with that set, it would be safer – and more considerate to Pedar – to have her re-shod in front. The visiting blacksmith would have no Peggy-sized shoes with him (and wasn't due till the afternoon anyway) but Rosemary gave me his address and phone number. Imagine, a blacksmith with a phone! I had come a long way from the west. In fact, I was noticing all sorts of differences between the prosperous heartlands and the economically depressed regions of Kerry and west Cork. For one thing, there was a greater variety of houses here; instead of the uniform yellow rectangular bungalow or coloured terraced house, there were manors, architect-designed houses and old cottages all mixed together. Earlier, I'd been tickled to pass a cottage with a goat balanced on the windowsill only a mile from a house with a peacock perched on the windowsill.

More prosperity meant more cars, so I took the back roads to my next destination, the Rock of Cashel. This is arguably Ireland's most important religious site and I planned to return and do it properly the next day. I'd already arranged a field with friends of my Lismore contact as well as of Harry and Rosemary. It's a small world, that of the Anglo-Irish. I passed the Rock with its castle magnificently silhouetted against the evening sky and matching the poem I'd copied out from one of Dervla's books.

Royal and Saintly Cashel! I would gaze upon the wreck of thy departed powers.

Not in the dewy light of matin hours,

Nor the meridian pomp of summer's blaze,

But at the close of dim autumnal days,

When the sun's parting glance, through slanting showers,

Sheds o'er thy rock-throned battlements and towers.

Such awful gleams as brighten o'er decay's

Prophetic cheek. At such a time, methinks,

There breathes from thy lone courts and voiceless aisles

A melancholy moral such as sinks

On the lone traveller's heart, amid the piles of vast Persepolis on her mountain stand,

Or Thebes half buried in the desert sand.

(*The Rock of Cashel* by Sir Aubrey de Vere 1788–1846)

The parting glance of the evening sun upon the rock-throned towers exhilarated me, but this lone traveller's heart was struck not by 'melancholy moral' but by Peggy's pleading neigh to stop messing around with a camera and find somewhere for the night.

At the next Big House I was given a luxurious campsite near a spring where the local Girl Guides learn the art of rural survival. Peggy shared a field with Brownie. We felt they'd find a lot to talk about since Brownie too had pulled a trap and travelled around Ireland with a lone adventuress (in this case the au pair) until a broken trace put an end to their journey.

I joined the family for coffee and stories about Tipperary in the old days. My hostess had grown up in the area and remembered the threshing parties in the days before combine harvesters. "Everyone in the village came to help and when it was all done, they feasted on a huge pot of potatoes. There was lots of laughter and merrymaking."

Cashel deserves its tourist rating. So often, a ruin that is impressive from a distance is disappointing when seen at close quarters, or a once-magnificent place is spoiled by tourist gimmicks. Not so the collection of buildings that comprises the Rock of Cashel. The cathedral, chapel and round tower date from the 12th and 13th centuries and had that aura of spirituality that makes you lower your voice, even in a ruin. There is lots to see: Cormac's Chapel, consecrated in 1134, is said to be the finest Romanesque church in Ireland, and there is an abundance of primitive and altogether delightful carvings.

This was the seat of Munster kings from the 4th century to the beginning of the 12th when it was presented to the Church. Indeed, it was said to be the place that St Patrick converted Aengus, the King of Munster, to Christianity. Those medieval stonemasons must have felt close to God as they built their masterpiece so high above the surrounding town. Yet their peasant blood shows in the dumpy Irish Marys portrayed on each side of the cross (you half expect them to be wearing aprons) and the Celtic quality of the stone heads.

I left unsatiated, but aware of Peggy's pleading calls and the need to be at the blacksmith's in time for our afternoon appointment. When I arrived, having trotted much of the way, he was still sweating over the huge hooves of a heavy horse. The owner and I exchanged horse lore while the new shoes were nailed into position, then it was Peggy's turn. She had a newly developed interest in bottoms – I'd had to smack her nose for the nip she'd given me when I mounted that morning – and I just pulled her head up in time as she aimed at Paddy's colourful Y-fronts showing provocatively above his trouser band as he bent over her hoof. He was extraordinarily quick. The old shoes were off and the new ones on in about fifteen minutes. No hot-shoeing here.

◡   ◡   ◡

My next hosts lived five miles away. They were expecting me so I was only slightly surprised to be greeted by a red-haired man and two boys who emerged from the woods some distance from the house. They were searching for some missing calves, they told me. My arrival must have been hideously inconvenient; the previous day they had been host to the riding part of a tetrathlon and on the following day two of the five children were returning to boarding school. This was Ireland, however, and here was another deeply religious, warm, entertaining and relaxed family who effortlessly incorporated my new face at the dinner table.

Two more new faces turned up while we were eating: a rather formidable French couple who were doing something with horses in the next valley. On being introduced, the woman lowered herself down next to me like an eagle landing on its eyrie, twisted sideway so she could stare into my face and said:

"How old are you?"

"Forty-three."

"*Mais non*, that is not true!"

"Yes, it is."

"No!"

Above: View from the Ring of Kerry
Below: I cook soup and Peggy catches up on her grazing while tethered by a hind leg

From Kerry to Cork

Above: The green road over the pass to Co Cork
Below: The Sheep's Head peninsula. My last bit of coast before turning inland.

Into Co Waterford

Above: Author Dervla Murphy and her daughter Rachel – and Orlando the goat
Below: The lonely sheepdog on the road into the Knockmealdown Mountains

The end in sight

Above: The Comeragh Mountains
Below: Our last day together

"All right then, I'm twenty-six."

"No!"

Fortunately her husband then called her away; I had a nasty feeling she expected me to say 60 so she could talk about grandchildren.

I was summoned to breakfast next morning by one of the boys driving a 1950s' tractor. Though only 15 he had a passionate interest in fixing up antique vehicles and was a dab hand at welding. I was back in mushroom country so breakfast was one of those marvellous black-stained fry-ups with lots of brown bread. I left with my saddlebags bulging with a picnic lunch and instructions for my final diversion through the Glen of Aherlow and into the Galty Mountains. I'd first heard about the Galtys from the man who chatted to me at the Mt Melleray monastery. He thought it the loveliest place in Ireland (so did Arthur Young, writing 200 years ago: 'Those who are fond of scenes in which nature reigns in all her wild magnificence, should visit this stupendous chain').

The old Celtic gods and heroes were busy around here and the largest of the corrie lakes, which are a feature of the Galtys, is said to have been formed when the ground opened up under the spell of harp-playing Cliach who was trying to win the heart of Princess Baina, daughter of the king of the fairies. Despite his sitting on top of the mountain for a year, working on two harps simultaneously, she never succumbed to his charms so the earth received him into its bosom. Or possibly into fairyland. Or maybe they're the same thing. Hard to tell, sometimes.

It was to Lough Muskry that I set off rather reluctantly on the grey morning of September 2nd. The weather was unpromising for a mountain excursion and I was suffering from that mixture of depression and anticipation that, for me, marks the end of a trip. Part of me was looking forward to going home and part of me dreaded parting with Peggy whose daily demonstrations of affection – or dependency – made it even harder. But the part that hated leaving Ireland told me I'd regret not seeing as much of the Galty Mountains as possible, so I took the sign-posted track through the conifers, opened a gate, and followed a good path to a stream. The view was pleasant and, in sun, would probably have been inspiring. But I was spoiled; I'd seen too many superlative mountain scenes and a river and some brown-green hills under a chill sky were not good enough. I sat by the stream, ate my ham sandwiches, and let the cloud of melancholy settle over me.

"Excuse me. Is it safe to pass your pony?" The English couple had come down from the lake. I asked them about the trail. "I don't think the pony will make it up there, it's a bit of a scramble." Having come so far I thought I ought to have a look, so I unbagged and unsaddled Peggy and tethered her for a prolonged lunch hour. As I climbed up in drizzle through the coarse grass I saw a rather large horse grazing further up the mountain not far from Peggy. Suppose it heard Peggy – it would be just like her to give an experimental neigh – and galloped over and broke its legs on the tether chain? Suppose it was a stallion and tried to have its wicked way with her? Climb, climb, worry, worry. It was further than I expected (it always is) to the ridge, but worth the effort. Sheep scattered as the lake came suddenly into view. A black, grim lough scooped out by glaciers below the wet, grim brown-grey cliffs. In sun, it's probably a blue lake under golden sandstone. I rather liked it grim.   ·

The two horses were still unacquainted when I got back to the stream. We jogged briskly down through the woods, with Peggy nurturing her little victory of not having climbed to the lake, and headed west along the road. A car full of giggling nuns drew up.

"Have you heard the results?"

"What?"

"Now how would she be hearing the results?"

They all collapsed in delighted laughter. "Hurling. It's the big match. You didn't know?"

⎗ ⎗ ⎗

I was heading for Ballinacourty House. The estate once owned much of the Glen of Aherlow, then, under the Land Reform Acts, most of the acreage was handed over to the tenants and finally in 1922 the Big House was burned. All that remains are the stables which were occupied by Eamon De Valera and his troops during the civil war. They had been converted into a rather posh bed-and-breakfast place with the grounds serving as a camp and caravan park. I'd been told about Ballinacourty by a couple of people, so it was an obvious choice for that night. Besides, Peggy had become such a snob she automatically turned into Big House drives.

Jennie La Haye was quietly amused by my request. She called her husband and said, "This visitor wants bed and breakfast." He looked at me, unimpressed. "Go on, look outside." Peggy and Peter had different ideas of what constitutes luxury horse accommodation. I knew Peggy would prefer a field, Peter was sure a well-appointed stable was everything her equine heart could desire. There was no field anyway, so Peggy was led to a Stately Stable where she contrived to look as pathetic as possible, propping her nose on the high door, whinnying to be let out, and refusing at first to eat the considerately provided hay and horse nuts. She was by now such a mistress of manipulation that I spent the evening (reserved for finishing my book) trailing up and down the drive so she could eat grass, answering questions from a gaggle of children, and lifting them onto her bare back.

I was half woken in the early morning by a blackbird singing a very sweet, very leisurely solo from a branch immediately above the tent. Then, as the chatter and clamour and tantalising bacon smells from the other campers began to permeate my world, I reached for my cup and saucepan and started boiling the water for tea.

Peggy was touchingly pleased to see me. I could see from the particles of sawdust sticking to her sides that she did at least lie down during the night so couldn't have been too miserable. I led her into the campground and, under the eyes of a dozen or so campers, groomed her, saddled up, bagged up and set off towards my final bit of sightseeing: Lough Gur. This lake and its surroundings were described in my guidebook as having 'a remarkable number of Stone Age dwellings and burial places' and I'd been urged by Pat Melody to see it. It was also on the way to Boher, where I had to leave Peggy for Pedar to collect. The morning was cloudy and blustery with rain promised by the Met man. At least, for once, I was prepared, with all my waterproof gear in an accessible place in the saddlebag. The first drops fell shortly after I'd left the campground, and soon Peggy was as black and slippery as a sea lion, but without its cheerfulness. She plodded along with her head down and sideways and ears back. I hunched myself in my anorak and felt the rain gradually trickle into my boots via my socks. I'd had a choice: rain trousers which kept my bottom dry and feet wet (because they're too short) or rain chaps which allowed me dryish feet but a clammy wet bottom. I'd chosen the former. Shortly after noon, I passed a lone pub. It was called the Welcome Inn. On the side was painted in bold black letters 'You are welcome in'. We plodded by. After a hundred yards I turned Peggy round towards the welcome. What the hell, it was nearly lunchtime and a Guinness under cover would be much nicer than marmite sandwiches and water on a rain-soaked saddle-table. I tied Peggy to a telegraph pole and went inside. The bar was empty. I stood and dripped onto the multi-coloured carpet until an elderly woman sidled in and looked at me suspiciously.

"I'd like a drink, please," I said cheerily. Silence. She regarded me balefully.

"What sort of drink?"

"Oh, a Guinness will do nicely. A bit wet isn't it? But I suppose we mustn't complain, the farmers will be happy." I burbled on.

"You on a bicycle or something?"

"No, a horse."

"Well, for God's sake!" She padded to the door and looked at Peggy then disappeared into the public bar to haul out the only other customer for a view. The atmosphere warmed, conversation began, and soon a complimentary plate of sandwiches had joined my Guinness. The other customer, a very portly man, was evidently a semi-professional pubber. He had a small stock of jokes which he produced and which I laughed at, I hoped in the right places since I didn't understand them.

The conversation moved on to witchcraft and Biddy Early. "You don't know who she is? They called her the Witch of Clare. She could talk to the *sidhe*. You know, the fairies." His grandfather remembered her; she died in 1874. "Oh yes, she could cast spells all right. But she cured people as well, mind you." Apparently Biddy had a great way with herbs and was as successful with animals as humans. The talk turned to a local woman who had a cure for shingles. Ears pricked for some gem of folk medicine, I asked what exactly she did. "Oh, she gives them a few sips of 7-Up and says something."

Before I could ask him to elaborate, I heard a neigh. Reluctantly, I peeped out of the door at Peggy's back view but she seemed all right so I returned to the bar. Another louder, longer neigh. Peggy's head was turned towards the pub entrance as far as her short rope would allow, and she was demanding my return. Overcome, as usual, by remorse at my boozy ways, I asked for a bucket of water and a piece of bread, paid for my drink and left.

At least the rain had stopped and we continued through pleasant scenery towards Lough Gur. I pulled out my book from the saddlebag and read the last couple of chapters, letting Peggy find her own way and return the astonished stares of passing cyclists.

Since we'd made an early start I told Peggy she could stop at 6. I selected a freshly painted yellow farmhouse set inside a frame of green fields with a long gravel driveway. My toes curled with anxiety as a group of Alsatians and Dobermans leapt up at my approach, followed by a large unfriendly-looking man. I put the usual question. "I wouldn't say we had." I smiled sweetly, thanked him, and turned the reluctant Peggy round. The next farmhouse was by the road and not as smart. There was no reply when I knocked on the door. Peggy neighed, and I could hear a shuffling and key clanking and a "Who is it?" Always a hard question to answer, but the door was cautiously opened. An elderly woman wearing one purple stocking listened to my request. "I don't think so, but I'm not the boss." She directed me to the farmyard where an old man emerged from the cowshed at the same time as his purple-stockinged wife came out of the back door. While waiting for their son, the boss, to arrive they looked me over appraisingly.

"Are you on your own?"

"Yes."

"Single?"

"Yes."

"Do you want to get married?"

"Well, not tonight."

The good-looking son appeared and said, "'Tis no problem. Which field would you like?" He suggested a paddock, three gates further down the road, almost overlooking Lough Gur, and with piped water for Peggy and me. He also gave me some milk and offered his phone so I could let Mr O'Connell know that I would be delivering Peggy tomorrow.

It was a pleasant paddock with some excitable cattle bellowing from a neighbouring field and high hedges providing protection from the wind. The grey cloud had rolled away leaving the usual Irish green-blue evening sky. This would be my last night camping with Peggy and I sat outside the tent watching her before I prepared my evening meal, pinning a picture in my memory. I'd told Pedar that I would bring her back a better pony, and I was right. Her Guinness-coloured coat shone in the evening sun, her sides were plump, her quarters well-rounded and she looked superbly fit. Which she was. Her regime for the last seven weeks had been almost identical to the conditioning exercise given to young race horses; hours of walking and slow trotting. Although a daily feed of oats might have given her more pep, she had obviously thrived on her diet of grass which had almost always been green and succulent despite the drought. And what luck I'd had with the weather! The downpour today – only a few hours in fact – served as a reminder of how little rain I'd had. I'd never been drenched to the skin, and in the whole 2 ½ months of the journey there had been only about five wet days. And this in the west of Ireland, one of the wettest regions in Europe. As one old Irishman put it, it had been 'the driest summer that came since the history of time!'.

ʊ   ʊ   ʊ

My plan for the last day was to arrive in Boher around noon and hope to get a lift into Limerick so I could catch the evening train to Dublin, but my subconscious had its delaying tactics and it was nearly 6 o'clock before I turned into Ted O'Connell's farm. I had found Lough Gur more interesting than expected.

The first archaeological site I'd come to was 'The Giant's Grave'. This was marked on my map and looked worth the short diversion. If a giant is buried there he must have been in two sections since the grave has two chambers. In fact it's a 'wedge-shaped gallery grave' which was the prehistoric (around 2000BC) resting-place for eight adults and four children. It was not hard to believe that a giant was involved in the construction of it, though. The sides were composed of a double wall of stone slabs with five massive stones resting on top, one of which is reckoned to weigh fifty tons or more. The grave overlooked the lake which must have been of special significance to the Bronze-Age Irishmen. They built their rectangular and circular houses around the shore, a *crannog* (small defended artificial island) in the lough, and also an impressive stone circle like a junior Stonehenge and roughly the same age, keyed to the summer solstice.

Lough Gur was a settlement as far back as 3000BC and the stone circle was built by the 'beaker folk' at the beginning of the Bronze Age. That metal, an alloy of copper and tin, was worked in Ireland between about 2000BC and 300BC when it was replaced by iron. One particularly fine piece of bronze workmanship was found here. Known as the Lough Gur shield it was discovered in 1872 in the marshy fringes of the lake, and sold for 30 shillings. There's a copy of this circular shield in the visitors' centre which was my next stop. Thought to date from 700BC, it's decorated with raised rings and bumps which, the label explains, reduced the impact of a sword. An undecorated bronze disc thick enough to withstand a slash from a sword would have been too heavy. The original Lough Gur shield is in the National Museum in Dublin, along with a mind-boggling display of gold artefacts dating from the same period. After visiting Lough Gur and following it up with a trip to the museum in Dublin, no-one could call the Irish a backward nation. Irish accomplishments in craftsmanship nearly 3,000 years ago surpass those of Britain. How much had we set these creative people back by colonisation and oppression, I wondered?

I spent quite a time at the visitors' centre knowing that Peggy was happily tethered on the picnic site, cropping the short but very sweet grass. I also wryly noticed that although she'd given one of her affectionate whinnies when I'd returned from the Giant's Grave, I only merited a sour look when I interrupted her lunch to continue our journey. I'd had my own midday meal with Desmond and his wife Mary, after he'd stopped his car to talk to me, happily accepting his invitation for tea at their house just down the road. He was an interesting man, having been a National Hunt jockey, a stunt rider in Hollywood, a long-distance lorry driver, and a breeder of mountain lions (pumas), of all things. He was now trying to get permission to set up a wildlife park in the grounds of a stately home that had recently been bought by Arabs.

By the time I rode away from Lough Gur it was mid afternoon. I sat on Peggy with my aching bottom and an aching heart. I looked at her sweet little ears, sharply pricked with their foamy markings around the base, and thought how empty the view of future lanes would seem without this familiar foreground. I also realised that she no longer carried herself like a carthorse. Her head was now high and her neck arched. Pretty as a picture, she was.

According to my map, Boher was just across the main road and over a railway line. Sure enough, I soon came to a church and the scatter of houses that I'd been told was the centre of town. Someone directed me to the O'Connells. I'd expected a crumbling run-down farmhouse and was impressed – and intimidated – by the long drive leading to a large white house. It looked deserted. I tied Peggy to a tree where, to her disgust, she couldn't eat, so added her neighs to my timid knocks. As I expected, there was no answer so I led Peggy back to a grassy area to graze while I made some further investigations. Then I realised that only the front of the house looked deserted. Around the back I found cars and an open door.

A girl was cooking dinner in the kitchen. I explained who I was and a young man appeared to show me where I could put Peggy for the night. He told me I could pitch my tent on the lawn outside the house.

"But I want to sleep in the field with the pony," I said, struggling to keep my voice steady, "it's our last night together."

"Well, I suppose it'll be all right," he said, as we led her through gooey cow dung in the farmyard and into a paddock already occupied by an inquisitive piebald gelding.

While I was unloading the bags, father Ted appeared on the scene and questioned why I was not pitching my tent on the lawn.

"She wants to sleep with the pony" said the son, rolling his eyes. Ted thought this plan absurdly sentimental. Out of the question, in fact.

"You can sleep in the house or in your tent near the house, and you can visit the pony at hourly intervals throughout the night if you want."

Watching Peggy and the piebald having a kicking match, I agreed that maybe it would be more sensible to camp on the lawn after all, so together we heaved the luggage back.

I was invited in for tea and stayed to help peel – and eat – six buckets of mushrooms. I'd seen no mushrooms since my bonanza in west Cork but Co Limerick seemed to be carpeted with them. My eyes and fingers itched to do some picking, so I was pleased when Sean, one of the sons, said that I could collect my own the next morning. They'd make a nice present for my friend Dorothy, who I would stay with in Dublin before catching the ferry back to Holyhead. "Go to the third field over there," he said pointing, "and you'll be tripping over them."

I got up early next morning and packed up for the trip home. The saddle had to be stripped of its girth and stirrups and put in a bag, and a handle devised so I could carry it. I sorted through the saddlebags, throwing out all my 'keep in case I need them' bits and pieces and giving useful heavy things like the tether chain ("Lovely, that'll be just right for the bull") to the farmer and tied the bags up into a bundle with the reins. Then I picked up the plastic water-bucket and headed for the fields for my final fungus foray.

I thought I'd understood where the good mushroom field was, but each meadow I walked across was a smooth expanse of green with not a white blob in sight. Or they were full of thistles and rushes, or calves which latched onto this promising-looking woman carrying a bucket, with enthusiasm. There didn't seem to be many gates and I had to scramble through barbed-wire fences, or slide down muddy banks into water-filled ditches then haul myself up the other side. I began to regret my mushroom greed and looked anxiously at my watch. I'd been offered a lift into Limerick "sometime in the morning" and didn't think it polite or expedient to be gone for too long. I'd set out before 8 and it was already nearly 9 o'clock. Then I saw them. A green field so densely dotted with white it looked like a spotted tablecloth. I was indeed tripping over mushrooms. After a few minutes I became so selective I was only picking perfect white domes with pink gills and ignoring the older or slug-nibbled specimens. It didn't take long to fill the bucket and start back towards the farm which was, after all, only three fields away. But the hedges were high and I couldn't actually see the house. I crossed several fields, none of which seemed to have a gate. One meadow had a very large, very menacing bull in it; I sidled round the edge wondering if bright-yellow plastic is as inflammatory to a bull as a red cape. Finally, to my great relief, I saw the farm buildings, with a nice boreen leading to them. When I arrived in the farmyard, however, I realised things weren't quite right. "Oh God, this isn't the right farm," I thought, as a small dog rushed out from behind a wall with its tail between its legs, followed by a flying wellington boot. Then came the farmer's wife who didn't seem in the least put out to discover a guilt-ridden English woman clutching a bucket of mushrooms in her farmyard. "Oh my, you have got a lot!" she said pleasantly as I muttered my apologies for trespassing. "You want the O'Connells? It's not far, just a couple of houses that way. You can't miss it."

I walked up the long drive towards the road and wondered where the hell I was. The road didn't look familiar and a few tentative steps in the direction she'd indicated confirmed my suspicions that it was the wrong O'Connell. I started jogging in the direction I felt was right, then realised the stupidity of relying on my 'sense of direction' and knocked at the door of a bungalow. It was opened immediately by a fat, greasy but very friendly old man who'd obviously been watching my progress through lace curtains since he directed me "the way you were going, but it's quite a way." He added, "Well over a mile." I looked at my watch. I'd already been gone two hours. "Typical!" I thought to myself sourly, "I go over a thousand miles without getting seriously lost, and look how I finish." Switching the mushroom bucket to my less aching left hand I set off down the road.

All that was left now was to say goodbye to Peggy. I could procrastinate no longer. When I arrived at her field she threw up her head, whinnied and walked towards me with pricked ears. Her piebald friend then trotted up for his share of the titbits. Peggy wasn't having this and ran at him with ears flattened and teeth bared. He turned round to kick her, she squealed, and my oft-rehearsed goodbye scene dissolved into equine squabbles. I couldn't hug her, I couldn't give her a kiss on the nose, I couldn't even stroke her. I just said, "Goodbye, Peggy. And thank you," and walked away, wiping the tears from my cheeks.

The Dublin taxi driver who took me to the coach station was talkative. What had I been doing in Ireland, he wanted to know, and how long had I been here? I told him, trying to keep the pride out of my voice and to assume tones of appropriate modesty. "You came over just to ride a horse around?" he asked incredulously, "No other reason?"

Epilogue

That was it. I never saw Peggy again, nor tried to keep in touch with Pedar. I didn't want the heartache of failure. And I knew she would be all right. After a holiday in Boher she would be taken back to Dingle and resume her job pulling Pedar's gig. She would sleep in the same field each night, with the same horse companions. And that would be enough; horses, like all animals, need routine to keep them happy.

I had taken Peggy out of her comfort zone and she had responded heroically. In the place of other horses she had bonded with me, as I had with her. But it took over 30 years of hindsight to appreciate just how much I owe her.

When I started the trek, with Mollie, I was still in the mindset that the most important part of horse management was control. Was the pony obedient? Could I make it do what I wanted? By the end of the journey I had learned that it was as important for me to understand what the pony was trying to tell me, as it was to impose my will on the animal. Peggy was the catalyst in that transition. As I'd remarked when I first had her, I'd never known such an extrovert, sociable horse. Communication was her thing, so communicating with me came naturally. I am ashamed, now, at how slow I was to learn that any strange behaviour was her attempt to tell me something, rather than sheer naughtiness.

Horses are perhaps unique in our animal-doting world. We love them, we try to bond with them, and then we sell them on. A talented horse will have several owners during its 30-year lifetime, and goodness knows how many riders. Each time it changes hands it is expected to make the adjustment and respond with generosity. Most horses do. That is an extraordinary and deeply touching fact.

My thousand miles through Ireland changed me forever. I learned how to cope alone with triumph and disaster, how to enjoy my solitary state and to live in the present as time slipped by. I learned about generosity, about the old, old human attribute of hospitality to strangers. I learned about the history of Ireland and the uncomfortable fact of my country's oppression, and I learned that this is one of the most beautiful places in Europe. But, above all, I treasure that opportunity to get to know, and be friends with, Mollie and Peggy.

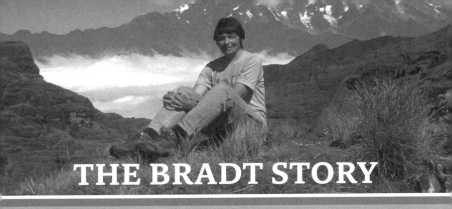

THE BRADT STORY

In the beginning

It all began in 1974 on an Amazon river barge. During an 18-month trip through South America, two adventurous young backpackers – Hilary Bradt and her then husband, George – decided to write about the hiking trails they had discovered through the Andes. *Backpacking Along Ancient Ways in Peru and Bolivia* included the very first descriptions of the Inca Trail. It was the start of a colourful journey to becoming one of the best-loved travel publishers in the world; you can read the full story on our website (www. bradtguides.com/ourstory).

Getting there first

Hilary quickly gained a reputation for being a true travel pioneer, and in the 1980s she started to focus on guides to places overlooked by other publishers. The Bradt Guides list became a roll call of guidebook 'firsts'. We published the first guide to Madagascar, followed by Mauritius, Czechoslovakia and Vietnam. The 1990s saw the beginning of our extensive coverage of Africa: Tanzania, Uganda, South Africa, and Eritrea. Later, post-conflict guides became a feature: Rwanda, Mozambique, Angola, Sierra Leone, Bosnia and Kosovo.

Comprehensive – and with a conscience

Today, we are the world's largest independently owned travel publisher, with more than 200 titles, from full-country and wildlife guides to Slow Travel guides like this one. However, our ethos remains unchanged. Hilary is still keenly involved, and we still get there first: two-thirds of Bradt guides have no direct competition.

But we don't just get there first. Our guides are also known for being more comprehensive than any other series. We avoid templates and tick-lists. Each guide is a one-of-a-kind expression of an expert author's interests, knowledge and enthusiasm for telling it how it really is.

And a commitment to wildlife, conservation and respect for local communities has always been at the heart of our books. Bradt Guides was championing sustainable travel before any other guidebook publisher.

Thank you!

We can only do what we do because of the support of readers like you – people who value less-obvious experiences, less-visited places and a more thoughtful approach to travel. Those who, like us, take travel seriously.

Bradt GUIDES
TRAVEL TAKEN SERIOUSLY